# Spiritual Lives

*General Editor*
Timothy Larsen

# SPIRITUAL LIVES

*General Editor*

Timothy Larsen

The *Spiritual Lives* series features biographies of prominent men and women whose eminence is not primarily based on a specifically religious contribution. Each volume provides a general account of the figure's life and thought, while giving special attention to his or her religious contexts, convictions, doubts, objections, ideas, and actions. Many leading politicians, writers, musicians, philosophers, and scientists have engaged deeply with religion in significant and resonant ways that have often been overlooked or underexplored. Some of the volumes will even focus on men and women who were lifelong unbelievers, attending to how they navigated and resisted religious questions, assumptions, and settings. The books in this series will therefore recast important figures in fresh and thought-provoking ways.

Titles in the series include:

**Woodrow Wilson**
*Ruling Elder, Spiritual President*
Barry Hankins

**Christina Rossetti**
*Poetry, Ecology, Faith*
Emma Mason

**John Stuart Mill**
*A Secular Life*
Timothy Larsen

**Leonard Woolf**
*Bloomsbury Socialist*
Fred Leventhal and Peter Stansky

# W. T. Stead

## Nonconformist and Newspaper Prophet

STEWART J. BROWN

OXFORD
UNIVERSITY PRESS

# OXFORD
## UNIVERSITY PRESS

Great Clarendon Street, Oxford, OX2 6DP,
United Kingdom

Oxford University Press is a department of the University of Oxford.
It furthers the University's objective of excellence in research, scholarship,
and education by publishing worldwide. Oxford is a registered trade mark of
Oxford University Press in the UK and in certain other countries

Published in the United States of America by Oxford University Press
198 Madison Avenue, New York, NY 10016, United States of America

British Library Cataloguing in Publication Data
Data available

Library of Congress Control Number: 2019940329

ISBN 978–0–19–883253–9

Printed and bound in Great Britain by
Clays Ltd, Elcograf S.p.A.

To Owen Dudley Edwards
'Charity never faileth'

# Preface

At the crowded Memorial Service for W. T. Stead on 25 April 1912 in London's Westminster Chapel, his close friend of over twenty-five years, the venerable Baptist Christian Socialist Dr John Clifford—with long, patriarchal white beard—delivered the main address. Stead, he said, was the most prominent British editor of the 1880s and 1890s, and he had transformed journalism. As a journalist, Stead was 'brilliant, rapid, unconventional, accomplished . . . his resources apparently exhaustless, and his energy without bounds'. And it was a journalism infused with a higher purpose. 'He was a journalist, but a journalist as Paul was an Apostle and Knox a Reformer, and woe to him if he did not preach and make potent the good news God gave him.' What was most important to Stead was God's divine plan for humankind; what defined him was his belief that God directly called him to serve that plan. 'To me,' Clifford declared, 'he was as a prophet who had come straight out of the Old Testament into our modern storm-swept life.' Stead had sought to proclaim God's will through journalism to an increasingly secular and materialist world; for him, the newspaper was 'a sword to cut down the foes of right-eousness, a platform from which to hearten and inspire the armies of the Lord, a pulpit from which to preach his crusades, a desk at which he could expound his policy for making a new heaven and a new earth. He was a man with a mission, and journalism was the organ through which he wrought at it.' Above all else, Stead 'was a prophet with a prophet's insight' and a 'prophet's fearlessness'.

William Thomas Stead, newspaper editor, author, social reformer, women's rights advocate, peace campaigner, and spiritualist, was one of the best-known public figures in late Victorian and Edwardian Britain. The son of a Congregational minister, Stead emerged to national prominence in the 1870s, when, as the young editor of the Darlington *Northern Echo*, he became a leading voice of the 'Noncon-formist Conscience', supporting the efforts of Protestant Dissenters to reshape British politics and society around Christian moral standards. In 1881, he became assistant editor of London's evening *Pall Mall*

*Gazette*, and then, from 1883, the newspaper's editor. At the *Pall Mall*, he pioneered what became known in Britain as the 'New Journalism', with emphasis on investigative journalism, sensationalist news stories, interviews of prominent figures, special 'extra' issues, moral crusades, bold headlines, and abundant illustrations. In 1885, he gained international prominence, and a prison sentence, for his highly controversial 'Maiden Tribute of Modern Babylon' newspaper campaign directed against the sex trafficking of girls and young women in London. In 1890 Stead left the *Pall Mall* and became founder-editor of the successful London-based monthly, *The Review of Reviews*, which provided readers with a digest of articles from the world's press, and promoted both global perspectives and the unity of English-speaking peoples. In 1893, he founded and edited *Borderland*, a quarterly journal to promote the study of psychic phenomena; his volume of *Letters from Julia*, first published in *Borderland* and described as messages from the afterlife, went through numerous editions and was translated into a number of languages. Stead became a major voice of the 'social gospel' in Britain and the United States following the publication in 1894 of his best-selling *If Christ Came to Chicago!* with its call for the redemption of the modern city. He was, moreover, a leading proponent and publicist of the Hague peace conferences of 1899 and 1907, and the arbitration of international disputes. Lauded by many for his journalistic crusades and Christian social ethics, he was despised by others for his sensationalism and self-promotion.

Stead's remarkable, often highly contentious public career has generated a rich biographical literature. Two highly sympathetic memoirs of Stead appeared shortly after his death: *My Father* (1913) by his daughter, Estelle, and *Stead: The Man* (1914) by his assistant, Edith Harper—both authors placing emphasis on Stead's spiritualism. The standard two-volume biography of Stead, Frederic Whyte's *The Life of W. T. Stead*, was published in 1925. A journalist who had worked under Stead, Whyte wrote a biography which was rich in insights on both Stead's journalistic career and the broader cultural context, although Whyte had little interest in Stead's Nonconformist roots, religious conceptions, or spiritualist writings. J. W. Robertson Scott, another journalist who had worked under Stead, provided a lengthy biographical study of Stead in his *Life and Death of a Newspaper* (a study of the *Pall Mall Gazette*), published in 1952. His account drew heavily from Stead's private journals and offered balanced assessments of Stead's achievements and character. In 1972 the historian Raymond L. Schults produced a thoroughly researched monograph on Stead's years at the *Pall Mall Gazette,* exploring his contributions to the 'New Journalism' and the development of the modern newspaper. In *The Invention of Telepathy* of 2002, the cultural historian, Roger Luckhurst, included a valuable chapter on Stead's interests in telepathic communications and engagement with psychical researchers. The literary scholar, Grace Eckley, published an impressively researched, highly laudatory biography of Stead in 2007. The centenary of Stead's death in 2012 brought a revival of interest, with a lively, engaging biography of Stead, *Muckraker: The Scandalous Life and Times of W. T. Stead,* by the journalist, W. Sydney Robinson; as the title suggests, Robinson emphasized Stead's sensationalist journalistic campaigns and alleged sexual liaisons. 2012 also saw an international conference at the British Library in London, which led to a volume of essays, *W. T. Stead: Newspaper Revolutionary,* edited by Laurel Brake, Ed King, Roger Luckhurst, and James Mussell. The essays mainly explored Stead's journalism, with some contributions on his spiritualism. The most important modern scholar of Stead was the historian, Joseph Baylen, who explored Stead's varied career in a series of well-researched, insightful, and authoritative articles. I had the opportunity to meet Professor Baylen when he was nearing retirement at Georgia State University and I was teaching at the University of Georgia, and I remember well his gracious manner and warm encouragement to a younger scholar. He did not, unfortunately, manage to complete the definitive biography of Stead for which we had hoped.

This book is a religious biography of Stead. What interests me as an historian of modern Christianity is how for Stead, and for many of his readers, the late nineteenth-century newspaper took on certain roles previously filled by the church, proclaiming a high social ethics, exposing and denouncing sin, seeking to discern the direction of the history and destiny of humankind, and forming participatory networks of readers for moral action. My biography gives particular attention to Stead's conception of journalism, at a time of growing mass literacy, as a means to communicate a social gospel, and his view of the editor's desk as a modern pulpit, from which the editor/preacher could reach a congregation of tens of thousands. The book

explores how his Nonconformist Conscience and sense of divine
calling infused his newspaper crusades, and it examines his efforts,
through forms of participatory journalism, to create a 'union of all
who love in the service of all who suffer' and what he called a 'Civic
Church'. It considers his growing interest in spiritualism and the
occult as he searched for the proof of an afterlife that he hoped
would draw people in an increasingly secular society back to faith. It
discusses his imperialism and his belief that the English-speaking
peoples of the British Empire and American Republic were God's
new chosen people for fulfilling the divine purpose, and it also considers how his growing understanding of other faiths and cultures, and
his moral revulsion over the South African War of 1899–1902,
brought him to question that belief. Finally, it assesses the influence
of religious faith on his later campaigns for world peace through the
arbitration of international disputes. To what extent can we discern
continuities in Stead's personal beliefs, as they move from the evangelical Nonconformity of his youth to those of a social gospel
reformer, broad church imperialist, and advocate of psychical exploration? How should we evaluate Stead's claims to be a prophet for a
new era, and a preacher in a newspaper pulpit? Stead, to be sure, was
not a serious theologian or profound religious thinker. Rather, he was
a gifted journalist and fluent, engaging writer, whose religious journey
reflected the challenges of preserving a Christian witness at a time of
increasing secularization.

I have many debts of gratitude to record. Timothy Larsen, the
general editor of the 'Spiritual Lives' series, welcomed my proposal for
a religious biography of Stead, and was consistently supportive. Sir
Brian Harrison first suggested that I write a religious life of Stead, and
David Bebbington encouraged the project and was generous in shar-
ing his expertise on both modern British evangelicalism and the
Nonconformist Conscience. The History of Christianity Research
Seminar at the University of Edinburgh and the Ecclesiastical History
Seminar at the University of Cambridge heard sections of the book,
and were helpful with comments and suggestions. My work on both
Stead and his historical context has benefited from the conversation
and suggestions of Emily Baylor, Duncan Bell, Clyde Binfield, Jane
Dawson, Susan Hardman Moore, Laura Mair, Hugh McLeod, Jolyon
Mitchell, Sara Parvis, Paul Parvis, Keith Robbins, Brian Stanley,

Stephen Sutcliffe, David Thompson, and Jowita Thor. All who work on Stead must express gratitude to Owen Mulpetre, who since 2001 has generously maintained the 'W. T. Stead Resource Site', providing scholars with access to a wealth of sources on Stead's life and work. The University of Edinburgh provided a semester's research leave and a research grant from the Moray Endowment Fund. Owen Dudley Edwards has read the entire text, and his comments and suggestions have been immensely helpful; it is with deep gratitude for the many years of friendship and support that I dedicate the book to him. My wife, Teri, and my family have borne with Stead, often with bemused smiles that Stead would have appreciated.

# Contents

# Abbreviations

| | |
|---|---|
| BL | British Library |
| Bryce Papers | Viscount Bryce Papers, Bodleian Library, Oxford, MS Bryce 140 |
| *NE* | *Northern Echo* |
| Novikoff-Stead Corr. | Correspondence of Olga Novikoff and W. T. Stead, Bodleian Library, Oxford, MS.Eng.misc.d.182 |
| *PMG* | *Pall Mall Gazette* |
| *RoR* | *The Review of Reviews* |
| Stead Papers | Stead Papers, Churchill College, Cambridge |

# 1

# A Voice of the Nonconformist Conscience, 1849–80

'I was a child of the manse', Stead wrote when in his mid-fifties. 'My father was an Independent minister, and both my parents were earnest, devoted Evangelical Christians. Independents sixty years ago were more Calvinistic than are their present-day representatives, and a sense of the exceeding sinfulness of sin and of the grim reality of the wrath of God permeated the atmosphere of our home.'[1] William Thomas Stead was born on 5 July 1849 in the old manse of the Presbyterian church in the Northumberland coastal village of Embleton. He was the second child of William Stead, then a minister in the Presbyterian Church of England, and his wife, Isabella. His father, born in 1814 in Crookes, near Sheffield, was the son of a cutler, or knife-maker. A pious lad with evangelical convictions, William Stead also became a cutler in Sheffield, but in 1839, at the age of twenty-five, he was accepted as a student of Airedale Theological College, a small, Independent dissenting academy in Bradford, where students received room, board, and tuition free of charge. Completing his studies in 1844, he was ordained minister of the Embleton Presbyterian Church in 1845. (At this time, English Presbyterian congregations were permitted to select ministers without a specifically Presbyterian training, provided the minister accepted the Presbyterian system of Church government.) The following year he married Isabella Jobson, the twenty-two-year-old daughter of a Northumberland farmer.

Late in 1849, William Stead returned to the Congregational denomination, accepting a call to become minister of the Independent church in Howdon, an industrial settlement on the banks of the Tyne, about five miles from Newcastle. He moved with his family to a modest manse in Howdon, and here he ministered for the next thirty-four years, until his death in 1884. It was, according to his son, a 'grimy spot, befouled and bemired, poisoned by chemical fumes, and darkened by the smoke of innumerable chimneys'.[2] The Independent, or Congregationalist denomination was broadly Reformed, or Calvinist in theology, with a respect for a learned ministry and a belief that each congregation should be self-governing, recognizing only Christ as head of the Church and seeking in worship to reflect the simplicity of the early Church. They were part of what was known as 'Old Dissent', Protestant Nonconformists who cherished a sturdy independence of character, disciplined lives, and hard work as a means of honouring God; they were heirs to the seventeenth-century English Puritans. In the mid-nineteenth century, Congregationalists were left-leaning Whig or even Radical in their politics, opposing the established Church of England and any connection of Church and State, as well as privilege or political favouritism.

As Congregational minister in Howdon, William Stead was active in home mission, including house-to-house visiting, organizing house prayer meetings, and visiting ships every Sunday at Howdon dock, with a group of helpers, to distribute pious tracts and invite the sailors to worship at his church. He served on civic bodies, and took a particular interest in extending popular education. Following the Education Act of 1870, he was elected to the Wallsend School Board and in 1878 he took the leading role in founding the Howdon's Mechanics Institute, an educational and recreational club for working men. 'He did not preach much about the obligation of doing our duty,' his son would later recall, 'he only made us feel that to neglect doing our duty was as flat a flying in the face of the law of the universe as the neglect to breathe.' 'He was emphatically a healthy man—healthy and whole-souled, with a sovereign hatred of shams and fine phrases, which was kept from being rancorous by a fine spirit of charity and a hearty human sympathy. I think he was the heartiest laugher I ever knew.' He had a great love of literature, with a good-sized library at his manse. His childhood poverty and limited formal education left him cautious, diffident, and self-effacing, as a labouring man now in a learned profession. He could be dismissed by his congregation if they became displeased with him, in which case he would have little hope of finding another position as a minister. 'The meekest and mildest of men,' his son observed, 'I have seen him bear insults which made me long, boy as I was, to smite the insulter to the ground... Modest and reserved, he never pushed himself.' Little is known of his theology, as he ordered that his several thousand manuscript sermons be burned a few days before his death. While not an eloquent or popular preacher, he earned respect as a dedicated pastor and he formed a congregation with a regular attendance of some two hundred people, along with a successful Sunday School for children. His income never exceeded £150 a year, but with a manse in addition to the income, he was able to support his family in reasonable comfort. Stead's mother, Isabella, said to have 'passed through much domestic affliction previous to her marriage', found consolation in a deep evangelical faith. She was known as a peace-maker, ever ready to intervene to mediate quarrels. One who knew her well described her life as 'very simple, very placid in its "deeds of weekday holiness"'.[3] Her influence upon him, Stead later wrote, 'was constant and abiding'.[4] She died after a brief illness in the spring of 1875.

## A Remarkable Nonconformist Family

William and Isabella Stead had nine children; of these three died in infancy or in their first years, while another, Joseph, died of scarlet fever in 1868 aged fifteen. The parents largely schooled their children at home and encouraged free and open discussions on most matters. For Sunday morning breakfasts, each family member would memorize a biblical verse and offer an interpretation, from which the conversation would then range widely over questions of religion and morality. They were a remarkable family. Of the five children who reached maturity, the eldest, Mary Isabella, born in 1847, became an educator, social welfare activist, temperance reformer, Liberal politician, and feminist. She co-founded the first Leicester branch of the Young Women's Christian Association, ran a mission to the poor at Balham in South London, conducted a soup kitchen in London during the bitter winter of 1894–5, co-organized a mission at Redcar in Yorkshire, and served as president of the Redcar Women's Liberal Association. The third child, John Edward, born in 1851, achieved an international reputation as a metallurgist, establishing a successful firm of analytical chemists, 'Pattinson and Stead', in 1876 and publishing numerous scientific papers. He was awarded the Bessemer Gold Medal of the Iron and Steel Institute (metallurgy's highest honour) in 1901, was elected a fellow of the Royal Society in 1903, and received three honorary doctorates. The fourth child, Sarah Anne, married George Strachan; she died in 1896, aged forty. The fifth child, Francis Herbert Stead, born in 1857, became a prominent Congregational minister, peace campaigner and social gospel activist. Educated at Owens College, Manchester, Airedale Theological College, Glasgow University, and several German universities, Herbert served for six years as a Congregational minister in Leicester, and then as warden of the Browning Settlement in a deprived district of London, where he worked for slum clearance, legislative help for the unemployed, national homes for the aged, old age pensions, women's rights, and international peace.[5]

In his early years, William Thomas Stead was taught at home by his father alongside his elder sister, with the two set in competition in learning their lessons. They were taught Latin from a young age, learning Latin grammar before English grammar. Their father also taught them to read, but not to speak French. Family life was on the whole happy, with games in the garden and long walks, but there was also a strict Nonconformist morality. 'I was born and brought up,' Stead later recalled, 'in a home where life was regarded ever as the vestibule of Eternity, and where everything that tended to waste time, which is life in instalments, was regarded as an evil thing.' 'Hence,' he continued, 'in our North Country manse a severe interdict was laid upon all time-wasting amusements which did not directly minister to the restoration of moral, or physical energy, and especially was the interdict severe upon those methods of dissipation which were so fascinating as to make them dangerous rivals to the claims of duty.' Of these temptations, he added, 'the first was the Theatre, which was the Devil's Chapel; the second was Cards, which were the Devil's Prayer Book; and the third was the Novel, which was regarded as a kind of Devil's Bible.'[6] He was, however, permitted to read Sir Walter Scott's novels, regarded as of a high moral standard.

His father's ardent sermons, the family's strict piety, and the difficulties in meeting the high moral expectations threw some dark shadows over Stead's childhood. In his father's faith, there was, alongside hope of salvation and everlasting life with Christ, also a real hell of everlasting torment, and a divine justice under which the reprobate should suffer eternal punishment. This faith could instil an uncompromising morality, but could also arouse terror. Stead recalled being struck at the age of eleven with an overpowering sense of his sinfulness and the conviction that 'I deserved to be damned'. 'I sobbed and cried in the darkness,' he remembered, 'with a vague sense of my own sin and of the terrible doom which awaited me.' His mother heard his cries, took him in her arms and comforted him with words about the love of God, until in time his terror passed. For the rest of his life he remembered that night as a 'thunderstorm'.[7]

## His 'First Conversion'

In July 1861, at the age of twelve, Stead was sent to Silcoates boarding school for Congregationalist boys, located near Wakefield. Its fifty boys were aged between ten and seventeen. The headmaster, Dr James Bewglass, a flamboyant teacher and an Irishman, roused the interest of the boys with accounts of the early battles of the American Civil War and the historic injustices of British rule in Ireland. Stead's arrival at the school coincided with the final stages of the evangelical revival movement that had been sweeping through Britain and Ireland since 1858–9, affecting hundreds of thousands. In August 1861, some of the Silcoates boys, including Stead, began holding prayer meetings and speaking earnestly about the state of their souls. Stead, who was homesick and distressed, now experienced what he described as an evangelical conversion, bringing a sudden conviction that he had always been saved from his sins by Christ's sacrifice, and giving him 'a sense of great peace and deliverance'. It was, at one level, a schoolboy episode, in which Stead and the other boys, enthused by the larger revival movement, tried to emulate its language and behaviour. But Stead believed that his conversion was a real change, with a lasting impact on his life. 'Whatever may be the objective reality of the altered relations which I then recognised as existing between my soul and its Maker,' Stead wrote in 1905, 'there is absolutely no question as to the abiding nature of the change it effected in my life. It is forty-three years since that Revival at school. The whole of my life during these forty-three years has been influenced by that change which men call conversion which occurred with me when I was twelve.'[8] Following this conversion, aged twelve, he joined the Congregational Church at Wakefield, and he remained a member of a Congregational church for all his life. 'Nor has anything,' he later wrote, 'occurred in all my subsequent wanderings, spiritual or otherwise, to lead me to wish to abandon that position.'[9]

His parents removed Stead from Silcoates School in June 1863, just before his fourteenth birthday, apprenticing him as a clerk with the firm of Charles Septimus Smith, a wine, spirits, timber, and leather merchant at Quayside, Newcastle-upon-Tyne, and Russian vice-consul. Stead had enjoyed his time at the school, writing for the school paper and developing a love for cricket. The two years at Silcoates were his only formal education, and he would be sensitive about this throughout his life, protesting (a bit too loudly at times) that his limited formal education had never harmed his prospects. His parents' decision to remove him probably resulted from financial pressures amid a general economic downturn. The American Civil War had brought a collapse in imports of raw cotton, which had a devastating impact on the textile industry and the British economy as a whole, presumably affecting congregational contributions to the Howdon church and thus his father's income. For a Congregational minister to apprentice his son to a merchant dealing in wine and spirits appears incongruous, but there is no evidence that the elder Stead was a total abstainer from alcohol, and Smith was a respected merchant. Stead, who soon rose to the position of salaried clerk, lived at home, commuted by train to Newcastle to work, and most of his earnings went to the family.

Shortly after leaving school, he felt his life transformed by Thomas Carlyle's *Letters and Speeches of Oliver Cromwell* (1845), with its emotive portrayal of Cromwell as the heroic 'God's Englishman', raised up by his religious faith and uncompromising morality, and imposing God's moral order upon a distracted and troubled people, who desperately needed a leader. Carlyle's Cromwell infused the young clerk with the hope of doing something extraordinary with his life. Stead venerated Carlyle's high moral tone, celebration of the heroic, energetic, sermonizing style, painstaking historical research, and ability to form an intimate personal connection with his readers. Carlyle was, according to Stead's biographer, Frederic Whyte, 'the writer who perhaps more than any other was to influence his whole life'.[10] Along with many Victorian Nonconformists, especially Congregationalists, Stead was also drawn to Carlyle's Cromwell as a champion against the perceived oppression of an established Church. 'The memory of Cromwell,' Stead wrote in 1899, 'has from my earliest boyhood been the inspiration of my life. That was not surprising, for I was the son of an Independent minister.' His admiration of Cromwell, 'the uncrowned king of English Puritanism', reached the level of religious devotion, which for a time overshadowed even his devotion to Christ. 'I can to this day remember,' he continued, 'the serious searchings of heart I experienced when I woke up to a consciousness of the fact that I felt a far keener and more passionate personal love for Oliver Cromwell, than I did even for the divine figure of Jesus of Nazareth. Cromwell was so near, so human, and so real.'[11]

## His 'Second Conversion'

Stead now immersed himself in reading on Cromwell, English Puritanism, and the English Civil War, and dreamed of literary fame as an historian of seventeenth-century English Puritanism. Reading late in the evenings, during lunch breaks and on the train, he gained an appreciation for history that remained with him for life. But a major history of Puritanism was too vast a project for a clerk, with little education, time, or library resources. In 1868 serious eye strain endangered his vision, and for a time his physician vetoed his reading outside the office. He took this threatened blindness as a sign from God that he 'must put away all idea of ever writing the book, or of making a name for myself, and must simply set to work and labour for those who were around me'.[12]

This perceived divine call to social service, and especially service to the poor, formed what Stead called his 'second conversion'. In embracing the call to service, he found special inspiration from another figure, who alongside Carlyle and Cromwell, would have a significant influence on his life. This was the New England poet, essayist, magazine editor, and Abolitionist, James Russell Lowell (1819–91). Stead was fifteen when he found by chance a 'yellow-backed shilling edition' of Lowell poems. A few years later, in 1867, his essay on Cromwell, signed 'W. T. Silcoates' and submitted to the *Boys Own Magazine*, won him some prize books, among which he chose another book of Lowell poetry.[13] 'That little volume,' he wrote in 1891, 'with its green paper cover, lies before me now, thumbed almost to pieces, underscored, and marked in the margin throughout . . . It has been with me everywhere; in Russia, in Ireland, in Rome, in prison, it has been my constant companion.'[14] 'In some of the critical moments of my life,' he noted, amid a telling juxtaposition of texts, 'I found in Lowell help such as I found in none other outside Carlyle's "Cromwell" and Holy Writ.'[15]

From Lowell, Stead derived an enthusiasm for humanity and sense of Christianity as a living force for good in the world. Lowell, Stead insisted, was 'a Puritan by heredity' for whom the 'moral fervour of the men of the *Mayflower* was wrought into the inmost fibre of his being'.[16] His Puritanism had brought Lowell to struggle for God's justice and righteous order, fighting through verse and prose to free America's black slaves. For Lowell, the Civil War and its many martyrs for freedom became 'God's new Messiah'.[17] Lowell's poetry celebrated a Jesus who had sacrificed his life in service to humanity, and who called his followers to do the same. 'It was in thus harmonising,' Stead explained, 'the broadest humanitarianism with the strictest orthodox theories of the divine mission of Christ that Mr. Lowell was most helpful to me; for he enabled me to hitch on all that was best and noblest in human endeavour to the old, old doctrine of Calvary. He has been, and long will be, the most potent preacher of the living Christ that this century has produced.' Stead believed that for Lowell the essence of Christianity involved the question: ' "What are you doing with the least of these my brethren?" Doctrine, ritual, sacrament—all these may be unimpeachably correct; but if these "little ones" are being crucified, what does it avail?'[18]

Through Lowell's influence Stead began to consider journalism as a career. Although Stead's father sometimes quoted the London Congregational minister, Thomas Binney, to the effect that if St Paul were alive in the mid-nineteenth century, he would edit a daily newspaper, Stead had not previously been attracted to journalism. Newspapers did not 'stir the sympathy of a lad full of daydreams from the poets and high imaginings drawn from the traditions of the Puritan and Covenanting struggles of the seventeenth century'. But Lowell's writings opened Stead's mind to the potential of journalism to bring social and religious change. He was profoundly moved by Lowell's prose preface to his poem, 'The Pious Editor's Creed', which portrayed the newspaper editor as a religious prophet, while regretting that most Christian preachers, 'instead of being a living force', merely vocalized 'certain theological dogmas' and adorned 'christenings, weddings, and funerals'. These preachers might reach a few hundred with their Sunday sermons. But newspaper editors preached to the masses and were becoming the prophets of the new, more democratic era. 'See what a pulpit the editor mounts daily,' Lowell enthused, 'sometimes with a congregation of fifty thousand, within reach of his voice.' 'And from what a Bible,' he continued, 'can he choose his text—a Bible which needs no translation, and which no priestcraft can shut and clasp from the laity—the open volume of the world, upon which, with a pen of sunshine or destroying fire, the inspired Present is even now writing the annals of God!'[19]

Outside his working hours, Stead threw himself into educational and social work, becoming a sort of 'unpaid curate' to his father in Howdon, while also active in voluntary philanthropic work in Newcastle. He taught in the Howdon Sunday School, was secretary of the Howdon Tract Society, led a cottage prayer meeting, and chaired a Young Men's Mutual Improvement Society, which included managing its cricket club. 'It was in those humble agencies,' he later wrote, 'and not in college class or university lecture rooms, that I learned all that I know of the art and science of human life.'[20] Years later, according to his sister Mary, local people would 'tell tales of the harum scarum lad who worked himself nearly to death to save the lads of the village'.[21] Stead was impressed with the formation in 1869 of the Charity Organisation Society, which promoted more rational and informed approaches to charity, including the careful investigation of applicants' need for relief and the formation of educational programmes designed to help relief recipients find employment and gain independence. Early in 1870, he helped to form a Newcastle Mendicity Society on this model and became its first secretary.

## Appointment as Editor of the *Northern Echo*

He also began writing articles on social and political questions for newspapers, especially the *Northern Echo*, a half-penny daily newspaper begun on 1 January 1870 in the northern town of Darlington, an important railway centre. The wealthy Quaker Pease family had promoted the formation of the newspaper and provided continuing financial support.[22] The proprietor was a former Methodist minister and Liberal journalist, John Hyslop Bell, and the first editor was an experienced London journalist, John Copleston.[23] The newspaper advocated advanced Liberal views and was priced for a mass market.[24] Stead was not paid for his articles, which included a series of short pieces on America and Americans. But Copleston gave him valuable guidance on journalistic writing, encouraging Stead to curb his Protestant zeal and adopt a more open and tolerant tone. 'You have a really powerful pen,' Copleston assured him in February 1871, 'and with very little practice you may command the attention of hundreds of thousands.'[25] Bell and Copleston, meanwhile, were not getting on, and in the spring of 1871 Copleston resigned as editor, moving to New York City later that year. Bell had liked the energetic style and Christian tone of Stead's articles, especially his 'Democracy and Christianity', which had portrayed the two movements as linked parts of the divine plan for the elevation of humanity.[26] He now took the risk of offering Stead the editorship of the *Northern Echo*.[27] For Stead, who had sent his articles by post and had never even been in a newspaper office, the unexpected invitation was a clear call from on high. 'To be an editor!' he confided to his journal on 16 April 1871, '... to think, write and speak for thousands.' 'Am I not,' he asked (thinking of Cromwell), 'God's chosen ... to be his soldier against wrong?'[28] After negotiating an arrangement by which there would be no Sunday work, Stead accepted the position and began work in July 1871. His initial salary was £180 a year, more than that of his father. At twenty-two, he was the youngest newspaper editor in England, aided by an experienced sub-editor, Mark Fooks, formerly of the *Northern Daily Express*.[29]

Shortly after accepting the position, Stead travelled to Leeds to meet another young journalist, Thomas Wemyss Reid, who in May 1870 had become editor of the *Leeds Mercury*. Seven years older than Stead, Reid was the son of a Congregational minister in Newcastle-upon-Tyne; their fathers were friends and had arranged for Stead to meet Reid and receive his advice. But if Reid had expected Stead to listen, he was soon disabused. Stead, Reid recalled, did most of the talking, and he talked on and on for hours, full of ideas of how he would conduct his newspaper. Stead's appearance was that of the 'ugly duckling', and his conversation 'distinctly eccentric', but there was also 'something that was irresistible in his candour, his enthusiasm, and his self-confidence'. Stead insisted that 'the Press was the greatest agency for influencing public opinion in the world. It was the true and only lever by which Thrones and Governments could be shaken and the masses of the people raised.' While Reid thought some of Stead's ideas 'ridiculous', he 'was staggered by the audacity of his schemes for revolutionising English journalism'.[30]

In 1871, William Stead was about 5 feet, 8 inches in height, with a slight build, and reddish-brown hair. He had a weak chin, which he filled out with a beard, and a disconcerting way of fixing his blue eyes on people in conversation. His difficulties with eye strain had ended. He wore ill-fitting clothes, lacked social graces and discretion, tended to sprawl over furniture, and was not shy about speaking his mind. He loved running, and would run everywhere, as fast as he could, including to and from church, which many found undignified. 'It was thought in the village,' he admitted, 'that I was a little daft.'[31] He was a romantic, loving the poetry of Coleridge, Byron, and Lowell, and the prose of Carlyle. When he was eighteen or nineteen, he was infatuated with a Scottish woman, ten years his senior, who had spent a summer with her brother in Howdon and apparently encouraged his attentions; she had returned to Edinburgh and, despite Stead's passionate letters, she married a naval officer. Now at the age of twenty-two he left the family home at Howdon with little formal education, but with immense self-confidence, a belief in a divine plan for his life, and lofty ideals and values, that would remain with him for life. Since his early twenties, Stead later wrote, 'I have learned a great many more facts, and [come] to know a great many more people, but my standpoint or outlook upon life, my conception of what is possible and of what ought to be done, in other words my ideal and objective were fixed by the time I was twenty.'[32] And his standpoint was essentially that of a Protestant Nonconformist, son of the manse, convert of the 1859–62 Revival movement, and member of a Congregational church, who viewed the Congregationalists 'as the heirs of Cromwell and Milton and the Pilgrim Fathers, and the representatives of extreme Democracy which knows neither male not female.'[33]

## The *Northern Echo* and the Nonconformist Conscience

With the support of the Quaker Pease family and the Methodist proprietor, Stead soon made the *Northern Echo* the leading north of England voice of what would become known as the 'Nonconformist Conscience'. It was a propitious time for a young Nonconformist editor enthused with high ideals for social and political change. The Protestant Nonconformist denominations were on the whole confident and rising in social status. The religious census of March 1851 had shown the number of Nonconformist worshippers to be nearly equal to those in the established Church, and some believed Nonconformist numbers were bypassing the number in the established Church by the early 1870s. Educational and income levels for Nonconformists improved in mid-Victorian Britain. Some achieved notable success in business, among them the Baptist Jeremiah Colman (1830–98), the 'mustard-king' of Norwich; the Quaker John Cadbury (1801–89) of Birmingham, producer of chocolates, especially hot cocoa drinks; the Primitive Methodist William Hartley (1846–1922) of Liverpool, producer of jams, and the Unitarian Joseph Chamberlain (1836–1914) of Birmingham, who by the 1870s was producing most of the metal screws in Britain.

Such Nonconformists would not accept being second-class citizens or tolerated outsiders; they demanded full political and civil equality. Since the 1830s, Nonconformist political agitation had secured the removal of most of their civil disabilities. In 1836, Parliament enacted the civil registration of births and deaths, removing the keeping of these records from the parish churches of the established Church. That same year, Parliament enacted the option of civil marriage, rather than requiring marriage according to Anglican rites in the parish church. In the mid-1850s, Parliament enacted legislation to permit Nonconformists to study for non-theological degrees at the ancient universities of Oxford and Cambridge; in 1871, theological degrees and most fellowships at Oxford and Cambridge were also opened to them. In 1868, Parliament passed William Gladstone's bill to abolish the compulsory Church Rate, or the tax levied in English and Welsh parishes for the maintenance of the parish church, which Nonconformists, as well as adherents of the established Church, had been required to pay.

The Second Reform Act of 1867 had expanded the parliamentary franchise in England and Wales, significantly increasing the number of voters, especially among the lower middle classes and the skilled artisans. About a third of all adult males over twenty years of age in England and Wales could now vote. Many of the new voters were Nonconformists, who now felt increasingly empowered to work not only to redress their remaining grievances, but also to reshape British national and imperial policies around their religious and moral convictions. With their emphasis on individual responsibility, self-discipline, and self-help, most Nonconformists were drawn to the Liberal Party that was emerging in the 1860s from an alliance of Whigs, radicals, and moderate reformers. The number of Nonconformists in Parliament steadily grew. As David Bebbington has shown, 14 per cent of the Liberal MPs were Nonconformists following the general election in 1868, 19 per cent following the general election of 1874, and 24 per cent following the general election of 1880.[34]

Soon after his arrival in Darlington, Stead became engaged to a Howdon woman, Emma Lucy Wilson, whom he had known since childhood. She was a devout Congregationalist, slightly older than him, the daughter of his mother's friend and a close friend of his older sister. They were married on 10 June 1873. They had prepared a special wedding service 'adapted to modern requirements', which at Emma's stipulation omitted the term 'obey' from the wedding vows. They rented a house, Grainey Hill, surrounded by trees and three acres of arable land, and located a few miles outside Darlington. Stead rode to and from the newspaper office on a small pony. He and Emma attended the Congregational church on Union Street in Darlington, where the minister, Henry B. Kendall, was a friend of Stead's father and also took a keen interest in collecting ghost stories.[35] At Grainey Hill, Stead adopted the persona of a small farmer, doing a little gardening, living close to nature, avoiding society and its artificial distinctions, independent of mind and beholden to none—like Cromwell on his farmstead at St Ives, or Carlyle at the country cottage at Craigenputtock. 'I live like a hermit—married hermit of course,' he explained to Olga Novikoff (of whom more later), in October 1877:

> I live two miles from the town, riding in to it every night, & doing all my
> work as far as possible in the silence & solitude of the country. I have no

neighbours. The little household is complete in itself, & around it, are no living things save my pony, the cow, the dogs, the poultry, the bees, & the birds, whose music in the summer morning, when I return tired & exhausted from work, is worth more to me than all the orchestras that exist in Europe. The nobles, the grandees, ignore our existence, as completely as I ignore them—well never mind! But you see I am not of their caste.[36]

Children followed: William was born in 1874, Henry in 1875, Alfred in 1877, and Emma Wilson (known as Estelle) in 1878. For Stead, it was an idyllic home—'the Garden of Eden plus the children', as he later recalled[37]—though his young wife, with most of the responsibility for raising the children, became depressed by the isolation.

The *Northern Echo* had a circulation of about 10,000 when he began his editorship, and this increased to about 13,000 by 1875. After March 1873, the newspaper became available in London through W. H. Smith newsagents, with copies arriving by rail before 10 am.[38] Along with editing the paper, Stead wrote six lead articles (editorials) and various short reports each week. Stead's *Northern Echo* promoted Nonconformist support for the Liberal party, and called for high moral standards in public figures, an eight-hour working day for coal miners, home rule for Ireland, a responsible imperialism, Anglo-American friendship, expansion of national education, temperance reform, and arbitration of international disputes. As Joseph Baylen observed, 'Stead gave the *Northern Echo* a sense of purpose and urgency, which most of the British daily press lacked, and made the *Echo* one of the most readable newspapers in Britain. In virile and vehement prose, Stead produced a torrent of acute leaders and personal commentaries on public affairs.'[39] The tone and style of his editorials were those of a Nonconformist preacher; he was his father's son, giving impassioned sermons on various topics six days a week to a 'congregation' of thousands of readers. 'Newspapers,' he insisted in an editorial promoting 'Religious Revival', 'are not mere chronicles of passing events; they are the teachers of the age.'[40] As Simon Goldsworthy has observed, 'the style of successful nonconformist preaching—the use of powerful language, vivid, often emotional material, and eye-catching examples to draw moral lessons while attracting and holding the attention of a congregation—lent itself to the new journalism which Stead in particular was to pioneer.'[41]

The early and mid-1870s were a time of intense religious conflict in the United Kingdom, with campaigns for disestablishment, religious controversies surrounding the Education Act of 1870, conflicts over Anglo-Catholic ritual within the Church of England, and clashes over the Vatican Council of 1869–70 and the doctrine of papal infallibility. Disestablishment was an especially pressing question. Gladstone's Liberal Government had carried the act disestablishing the Protestant Church of Ireland in 1869 (with the act going into effect in 1871), and many Nonconformists hoped this would be a precedent for disestablishment throughout the United Kingdom, ending the connection of Church and state and placing all denominations on an equal footing under the law. There were large-scale disestablishment campaigns in England and Wales from 1871 and in Scotland from 1874, and motions for disestablishment were introduced in the House of Commons in 1871, 1872, and 1873. The Nonconformist *Northern Echo* had championed the cause of disestablishment from its formation.[42] Stead was a strong advocate of disestablishment, believing, as he wrote in a private memorandum, that 'the Established Church is an anomaly, an injustice and inconsistent with religious equality, out of place in a democratic State where its faith is repudiated by a large proportion of the people'. The established Church, he added, 'lowers the standard of Xtian citizenship. Its influence is always on the selfish side, in favour of high-handed wrong, against justice, against right.'[43] His disestablishment fervour was influenced by his Congregationalism and his admiration of Cromwell, and his *Northern Echo* editorials were scathing about the established Church. Every Liberal, he wrote in an editorial, 'The Curse of the Church' (6 April 1874), must 'ask himself how long the Upas tree of the Establishment is to be permitted to curse with its poisonous shade the Christian graces which should distinguish the English Church'. He was appalled by how many Anglican clerics would insist on their legal rights over parish burial grounds, refusing to allow Nonconformists to bury their dead with their own burial services and thus seeking to 'perpetuate their supremacy beyond the tomb'.[44]

His editorials denounced the Anglo-Catholic ritualism that was growing in influence within the established Church of England— with its stone altars, lighted candles, rood screens, crucifixes, incense, priestly vestments, and mixing of water and wine in the chalice.

Ritualism, he insisted in August 1873, was the 'resurrection of the theology and fashions of the dark ages', and an attempt by Anglo-Catholic clergy to subvert the established Church and reimpose 'the yoke of Rome'. 'When Ritualism, by its seductive arts, has permeated our parishes with its effete superstitions,' he predicted, '... the line dividing Anglicanism and Romanism will be so fine that at no distant date the [Pope] will count the Church of England as among the most faithful children of the Church of Rome.'[45] Ritualist clergy were guilty of the 'deadly sin' of 'identifying Christianity with the most hateful intolerance and parading as the spirit of the Church of Christ the very spirit of those who crucified the Saviour'. The ritualist *Church Herald* was nothing less than the 'organ of Antichrist'.[46] In 1874 Parliament sought to curb ritualist innovations with the controversial Public Worship Regulation Act, but Stead insisted the Act would bring no benefit. For while the Act curbed extreme Anglo-Catholic ritual, it still allowed the bishops to enforce existing High Church forms of worship which Stead viewed as abhorrent.[47]

Stead's *Northern Echo* expressed mixed views on the Education Act of 1870. Stead praised its aim of bringing primary education to all children in England and Wales through the introduction of elected school boards and rate-supported board schools, but he criticized the continued state grants to Anglican schools.[48] That said, he insisted that Nonconformists should not break with the Liberal party over the Act, as some Nonconformists demanded.[49] Stead's *Northern Echo* warmly supported the United Kingdom revival of 1873–5 led by the American evangelists Dwight L. Moody and Ira D. Sankey.[50] The American evangelists, Stead maintained, were free of sectarianism, with a democratic emphasis on the essential equality of all people before God, and a simple gospel message that attracted vast crowds in England, Scotland, Ireland, and Wales. His only regret was that there was so little opposition to their revival movement. In his view, genuine religious faith meant struggle against a world steeped in sin, and 'real lasting good is seldom accomplished so easily, so quietly'.[51] The *Northern Echo* applauded the revived interest in the Protestant overseas mission movement following the death in 1873 of the African missionary-explorer, David Livingstone, and his burial in Westminster Abbey. For Stead, the numerous missionary societies, with branches 'in every English village', their May meetings in Exeter Hall and their religious and humanitarian concern for the welfare of other peoples, elevated the British nation with a higher moral purpose. The missionaries and their supporters at home represented a responsible imperialism, and promoted within the United Kingdom 'the civilising mission with which she seems to be entrusted by the RULER of the world'.[52]

## Josephine Butler and the Contagious Diseases Acts

Along with most Nonconformists, Stead passionately opposed the state's attempts to regulate prostitution through the Contagious Diseases Acts; these Acts, he later observed, formed 'one of those subjects upon which I have always been quite mad'.[53] Parliament had passed the Contagious Diseases Acts in 1864, 1866, and 1869, to combat the alarming spread of venereal disease among soldiers and sailors. The Acts forced suspected prostitutes in a number of British towns to undergo testing and licensing, and if found to be infected, to be incarcerated and required to undergo medical treatment—or, as Stead put it, 'if healthy, she is certified as fit for vice; if diseased, she is locked up in a hospital gaol'.[54] The police were given extensive powers to arrest suspected prostitutes, and the medical tests were highly invasive and humiliating. For their supporters, the Acts were necessary for public health and the effectiveness of the armed forces. For their opponents, the Acts imposed a double standard, subjecting women but not men to forcible testing and mandatory treatment, while their enforcement resulted in injustices, with non-prostitutes, usually working-class women, being taken up, forcibly tested, and licensed as prostitutes. But more distressing, the Acts meant the state licensing and regulation of prostitution, undermining the foundations of social morality.

A National Association for the Repeal of the Contagious Diseases Acts was formed in 1869, gaining strong support from within the Nonconformist Churches. That same year, a Ladies National Association was formed; it was soon led by Josephine Butler, an Anglican clergyman's wife. Beautiful, intelligent, and charismatic, Butler had in 1864 experienced the accidental death of her young daughter, which drove her to seek consolation in compassionate work among poor women, including prostitutes, in Liverpool. Feeling a personal call from God, she proved an effective orator and led a women's campaign against the Acts, including public meetings and demonstrations, and the issuing of tracts and petitions to Parliament. The female campaigners were bitterly denounced for speaking publicly on sexual matters, and gangs of thugs violently attacked their meetings.

Stead admired Butler, viewing her campaign as a struggle for womanhood, purity, and freedom. In this he was influenced by his mother. 'My earliest recollection of the agitation,' he later wrote, 'was that, in 1870, my mother and the mother of my future wife canvassed the women of our village for signatures to a petition for Repeal. It was the first time I had ever seen my mother promote a petition to Parliament... and I remember feeling a horror of great darkness, together with a kind of wondering marvel, at the women's protest against the... abomination.'[55] Butler fought not simply to 'beat back' the manifold evils of the Contagious Diseases Acts, but to testify to divine sovereignty over the world, and 'to help realize the fulfilment of the great prophecy, [that] the kingdoms of this world are to become the kingdoms of our God and of His Christ'. Confronted by these Acts, Butler and her supporters 'were compelled to lay the axe to the root of the whole congeries of doctrines as to the necessity of vice, the impossibility of male chastity, and the creation of woman as a mere vessel... for the brutal instincts of man'.[56]

Stead introduced the theme of the Contagious Diseases Acts into the pages of the *Northern Echo* in late October 1871, with a lurid editorial on prostitution in Manchester, where some 3,000 women supposedly made their livings in the sex trade, some as young as fourteen years of age. Many became dependent on drink; their lives, he insisted, were a 'slow suicide'. An estimated three-quarters of the women, it was said, had once attended Sunday Schools, and yet these daughters and sisters were now 'offered to the lusts of mankind', treated as outcasts 'to be spurned by the world', and consigned to early deaths, while the men who used them, often 'men of wealth and respectability', suffered no loss of social status. 'The existence of a hell has been somewhat disputed of late,' he observed. 'As long as women are sacrificed to the lusts of men, so long will a hell be absolutely indispensable, if divine justice has to be more than a miserable sham.'[57] In using such language, Judith Walkowitz has argued, Stead reflected older melodramatic literary traditions, including fictional stories of innocent lower-class girls seduced or raped by wealthy aristocrats, and of the fallen woman as object of pity and sympathy.[58] He also drew on the older traditions of sin, ruin, and hell in Nonconformist preaching.

Over the following years, Stead provided extensive coverage of the campaign against the Contagious Diseases Acts, which he equated with state-regulated and state-sanctioned prostitution. While the subject was an 'ugly' one, it was the duty of every citizen in the United Kingdom's emerging democracy to recognize and confront social evils. 'In a country like ours, what the State does, we do; and every individual is individually responsible for its actions unless he protest against them.'[59] In an editorial of April 1876, he christened Butler and the campaigners against the Acts the 'New Abolitionists'. The earlier abolitionists, including James Russell Lowell, had revealed the real nature of slavery and fought bravely to end it. The New Abolitionists were struggling to reveal the true extent of sexual abuse and to free prostitutes from a state-regulated 'bondage of hell', which, because prostitutes were stigmatized for life by the state licensing system, meant a 'life-long servitude'.

There was for Stead a vital difference between the Old and New Abolitionists. While black slaves in the American South, Stead maintained, had been held in physical bondage, they had Christian consolations of recompense in the next life. But prostitutes were cast off by churches and Christian society, and many believed (however wrongly) that they would be damned for their sins in the next life. 'Even in the worst days of American slavery,' he wrote, 'a negro could always call his soul his own. It was not absolutely impossible for the slave to be supported and sustained by the sublime consolations which Christianity imparts to the down-trodden and oppressed.' 'But into the prison-house of Prostitution,' he continued, 'gleams no ray of hope athwart the darkness of despair. Its only light is the lurid glare of Hell.' To their immense credit, Butler's New Abolitionists were prepared to descend into the darkness of the brothels, embrace the untouchables and help them regain their humanity: 'Mrs Butler has consecrated her life to the service of those of her own sex from whose touch most women recoil as if it were pollution.'[60] About this time, Stead wrote his first letter to Butler, suggesting her movement needed a work of imaginative literature, like Harriet Beecher Stowe's anti-slavery novel, *Uncle*

*Tom's Cabin*, to bring the human costs of the Contagious Diseases Acts
and state-regulated prostitution vividly before the public.[61]

In his editorials on this theme, Stead was very much the Nonconformist preacher, asserting an uncompromising morality derived from
Scripture and Christian teachings. The Contagious Diseases Acts
were expressions of collective sin, of national apostasy, and threatened
to bring the wrath of God upon a guilty nation. They institutionalized
evil, and there must be no compromise with evil. He reduced the
complexities of the public health measures aimed at curbing venereal
disease to a matter of simple right and wrong. His condemnations of
state-regulated prostitution appealed to many fellow Nonconformists,
who had grown up with stories of the struggle to end the slave trade
and slavery in the British Empire by the acts of 1807 and 1833
respectively, and had witnessed from afar the American Abolitionist
movement and God's 'terrible swift sword' during the American Civil
War. Stead's rage against the Contagious Diseases Acts was genuine,
rooted in his religious faith. The *Northern Echo* played no small part in
the agitation that convinced Parliament to suspend the Contagious
Diseases Acts in 1883 and finally to repeal them in 1886. Stead
would remain on close terms with Josephine Butler for the remainder
of her life.

Stead's editorship was proving successful. The *Northern Echo*'s circulation was steadily increasing and by July 1874 his income had been
raised to £300 a year. Yet, he also felt he was not achieving what he
had been called to do. He had not become the prophet that in 1871 he
had envisaged himself becoming. Preparing the newspaper was
becoming routine. He worried in a private journal entry in July
1874 that he was 'already regarding the daily sermon to 10,000
persons as if it were a literary exercise, the chief point its creditable
performance from a professional point of view. I am less of a prophet
and more of a journalist.' He was, to be sure, producing racy editorials
on a variety of religious and moral subjects; the newspaper's proprietor and financial backers were content. But Stead was dissatisfied and
restless. 'I have a dread,' he confided to his journal in December 1875,
'... that I may sink into a hulk rotting in port instead of being a
God-sent messenger to the age in which I live.'[62] In the spring of 1875,
his mother died, aged only fifty-one, after a short illness, and on
her deathbed, she had told him three things. First, he was not to

'domineer' over his wife, Emma, suggesting that all was not well in his marriage. Second, he was not to 'overtax' his strength. Finally, he was to submit his will 'in *all* things to God', as she thought that his excessive 'nervousness' (or restlessness) resulted in a 'great part from not doing so'. Then in the summer of 1876 he found a cause worthy of Cromwell, Carlyle, or Lowell; it led to what some would view as his greatest achievement.

### Stead and the 'Bulgarian Atrocities'

'The Bulgarian agitation,' Stead later wrote, 'was due to a Divine voice. I felt the clear call of God's voice, "Arouse the nation or be damned". If I did not do *all* I could, I would deserve damnation.'[63] In the summer of 1875, various Christian populations in the Ottoman territories in the Balkans rose in rebellion. They were suffering under the burden of crippling taxes and years of misgovernment, and they were also inspired by nationalism and pan-Slavism. Lord Beaconsfield's Tory government feared the risings would provide an occasion for Russian military intervention in support of the Balkan Christians, their kindred people, sharing their Orthodox faith and Slavic identity. A Russian military victory over Turkey would give Russia control over the Balkans, Constantinople, and the eastern Mediterranean, threatening the Suez Canal and Britain's key Mediterranean route to India. Britain had fought the Crimean War of 1854–6 in order to defend the Ottoman Empire against Russian expansion, and the preservation of the Ottoman Empire remained fundamental to British foreign policy. In the early summer of 1876, Beaconsfield's government sent a fleet of ironclads to the Dardanelles to demonstrate its resolve to support the Ottoman Empire.

The Turks had by now moved to crush the risings. In eastern Rumelia, they used regular troops and local Muslim militias against the Orthodox Christian Bulgarians, and these forces, especially the militias, acted with extreme cruelty—destroying some seventy villages and massacring an estimated 15,000 men, women, and children. There was widespread rape and torture, many victims were burned alive in churches or barns, and survivors often sold into slavery. Early in June, the first reports of the Bulgarian atrocities appeared in British newspapers, and in August, the Irish-American journalist, Januarius

MacGahan, published graphic accounts in the London *Daily News,* including descriptions of the massacre in Batak, where some 5,000 men, women, and children had been tortured and murdered, and where corpses lay unburied and rotting. Much of the British public was sickened, while the British fleet in the Dardanelles poised to support the Ottoman state implied that Britain was complicit in the massacres.

Stead had studied Russian history and culture since working as a clerk for the Newcastle merchant and Russian vice-consul in the 1860s. From 1875, Stead's *Northern Echo* supported the popular risings in the Balkans, portraying them as a liberation movement.[64] As reports of the massacres reached Britain, he seethed with righteous fury against Britain's support for Ottoman control over the Balkans. In April 1876, the *Northern Echo* denounced Beaconsfield's government for propping up the 'loathsome tyranny of the SULTAN' and enabling 'the decrepid Empire to maintain its hold upon the writhing provinces'. The government had implicated the whole British people in the Ottoman Empire's massacres of peoples wishing to be free. 'As we have shared in her crimes... upon our heads will be visited the retribution for our sins.'[65] In the summer of 1876, as more reports of the Bulgarian massacres reached Britain, the subject became increasingly visceral for him. Along with many Nonconformists, what most distressed him were the reports of gang rapes of Bulgarian women and girls.[66] His personal friend, the Rev Benjamin Waugh, thought Stead was tormented by a vision of the rape and murder of Bulgarian women 'in the form of his own mother, with long hair like hers, and feelings, and fountains of tears'.[67] 'It was like a Divine possession,' Stead later wrote, 'that shook me almost to pieces, wrung me and left me shuddering and weak in an agony of tears.'[68] 'A war of extermination is being carried on against the Christians in Bulgaria,' thundered the *Northern Echo* on 24 June, resolutely recounting the 'sickening' accounts of women burned alive and children butchered.[69] For Stead, the Slavic Christians were struggling to gain their freedom, both political and religious, and the British people had a sacred duty to support their struggle. He insisted that Conservative politicians and the London elite supported the British alliance with Ottoman despotism in the Balkans from their narrow conceptions of British self-interest. But he believed that ordinary people, especially in the provincial north, had higher notions of freedom, religion, and morality. For them, the horrors in the Balkans recalled memories of England's popular struggle for political and religious freedom in the seventeenth century. 'We believe,' he wrote on 13 July 1876, 'that the cause for which CROMWELL fought and HAMPDEN died is worthy of the sympathies, the prayers, and the assistance of every one worthy of the name of man.' However strange it might seem to the Conservative London elite, 'we in the North here esteem the liberties of men and the honour of women to be worth fighting for, and hence we regard with unfeigned sympathy the efforts which the Christians of the East are making to win the one and protect the other.' During the American war to end slavery, it had been the 'honest hearts of England's working people' that 'remained true to the good cause'.[70] His commitment to the Bulgarian agitation, Stead later wrote, was profoundly influenced by the example of the Abolitionists and the American Civil War, especially the Abolitionist poet, James Russell Lowell. 'For slaves read Slavs,' he observed, 'and the fiery appeals of the American abolitionist fit to a nicety the mood of the champions of Bulgarian independence.' 'For me at least, Lowell supplied the psalms of the Crusade of 1876–8.'[71]

Stead revered William Ewart Gladstone as a man of faith and principle, and had regretted his retirement from the Liberal Party leadership in 1875. When Gladstone denounced the government's Eastern policy in the House of Commons on 31 July 1876, Stead welcomed the intervention from 'the custodian of the English conscience' and the 'incarnation of duty'.[72] The agitation against the Bulgarian atrocities was now gaining some influential Christian support. Nonconformists, especially Congregationalists, were most active in the protests.[73] But High Church and Anglo-Catholic clerics within the Church of England also became prominent, among them Henry Parry Liddon, canon of St Paul's Cathedral and professor of exegesis at Oxford University, Malcolm MacColl, a London parish priest, and R. W. Church, dean of St. Paul's Cathedral. High Church and Anglo-Catholic clerics had long been attracted to the liturgy and theology of the Orthodox Church, and now felt a special sympathy for endangered Orthodox Christians in the Balkans. Nonconformists and Anglo-Catholics drew together in protesting the atrocities, in what the primate of the Church of England, Archbishop A. C. Tait (no friend to the protestors), called an 'unholy alliance'.[74] Stead, whose *Northern Echo* had for years denounced the established Church of England and Anglo-Catholic ritualists, now reconsidered his views; on 28 August 1876, for example, he praised the 'fearless intrepidity' of the High Church Liddon in speaking out against the massacres.[75]

From late August 1876, Stead helped organize and publicize a series of public protest meetings across the northeast of England, to rouse popular opinion over the Bulgarian atrocities and to oppose any government moves to draw Britain into war against Russia in support of the Ottoman Empire. The first was held on 25 August 1876 in Darlington; at this meeting the Quaker Pease family, financial backers of the *Northern Echo*, played a prominent role. The meeting, according to Stead, was 'crowded, indignant and unanimous'. The next day, Stead sent his report of the meeting to Gladstone, assuring him that 'more than one speaker ventured to express a hope that you may yet consent to resume office in order to complete the work of the Crimean War, by the emancipation of the Christians from the Turkish yoke'.[76] During the coming month, the *Northern Echo* reported on forty-seven protest meetings held in the northeast.[77] Stead wrote dozens of letters each day, 'appealing, exhorting, entreating', and took the leading role in 'rousing the North'.[78] Many had wept over MacGahan's reports of the Batak massacres, and now welcomed the chance to voice their outrage. Although frequently organized on short notice by a few local individuals, the protest meetings often attracted large attendances. For Stead, the meetings were democratic declarations, showing the essential decency of the British people. They formed 'the first agitation in the long annals of England in which the Democracy sprang to its feet by an instantaneous impulse without waiting for the guidance of its leaders.' 'If ever,' he added, 'there was a case in which the old adage held true, *Vox populi, vox Dei*, this was the time.'[79]

Gladstone was troubled in conscience by the massacres and pro-foundly moved by the popular protest movement. According to his biographer, Colin Matthew, sometime between July and the begin-ning of September, 'Gladstone experienced a conversion of evangel-ical intensity.'[80] This culminated, on 5 September 1876, in the white heat of his impassioned pamphlet, *The Bulgarian Horrors and the Question of the East*, with its outrage over both the atrocities in the Balkans and Britain's complicity in the crimes. The Ottoman Empire, he insisted, had forfeited any moral claim to govern its European provinces and must now be forced to leave those provinces. It was 'the only reparation we can make to the memory of those heaps on heaps of dead; to the violated purity alike of matron, of maiden, and of child'.[81] The pamphlet sold some 200,000 copies by the end of September, further inflaming the protest movement. Stead wrote Gladstone to express gratitude. 'You have justified and more than justified the unshaken devotion which the north has placed in your leadership. You have once more taken your proper place as the spokesman of the national conscience.' His only criticism was that Gladstone had not appealed for concerted action by the Churches. 'Can you not also show,' he asked, 'that England's Christianity as organized in the churches is as real as it was in the days of the [Cromwellian] Commonwealth?'[82]

On 9 September, a mass outdoor protest meeting was held on Blackheath Common, in Gladstone's London parliamentary constituency of Greenwich. Despite torrential rain, an estimated 10,000 people heard Gladstone denounce the atrocities and the government's Eastern policy. It had the feel of a religious revival meeting. Stead travelled by train to London for the meeting; it was the first time he heard Gladstone speak. For him, Gladstone's words of condemnation seemed to come from the very heavens. 'There was,' Stead later recalled, 'a rhythm almost of a chant in the way in which Mr. Gladstone pronounced those solemn words that carried awe into every heart. It was as if the High Priest of humanity were pronouncing the doom which was impending over the guilty Empire.' Of Gladstone's address on Blackheath Common, Stead recalled thirty years later that 'I have seen no finer, more inspiring spectacle in my time.'[83]

The protest meetings continued through the autumn of 1876, sending 455 memorials or petitions of protest to the government. Nonconformists continued to play the predominant part in the movement, and Stead's *Northern Echo* vigorously promoted the protest meetings. In September, Stead tried to arrange a 'Bulgarian Sunday', which would follow the example of the Cromwellian Commonwealth, when in 1655 special services were held in all the English Churches to anathematize the massacres of the Waldensians in Piedmont. Stead called for a Sunday to be set apart by the nation for special services, prayers of intercessions, and collections on behalf of the 'sufferers in

Bulgaria'. 'The Churches of the [Cromwellian] Commonwealth,' he wrote in the *Northern Echo* of 14 September, 'were found capable of giving adequate expression to the generous enthusiasm of the nation. Are the Churches of to-day less able to give vent to the emotions which throb in the national heart?' For, he insisted, 'never before in the course of this century has the heart of the nation been so deeply stirred.'[84] Although his proposal received some influential support, and many individual churches held special collections, Stead's call for a national 'Bulgarian Sunday' was unsuccessful.[85] The agitation of 1876 culminated on 8 December with a large demonstration in St James Hall, London, with Gladstone the principal speaker. While Stead thought Gladstone's speech lacked the tone of 'outraged conscience' that had been so pronounced at Blackheath, he was impressed by Gladstone's quiet resolve that dominion in the Balkans 'should be taken out of the hands of the Turk'.[86] Stead believed himself to have been the major influence in drawing Gladstone into the cause, and that in doing so he had been God's instrument. 'I am inclined to attribute,' he noted in his private journal on 14 January 1877, 'some of Mr. Gladstone's evident desire to please me to his consciousness that I was the first to sound in his ears the summons which God had already spoken to his soul.'[87]

Stead was by now arguing in the *Northern Echo* that Britain must not only cease its long-standing policy of supporting the Ottoman Empire, but must go further, reverse decades of official policy, and ally itself with Russia to liberate the Balkan Christian peoples by military force if necessary. He applauded the Russian volunteers who were rushing to fight alongside the Slavic Christians in the Balkans. Then, in April 1877, the situation changed dramatically when Russia declared war on the Ottoman Empire, invading the Ottoman Balkans with regular troops. The British public mood quickly shifted from outrage over Bulgarian atrocities to fear of Russian conquest of the Balkans and Constantinople. Many demanded war against Russia in support of the Ottoman Empire, as in the Crimean War. Some were enthusiastic for war, and a popular pro-war music hall song added a new word to the language, 'jingoism'. Tories denounced sentimental concerns over suffering Bulgarians and called for military action to defend Britain's interests in the Eastern Mediterranean. Tory newspapers argued that Russian occupation of the Balkans would simply mean more atrocities, only now perpetuated by Russian soldiers and Serbian or Bulgarian nationalists against Muslim civilians.[88]

Stead's *Northern Echo* continued calling for a British alliance with Russia against the Ottoman Empire, but with the rising anti-Russian jingo fervour, he was becoming isolated. As calls for war against Russia grew louder, and a populist nationalism in Britain was inflamed, Stead became hated in many quarters. He feared that he might be killed by a jingo mob, but remained resolute. 'I saw myself,' he noted in his journal in early 1877, 'mobbed, murdered, and I thought, all this may be, nay probably will be if you determine to resist the war passion with whole-souled energy. And then I thought the welfare of untold generations depends on this. Millions of fellow creatures may be saved if you do your duty.' But despite the fears, these were heady days for Stead; he had never felt so alive. His daily editorials were being read across the country, and he was corresponding with leading politicians and public intellectuals. 'I was only twenty-seven,' he wrote in 1892, 'and it was the first occasion I had ever been at the centre of things.'[89]

### Madame Olga Novikoff

In mid-September 1877, Stead heard from a wealthy, enigmatic, well-connected, London-based Russian, Madame Novikoff. She had been reading his *Northern Echo* editorials, and was impressed with this English journalist who wrote as though he were Russian. She invited him to her salon at Symonds' Hotel, Brook Street, London (she would later move to Claridge's), where she regularly entertained influential British politicians, authors, and artists. Olga Novikoff, née Olga Kirieff, had been born in 1840 in Moscow, one of five children of a Russian landowner and decorated army officer. She was a god-daughter of the Tsar, had been taught English from an early age, and in 1860 had married Ivan Novikoff, an army officer who was twenty years her senior, with whom she had one son, born in 1862. She had become involved in Slavophile circles in Moscow and St Petersburg, passionately embracing the cause of the unity of the Slavic peoples, including those of the Balkans, under Russian leadership. She had visited England in 1868 and 1873, developing friendships with Gladstone and other public figures. In July 1876, her younger brother,

Nicolas Kirieff, was among the first Russian volunteers killed in the Balkans, shot while leading an attack by Serb militia. Devastated by her brother's death, she returned to England in the autumn of 1876, taking rooms at Symonds' Hotel, and using her influence to defend Russian policies and oppose British military action in support of the Ottoman Empire. For some, she was an attractive, intelligent, cultivated, charming, forthright, and impassioned Russian patriot. For others, she was pushy, vulgar, had 'the manners of a second-rate adventuress', and was probably a paid Russian agent, using her charms with British politicians to gain influence and information.[90]

On receiving her letter in September, Stead, who was unacquainted with London society, made inquiries. He 'heard her darkly alluded to as a kind of Russian Loreley who lured English statesmen to their destruction by the fascination of her song'.[91] Yet he was also moved by the stirring account of her brother's death in Serbia written by the eminent English historian of the Crimean War, Alexander Kinglake.[92] On 10 October 1877, Stead wrote to thank her for her letter, reaffirm his support for Russia's Balkan policy, and convey his condolences for the loss of her brother, the 'sainted Kirieff'. As for visiting her in London, he confessed that he was unacquainted 'with ladies' salons' and tended to shrink from society, but if she was ever in the north, he hoped she might visit his home: 'I feel sure that Nicolas Kirieff's sister will not despise the hearty homage which I venture to pay to her as the representative of the chivalrous love of those who have . . . yielded up their lives in order that the oppressed might be freed.'[93] She responded by thanking him for mourning her brother—'the most generous, chivalrous creature that ever lived'—and telling him that her widowed sister-in-law was now serving as a sister of charity with the Russian army.[94]

They continued to correspond. She told him she had subscribed to the *Northern Echo* when living in Russia, and she sent him her photograph, which Stead assured her on 15 October 'proves to me that my correspondent is as fair as she is noble, & that her features are worthy of the sympathies of her heart'. Stead told her of how he dreamed of an alliance of the British and Russian peoples, and revered the sacrifices being made by Russian soldiers for the liberation of the Balkan peoples. 'My hopes & prayers could not be more fervent for the success of the Russian armies if instead of being Russian they were

English . . . To what horrible fate have so many thousands gone forth.'
'But as you say,' he added, 'all great causes demand great sacrifices &
the progress of our race is over the graves of heroes.'[95] On 19 October,
in 'the longest letter I have written since the days when I wrote
love letters to my betrothed', he described his home and manner of
living, and conveyed his insecurities about his social status. 'You will
understand,' he confided, 'that though Dukes & such like creatures,
read what I write & sometimes write to me . . . they do not mix
with such humble people as newspaper editors'—especially the mere
'editor of a halfpenny paper in the North of England'.[96]

Stead found corresponding with this mysterious, aristocratic
Russian woman exciting. 'Your letters,' he confessed on 18 October
1877, 'add a new charm to my existence.'[97] But it was more than that.
He had been under immense personal pressure for over a year,
conducting a highly emotive, demanding popular campaign for a
new, pro-Russian Eastern policy that he fully believed would save
tens of thousands of lives. He was exhausted, stressed, and often
unable to sleep. He knew that, while many had supported his condemnation of the Bulgarian massacres, relatively few supported his
calls for an alliance with Russia to end Ottoman rule in the Balkans.
On the contrary, his support for Russia in the war was highly unpopular in many quarters. He could not confide in his wife, for 'nearly all
my wife's relations are Turkophil' and his views had resulted in
'painful' family tensions.[98] But in Madame Novikoff he found a
woman, a Russian aristocrat with a sensitive soul, who shared his
feelings, who had suffered the heroic sacrifice of her brother, who
admired and respected Stead, and who assured him that his lonely
struggles were not in vain. He confided his inner thoughts to her,
seeking not only comfort, but also reassurance that his protest movement of the past year had a higher purpose. His feelings for her, or
rather for his idealized vision of her, were growing strong (they had
still not met), and their correspondence grew more intimate.

She told him of how her brother's death had enhanced her Russian
Orthodox religious beliefs, giving her a more serious perspective on
life and recalling her to a 'conscientiousness of the eternal reality'. He
responded on 22 October with a long letter, marked 'private', in
which he poured out his own personal confession of faith. He was
touched that she should bring religion into their correspondence. 'It is

only in such generous confidences that there is real communion of
souls, & you are kind indeed in permitting me as it were to worship by
your side in the inner sanctuary of your faith.' He confided that in
matters of faith he was not concerned with theological doctrine or
outward expressions of piety. For him, true religion involved compassion for others, and a willingness to sacrifice for their welfare. Compassionate sacrifice had been the essential teaching of Christ, and it
was to compassionate sacrifice that Christ called his followers. As
Christ's sacrifice on the Cross had transformed the world, so the
Christ-like sacrifices of those like her brother continued to elevate
humanity. 'Your brother's death,' he told her, 'vividly brought back to
my memory the sublime story of Calvary, and your letter speaking of
the "great change" produced in you by the terrible event in Servia
confirmed me in impression that Christ was speaking to us through the
heroic Christlike death of Nicolas Kirieff.' 'In all the acts of heroism,
in all the works of self-sacrifice, in all the holy, self-denying lives lived
on earth I see the reflected rays of the holiness of Christ, & ... the
working of the same Almighty spirit which called a world sunk in
corruption & sin around the stainless life of the Divine hero who came
to earth to live and to die to save us from our sins.' He proceeded to
share his belief in a triune God of compassionate sacrifice. 'I believe,
do you not,' he wrote:

> in God the Father of all beings in this wide world, loving us with a
> yearning love greater than that of a mother for a child, chastening us
> only as affection, & leading each of us some place higher & higher—on
> which Mazzini called the infinite ascending spiral by which mortals
> reach the skies. I believe, do you not, in God the Son, Jesus Christ, the
> Crucified, in whose stainless life, and bitter death, we see personified
> the purity, and the comparison of God the Eternal. In God the Holy
> Ghost, whose sacred influence touched your heart with the story of
> Nicolas's sacrifice as it did on the day of Pentecost's those of apostles
> with the story of the death of the just one for us the unjust.

Christ continued to call us, Stead insisted, to sacrifice our selfish interests
for others. In his own struggle against Bulgarian atrocities, and now for
Balkan liberation, he was sure he was following Christ. 'In embracing
the cause of the oppressed Slavs of Eastern Europe, we accept Christ
anew'—not because the Slavs were Christian and the Turks were

Muslims, but because the Slavs were an oppressed people, struggling for their freedom, and supporting them, for Stead, meant placing principle above national self-interest. And because 'every time we yield to temptation to live for self instead of for others, we reject Christ.'[99]

In late October 1877, he travelled to London to meet Olga Novikoff, and was captivated. She was nine years his senior, very attractive, well travelled, experienced with the world, confident in society, with a warm sense of humour, and full of passionate conviction. She had a 'presence' and a beautiful singing voice, 'full of fire and fervour'. And she seemed to know everyone. At her salon at Symonds' Hotel, she introduced him into London's literary and political society, and he now personally met eminent national figures he had known only in writing or seen from afar. 'It was there,' Stead later recalled, 'that I first met Mr. Gladstone, Mr. Kinglake, Mr. Froude, Mr. Stansfeld, Mr. Courtney, Count Beust, Mr. Matthew Arnold, and a host of other notables.' Then she offered one day to take him to meet Thomas Carlyle. 'Had she proposed to dine with the Apostle Paul,' he wrote, 'I could hardly have been more startled. Carlyle, from my earliest boyhood, had been as one of the greater gods in a shadowy Olympus. To call upon him as if he were an actual mortal seemed like a chapter out of fairyland.' Such was Novikoff's magic that a half hour later they were in Carlyle's home in Chelsea, discussing the Russian situation. Stead was impressed with how warmly Carlyle spoke of Madame Novikoff, with whom he regularly took carriage drives.[100] Stead visited Carlyle again at his home, and once he took Madame Novikoff's place on a carriage drive in Regent's Park. Sadness clouded those meetings, for Stead's childhood hero was now unwell and unhappy. 'There is no more work for me to do,' he told Stead on their last meeting in the carriage, 'I cannot write.' There was nothing left, Carlyle said, but to wait 'to meet the Eternal'.[101] Stead's first meeting with Gladstone at Novikoff's salon was more satisfying— with the great man relaxing in an 'easy-chair' and saying how much he admired the *Northern Echo* and how important Stead's protest movement in the north of England had been to the Liberal cause.[102] 'It was a great new world to me,' Stead would recall, 'to see the men whom I had been reading and writing about all my life face to face.' 'Still more important,' he added, 'was it to meet Mr. Gladstone ... and to come for the first time behind the scenes of English ... political life.'[103]

Stead also became acquainted with Novikoff's 'dear friend', Canon Henry Parry Liddon of St Paul's Cathedral, first meeting him in July 1878 in Oban, in the Scottish Highlands, where they were both on holiday. Their common friendship with Novikoff induced a long conversation which included their mutual antipathy to Beaconsfield's Tory policies, and their admiration for the Russian soldiers fighting to liberate the Balkan Christians. When Liddon invited Stead to visit him in London, Stead unthinkingly blurted out (as he told Olga) that 'I never go to London except to see Madame Novikoff!!!'[104] He and Liddon became close friends. Through Liddon, Stead developed a friendship with R. W. Church, the High Church dean of St Paul's. The dean and his wife invited Stead to be their personal guest at St Paul's for the consecration of J. B. Lightfoot as bishop of Durham on 25 April 1879; he took tea in the Deanery and sat in the dean's pew. Stead was charmed by these intelligent and cultivated High Church Anglicans who shared his Russophile sentiments. His Nonconformist zeal for disestablishment and his opposition to High Anglican doctrine and liturgy, which had been so central to his family's identity, now softened.

With Stead's assistance, Novikoff began publishing letters 'From a Russian Correspondent' in the *Northern Echo*, promoting Anglo-Russian understanding and the Russian cause in the war. She signed these 'OK' (for Olga Kirieff) and the first letter appeared on 19 November 1877. Her *Northern Echo* letters were published under the title, *Is Russia Wrong?* in 1878, with a preface by James Anthony Froude. Stead read to her James Russell Lowell's poetry, still so precious to him; they were both impressed with the parallels between the American Civil War to free the slaves and the Russian war to free the Balkans Slavs, and 'we both marvelled to find how exactly the circumstances of the war in the West were reproduced in the East.'[105] Stead travelled to London to be with her as often as possible. She sent his pro-Russian *Northern Echo* articles to her Slavophile circle in Russia, to be translated and published in Russian newspapers, establishing for him a reputation as an English friend of Russia. He told her what he learned as a journalist about the attitudes of British politicians towards the war. They formed a close partnership, focused on the liberation of the Balkans from Ottoman control through a future Anglo-Russian alliance. They were in many respects, Stead acknowledged, 'poles apart': 'She is Greek Orthodox, of noble family, and an autocrat by conviction. I am an English Nonconformist, born of the common people, and a Radical alike by temperament and conviction.'[106] She was also anti-Semitic, and he insisted he was not.

At some point in late 1877 or early 1878, they became lovers. He wrote to her as a guilty lover on 25 January 1878, begging her for reassurance of her love for him, agonizing over his treatment of his wife, and hoping that amid his conflicting feelings for her and for his family 'I shall not go insane.'[107] But he could hardly stay away from her, and the affair continued through most of 1878. His wife, Emma, became aware of the affair, and in October 1878 returned to her mother's home with the children. Stead now had to choose between his family and his lover. He wrote to Novikoff on 28 October, explaining the situation and saying he must end their love affair, though not, he hoped, their friendship. Clearly in agony, he begged her to write to him once more as his lover. Open up to him, he pleaded, 'for one last time your whole soul & your whole heart to me, tell me truly faithfully as the dearest friend I have on earth all that you wish to say. Never fear if it grieves me. Never mind the humiliation will do me good. Tell me where you see me inconsistent, mean, un-Christian, & weak. Warn me, be a better angel to me.' The end of the affair was torture for him; he felt his 'soul is tossed indeed with foaming waves'. A friendship he wanted to be noble, disinterested, and elevated, strengthening them both in shared sacrifice for the Balkan peoples, had resulted in selfishness and pain. 'I did hope once,' he assured her, 'to supply to some little extent the irreparable loss of your sainted brother. I fear I have failed, even my poor little prayer seemed blasphemy.' 'But dearest write to me for once without reserve, even if it were for the last time. Give me some assurances which I can cherish for the rest of my life, that I have not been a temptation & a curse to you.'[108]

His wife returned to him with the children, but his private journal entry of 5 January 1879 showed that his marriage was in danger. His wife was depressed and deeply unhappy, and he knew he had 'treated her cruelly'. The countryside home, which he had once seen as so idyllic, was now sombre and dark; 'it is almost as frightful,' he opined, 'to see a wrecked home as to look at a lost soul.' There were times 'when death, but for the poor children, seemed the only solution'.

He reflected on how, in Olga Novikoff, he had met 'another soul as surcharged with kindred thoughts' and how their 'existences mingled'. 'How large a place she has occupied in my life,' he wrote of her. 'How my life has broadened, my views widened, and intensified. What friends have I not made. What work have I not done.' 'But I do not wish,' he confessed, that 'I had married O.K.'[109] A year later, in January 1880, his home was still unhappy, but his agony over the end of the affair was easing. He tried to revive family worship at home with Emma and the children but it was, he confessed, a 'sad failure'. He remained friends with Olga, and continued to correspond with her about the cause of Anglo-Russian friendship. 'I am still deeply attached to her and would still do anything for her,' he confided to his journal, 'but I no longer love her with that sinful passion the memory of which covers me with loathing, remorse and humiliation . . . I love her intensely, but no longer as a second wife.'[110]

He knew he needed a change in his life. His wife wanted to leave the house at Grainey Hill where she felt isolated and depressed. He missed his frequent trips to London and being at the centre of national political life, and sometime before January 1880 he had a 'premonition' that he would be called to edit a major London newspaper. He was, in many senses, no longer the Nonconformist Radical he had been in 1871, and this was a reason for moving on from the *Northern Echo*. The campaign against the Bulgarian atrocities, in which he had played so prominent a role, had closed. The war between Russia and the Ottoman Empire had ended in 1878, and the great powers had met that year in Berlin at the invitation of Germany's chancellor, Otto von Bismarck. The Congress of Berlin had redrawn the map of the Balkans, loosening Ottoman control over its Balkan territories, but failing to placate Russia or the Balkan nationalists. Bulgaria had not won its independence, but neither had there been war between Britain and Russia. In 1879–80, the Liberal Party was reinvigorated by Gladstone's Midlothian campaign, demanding a more ethical foreign and imperial policy.

The general election of April 1880 gave the Liberal Party an overwhelming majority in the House of Commons, with Stead's *Northern Echo* contributing in no small way to the Liberal victory in the north of England. Gladstone, brought back as Liberal leader, formed a government. It seemed the birth of a new, more ethical political order, and Stead was elated. 'I will not attempt to express,' Stead wrote to Gladstone on 9 April 1880, '... my sense of our indebtedness to you for the brave part which you have played in the great revolt of the national conscience which began in 1876, and is now being crowned with such complete success.'[111] 'The explosion of popular sentiment which has destroyed Lord BEACONSFIELD'S majority,' thundered his *Northern Echo* editorial of 13 April 1880, 'was the protest of the national conscience against a policy which ignored the elementary principles of morality—to say nothing of the essential spirit of Christianity.' He was recovering his faith in Britain as a Christian state. 'Above all,' he added of the Liberal triumph, 'it proves that our national profession of Christianity is not a hollow farce and a ghastly sham.'[112]

In July 1880, Stead was invited, probably on Gladstone's recommendation, to become assistant editor to John Morley, the newly appointed editor of the *Pall Mall Gazette*, a London evening newspaper. Formerly a Conservative paper, the *Pall Mall* was taken over after the general election of 1880 by a Gladstonian Liberal proprietor, Henry Yates Thompson, who appointed Morley as editor and then was in touch with Stead. Interestingly, Stead sought advice on whether to accept from his two High Anglican friends, Canons Liddon and Church of St Paul's cathedral, and they both recommended that he come to London.[113] After negotiations, Stead accepted the appointment, at a salary of £800 a year, beginning in October 1880.

During his years at the *Northern Echo* he had matured as a journalist, developing an energetic, forthright, highly personal style. He had created a form of participatory journalism, calling on his readers, especially during the Bulgarian atrocities campaign, to attend public meetings and participate in political action. He made his editor's chair a pulpit, and his readers a congregation. He insisted that it was not enough for readers to read righteous editorials; they had to go forth into the world to act righteously. The Bulgarian atrocities campaign of 1876 made him a national figure, and his relationship with Olga Novikoff in 1877–8 introduced him to leading public figures in London and gave him international contacts in Russia. While he continued to portray himself as a Nonconformist Radical and heir to the Puritans, he was no longer so close to his Nonconformist roots. His friendships with the High Anglicans Liddon and Church softened his views on disestablishment and Anglican liturgy. He retained an

intense Christian faith, but was less concerned about doctrinal differences and more about Christianity as a call to sacrifice and service. He
was in many respects a chastened figure. His love for Novikoff had
expanded his horizons, but at the cost of great pain to his wife and to
himself; he knew he had done wrong to enter into the affair, and he
ended it. It is not clear how Novikoff viewed matters or Stead's
behaviour. She accepted the end of their affair, and they remained
friends for life and continued their political co-operation. Stead was
now thirty-one years of age, and with little formal education but with
valuable journalistic experience and an abiding sense of divine calling,
he was now second in command of an evening newspaper in the
capital city of the largest empire in the world.

## Notes

1. W. T. Stead, *The Revival of 1905* (London, 1905), p. 4.
2. W. T. Stead, 'My Father', *Jarrow Guardian* (29 February 1884).
3. Estelle W. Stead, *My Father* (London, 1913), pp. 4–6.
4. J. W. Robertson Scott, *The Life and Death of a Newspaper* (London, 1952),
   p. 92.
5. John S. Stevenson, *The Reverend William Stead and his Family: An Eulogy*
   (Newcastle-upon-Tyne, 1987), pp. 5–8.
6. Frederic Whyte, *Life of W. T. Stead*, 2 vols. (London, 1925), vol. ii, pp. 247,
   249–50.
7. Stead, *The Revival of 1905*, pp. 4–5; Stead, *My Father*, p. 18.
8. Stead, *The Review of 1905*, p. 10.
9. Stead, *My Father*, p. 24.
10. Whyte, *Life of W. T. Stead*, vol. i, p. 18.
11. W. T. Stead, 'Oliver Cromwell and the National Church', *RoR* (May
    1899), p. 425.
12. Stead, *My Father*, pp. 32–3.
13. 'A Biography of Oliver Cromwell', *The Boy's Own Magazine* 55 (1 July
    1867), p. 4.
14. W. T. Stead, 'James Russell Lowell: His Message and How It Helped
    Me', *RoR* (September 1891), pp. 236, 123.
15. Ibid., p. 235.
16. Ibid., p. 238.
17. Ibid., p. 240; W. T. Stead, *The Story that Transformed the World or the Passion
    Play at Oberammergau 1890* (London, [1891]), p. 158.

18. Stead, 'James Russell Lowell: His Message and How It Helped Me', p. 240.
19. James Russell Lowell, *The Biglow Papers* (London, 1865), pp. 94, 95.
20. W. T. Stead, 'Character Sketch: Sir T. Vezey Strong', *RoR* (December 1910), p. 547.
21. Mary Stead to W. T. Stead, August 1885, cited in Whyte, *Life of W. T. Stead*, vol. i, p. 176.
22. The political and social background to the founding of the newspaper is related in Owen Mulpetre, 'W. T. Stead and the New Journalism' (University of Teeside MPhil thesis, 2010), pp. 40–54.
23. W. T. Stead, 'A North Country Worthy', *RoR* (July 1894), pp. 85–8; Whyte, *Life of W. T. Stead*, vol. i, p. 22.
24. J. Hyslop Bell, 'Northern Echo Prospectus', W. T. Stead Resource Site https://attackingthedevil.co.uk (accessed 28 September 2017).
25. Whyte, *Life of W. T. Stead*, vol. i, p. 27; Joseph O. Baylen, 'The "New Journalism" in Late Victorian Britain', *Australian Journal of Politics and History*, 18 (1972), p. 368.
26. Robertson Scott, *Life and Death of a Newspaper*, p. 94; [W. T. Stead], 'Democracy and Christianity', *Northern Echo* (14 October 1870).
27. Mulpetre, 'W. T. Stead and the New Journalism', pp. 59–65.
28. Quoted in Baylen, 'The "New Journalism" in Late Victorian Britain', pp. 368–9.
29. W. Sydney Robinson, *Muckraker: The Scandalous Life and Times of W. T. Stead* (London, 2013), p. 18.
30. T. Wemyss Reid, *Memoirs of Sir Wemyss Reid 1842–1885*, ed. Stuart J. Reid (London, 1905), pp. 307–10, quotations on p. 309.
31. Robertson Scott, *Life and Death of a Newspaper*, p. 93.
32. Ibid., p. 92.
33. Stead, *My Father*, p. 24.
34. David Bebbington, *The Nonconformist Conscience: Chapel and Politics 1870–1914* (London, 1982), p. 12.
35. Irene Macleod, 'A Real Ghost: Verifying the Sighting of James Durham of Darlington', *News-Stead*, 20 (Spring 2002), pp. 18–19.
36. W. T. Stead to Olga Novikoff, 19 October 1877, Novikoff–Stead Corr., fos. 10–13.
37. W. T. Stead, 'My Son', *RoR* (January 1908), p. 24.
38. Robertson Scott, *Life and Death of a Newspaper*, pp. 100, 103; Mulpetre, 'W. T. Stead and the New Journalism', p. 68.
39. Baylen, 'The "New Journalism" in Late Victorian Britain', p. 370.
40. 'Religious Revival', *NE* (18 October 1873).

38 *W. T. Stead*

41. Simon Goldsworthy, 'English Nonconformity and the Pioneering of the Modern Newspaper Campaign', *Journalism Studies*, 7 (2006), p. 391.
42. 'The Work of Disestablishment', *NE* (5 January 1870); 'Disestablishment', *NE* (19 November 1870).
43. Robertson Scott, *The Life and Death of a Newspaper*, p. 109.
44. 'The Curse of the Church', *NE* (6 April 1874).
45. 'The Appeal to Protestants', *NE* (30 August 1873).
46. 'Sacerdotal Insolence', *NE* (16 April 1874).
47. 'The Regulation of Public Worship', *NE* (11 July 1874).
48. 'The Anti-Forster Ferment', *NE* (24 June 1873).
49. 'The Fallen Ministry', *NE* (14 March 1873); 'The Nonconformists and the Liberal Party', *NE* (1 September 1873).
50. 'Messrs. Moody and Sankey in Darlington', *NE* (18 October 1873); 'The American Revivalists', *NE* (27 October 1873); 'Moody and Sankey in London', *NE* (11 March 1875).
51. 'The Primate on Moody and Sankey', *NE* (23 May 1875).
52. 'The Missionary Meetings', *NE* (1 May 1874).
53. Robertson Scott, *Life and Death of a Newspaper*, p. 96.
54. W. T. Stead, *Josephine Butler: A Life Sketch* (London, [1887]), p. 24.
55. Ibid., p. 42.
56. Ibid., pp. 34, 36.
57. 'Bishop Frazer on the Social Evil', *NE* (27 October 1871).
58. Judith R. Walkowitz, *City of Dreadful Delight: Narratives of Sexual Danger in Late-Victorian London* (London, 1992), pp. 85–7.
59. 'An Ugly Prospect', *NE* (22 May 1873).
60. 'The New Abolitionists', *NE* (3 April 1876).
61. Stead, *Josephine Butler*, pp. 85–6; Whyte, *Life of W. T. Stead*, vol. i, pp. 41–2.
62. Private journal entry of 26 December 1875, 5 July 1874, cited in Robertson Scott, *Life and Death of a Newspaper*, pp. 103–4, 100–1.
63. Private journal entry of 14 January 1877, cited in Robertson Scott, *Life and Death of a Newspaper*, p. 104.
64. W. T. Stead, *The M.P. for Russia: Reminiscences and Correspondence of Madame Olga Novikoff*, 2 vols. (London, 1909), vol. i, pp. 380–1; Whyte, *Life of W. T. Stead*, vol. i, p. 44.
65. 'The Doomed Empire', *NE* (17 April 1876).
66. Bebbington, *The Nonconformist Conscience*, p. 115.
67. Benjamin Waugh, *William T. Stead: A Life for the People* (London, [1885]), p. 18.
68. Private journal entry of 14 January 1877, cited in Robertson Scott, *Life and Death of a Newspaper*, p. 104.
69. 'Our Policy in the East', *NE* (24 June 1876).

70. 'England and the Eastern Insurgents', *NE* (13 July 1876).

71. Stead, 'James Russell Lowell', p. 243.

72. 'England's Duty in the East', *NE* (3 August 1876).

73. R. T. Shannon, *Gladstone and the Bulgarian Agitation*, 2nd edn. (Hassocks, 1975), p. 166.

74. Ibid., pp. 83–5, 179; A. J. P. Taylor, *The Trouble Makers: Dissent over Foreign Policy 1792–1939*, 2nd edn. (London, 1993), p. 78.

75. 'The Duty of the Hour', *NE* (28 August 1876).

76. 'The North Country and the Atrocities', *NE* (26 August 1876); W. T. Stead to W. E. Gladstone, 26 August 1876, BL, Gladstone Papers, Add. Mss. 44303, fos. 230–1.

77. Shannon, *Gladstone and the Bulgarian Agitation*, p. 73.

78. Private journal entry of 14 January 1877, cited in Robertson Scott, *Life and Death of a Newspaper*, p. 104.

79. Stead, *The M.P. for Russia*, vol. i, p. 247.

80. H. C. G. Matthew, *Gladstone 1809–1898* (Oxford, 1997), p. 282.

81. W. E. Gladstone, *Bulgarian Horrors and the Question of the East* (London, 1876), p. 31.

82. W. T. Stead to W. E. Gladstone, 6 September 1876, BL, Gladstone Papers, Add. Mss. 44303, fos. 233–4.

83. Stead, *My Father*, p. 71.

84. 'A Bulgarian Sunday', *NE* (14 September 1876).

85. 'Bulgarian Sunday', *NE* (18 September 1876); Shannon, *Gladstone and the Bulgarian Agitation*, pp. 136–8.

86. 'The Result of the Conference', *NE* (9 December 1876).

87. Robertson Scott, *Life and Death of a Newspaper*, p. 104.

88. Stead, *The M.P. for Russia*, vol. i, pp. 296–305.

89. W. T. Stead, 'Character Sketch: April', *RoR* (April 1892), p. 352.

90. For accounts of Olga Novikoff, see Stead, *The M.P. for Russia*; Joseph O. Baylen, 'Olga Novikov, Propagandist', *American Slavic and East European Review*, 10 (1951), pp. 255–71; H. C. G. Matthew, 'Novikov [née Kireev], Olga (1840–1925), *Oxford Dictionary of National Biography* (Oxford, 2004), vol. 41, pp. 229–30; Kathleen McCormack, 'Sundays at the Priory: Olga Novikoff and the Russian Presence', *George Eliot—George Henry Lewes Studies*, 67 (2015), pp. 30–42.

91. W. T. Stead, 'Madame Olga Novikoff, née Kiréef, "O.K."', *RoR*, 3 (February 1891), p. 123.

92. Stead, *The M.P. for Russia*, vol. i, p. 382.

93. W. T. Stead to Olga Novikoff, 10 October 1877, Novikoff–Stead Corr., fos. 1–2.

94. Stead, *The M.P. for Russia*, vol. i, p. 382–3.

95. W. T. Stead to Olga Novikoff, 15 October 1877, Novikoff–Stead Corr., fos. 3–7.
96. W. T. Stead to Olga Novikoff, 19 October 1877, Novikoff–Stead Corr., fos. 10–13.
97. W. T. Stead to Olga Novikoff, 18 October 1877, Novikoff–Stead Corr., fol. 9.
98. W. T. Stead to Olga Novikoff, 19 October 1877, Novikoff–Stead Corr., fos. 10–13.
99. W. T. Stead to Olga Novikoff, 22 October 1877, Novikoff–Stead Corr., fos. 14–17.
100. Stead, 'Madame Olga Novikoff', p. 133.
101. Whyte, *Life of W. T. Stead*, vol. i, pp. 57–60.
102. Stead, *My Father*, pp. 72–80.
103. Stead, 'Madame Olga Novikoff', p. 133.
104. W. T. Stead to Olga Novikoff, 22 July 1878, Novikoff–Stead Corr., fos. 28–30.
105. Stead, 'James Russell Lowell', p. 243.
106. Stead, *The M.P. for Russia*, vol. i, p. 383.
107. W. T. Stead to Olga Novikoff, 25 January 1878, Novikoff–Stead Corr., fos. 20–2.
108. W. T. Stead to Olga Novikoff, 28 October 1878, Novikoff–Stead Corr., fos. 32–3.
109. Private journal entry of 5 January 1879, cited in Robertson Scott, *Life and Death of a Newspaper*, pp. 107–8.
110. Private journal entry of 11 January 1880, cited in ibid., p. 111.
111. W. T. Stead to W. E. Gladstone, 9 April 1880, BL, Gladstone Papers, Add. Mss. 44303, fos. 333–34.
112. W. T. Stead. 'What It Means', *NE* (13 April 1880).
113. Robertson Scott, *Life and Death of a Newspaper*, p. 115.

# 2

# To Be a Christ

*Striving for Righteousness at the* Pall Mall Gazette, *1880–8*

The 'ideal to be aimed at', Stead wrote in his private journal on 22 October 1880, is '"Thy Kingdom Come, Thy Will be done on Earth as it is in Heaven"'. God, he believed, had brought him to London and the *Pall Mall Gazette* for a purpose, and this must include hearing the divine command in 'every cry of the suffering' and being stirred to 'fresh exertion by every spectacle of sin and misery'. He observed how, according to James Russell Lowell, each man and woman had been made in Christ's image, and yet society corrupted 'Christ's images into paupers and prostitutes'. An editor, Lowell had taught, must help restore people as Christ's images, by encouraging 'every agency for good' in society. For Stead, his role as assistant editor of a major London newspaper must 'combine the function of Hebrew prophet and Roman tribune with that of Greek teacher'.[1]

On arriving in London, Stead leased a spacious home, 'Cambridge House', with a garden, in Wimbledon Park. He then stayed for several weeks at the home of John Morley and his wife, while renovations were made to the house. Writing to his sister on 12 October 1880, Morley described his new assistant as 'a queer child of virtue, but a nice and good fellow'.[2] Stead's wife and children joined him in January 1881. He and Emma joined the Wimbledon Congregational Church under the pastorate of Walter C. Talbot, who became Stead's close friend; under Talbot's leadership, a large neo-gothic church, with seating for over eight hundred, was built between 1883 and 1884 on Worple Road.[3] Emma seemed happier in London, and their marital difficulties continued to ease. In their first years in London,

Stead spent as much time as possible with his family. They kept a pony for the children and Stead shared in their studies and sports 'with the enthusiasm of a boy', while he enjoyed running with the children to church. He and Emma had four children when they moved to London, and two more would follow. The older four children were schooled at home, aided by a governess and later a private tutor; the younger two would attend a day school. Unlike many literary people, Stead was not a 'diner out', and he never joined a London club.[4] Nor did he conform to the image of the assistant editor of a leading London daily; he remained careless in his appearance, his linen was none too clean, he wore ill-fitting, unfashionable checked suits and an old sealskin cap, never mastered social graces, sprawled over furniture, and enjoyed running as fast as he could down central London streets. He continued to enjoy a close friendship with the High Anglican Canon Henry Parry Liddon of St Paul's Cathedral, and from 1880 to 1890, they took a long walk together every Monday afternoon that Liddon was in London, discussing theology, the Church fathers, social reform, or Liddon's sermons. 'It is very odd,' Stead observed in 1905, 'now I come to look back upon it, how familiarly the dear Canon would condescend—without appearing to condescend—to discuss every conceivable subject under the sun, and even over it, with a Radical Nonconformist editor who was twenty years his junior.'[5]

The *Pall Mall Gazette* was one of five evening daily newspapers in London, all of which sold for a penny. There were also six morning daily newspapers in London, dominated by *The Times*. The evening newspapers were intended for the end of the working day, when readers presumably had more time for reflection; their news articles were often shorter, there were more feature stories, and they included reviews of earlier press reports. They were directed mainly to educated middle- and upper-class readers. The *Pall Mall*, founded in 1865, was Conservative in its politics until 1880, when the new owner made it a Liberal paper. Its circulation in the early 1880s was about 13,000, while the morning *Daily Telegraph* boasted 250,000 and the evening *Echo* 100,000. The *Pall Mall* was produced on Northumberland Street, 'a mean-looking thoroughfare, more like a passage than a street', with the editorial offices in the upper part of the building, and the printing rooms in the lower part.[6] 'There may have been less convenient, darker, and grubbier daily paper offices in London,' one of its journalists recalled, 'than our old building in Northumberland Street, but I never heard of them.'[7]

## John Morley's Apprentice

Stead greatly admired his editor, John Morley, who was eleven years his senior and a respected essayist and literary critic. Opposites in many respects, their working relationship was sometimes tense, with their most serious differences involving religion. Before accepting the assistant editor post, Stead had been concerned about 'Morley's irreligion', fearing that he might make the *Pall Mall* 'an aggressive anti-Christian paper', which would force Stead's resignation.[8] Stead consulted his High Anglican friends, Liddon and Church, about this, and they advised accepting the appointment. 'We differed about everything,' Stead later recalled, 'from the Providential government of the world to the best way of displaying the latest news.' Yet they enjoyed the cut and thrust of their exchanges. They would start each working day with a half-hour discussion of current events, to help determine the content of the day's edition. The topics ranged widely and Stead learned much from these exchanges. Stead's home in Wimbledon was not far from Morley's home, and Stead recalled that 'we were for several years near neighbours and good friends.'[9]

Morley, like Stead, came from a northern Nonconformist background; he was born in 1838 in Blackburn into a prosperous Methodist family, and had a strict Nonconformist upbringing. His father, a successful surgeon, then joined the Church of England, decided that his pious son should become an Anglican clergyman, and sent him to Oxford. Morley, however, lost his belief in Christian doctrine while at Oxford. Enraged over this, his father cut off financial support, forcing him to leave Oxford in 1859 with only a pass degree. Young Morley moved to London and supported himself by teaching and journalism. He soon won respect as an author, contributing to the quarterly journals and publishing studies of Burke, Voltaire, and Rousseau. In 1867, he was appointed editor of the prestigious *Fortnightly Review*. He lived with Rose Mary Ayling, mother of two children from a previous, possibly abusive relationship. They married in 1870 and Morley adopted her children. But many looked askance at their cohabitation

before marriage and her social background, and the Morleys rarely
socialized. Morley grew cautious, reserved, and distant in manner, as
though telling people not to pry.

He was also generous, sympathetic, and compassionate. He became
England's leading interpreter of the liberal philosopher, John Stuart
Mill. Morley's religious views were complex. Rejecting Christian
doctrines, he pursued the ideals of freedom, morality, and progress
with a kind of religious commitment. As one biographer noted,
'Morley's Liberalism was Christianity minus the creeds.'[10] He
respected truly religious people, and believed religion, as an expression of transcendent truths and ethical values, was vital to national life.
'Those who know him and know his writings,' Stead wrote in 1890,
'have long ago recognised him as one of the potent influences which
make for religion and righteousness in this generation. By birth, by
habit of thought, and by natural predilection he is a puritan pulpiteer,
born in the nineteenth century, when our hot gospellers betake themselves to the press instead of to the pulpit.'[11]

By his friendship with Morley, Stead became close to one of
Britain's leading 'honest doubters'. From the 1840s, there were in
Christian Britain a small but growing number of influential thinkers
from upper- and middle-class backgrounds who openly rejected
Christianity. They included the novelist Mary Ann Evans (George
Eliot), the philosopher Herbert Spencer, the historian James Anthony
Froude, the poet Arthur Clough, the intellectual historian Mark
Pattison, and the art historian and critic John Ruskin. These 'honest
doubters' were serious people, often strong Christians in their youth,
who departed from Christianity after earnest reflection. They lost
their faith for differing, intensely personal reasons. Some were influenced by biblical criticism, some by Church histories, studies in
comparative religion, or discoveries in geological or biological science.
Perhaps most important were the moral questions raised by such
Christian doctrines as predestination, the atonement, or eternal punishment. Most honest doubters found their loss of faith painful, often
leading to agonizing breaks with family and friends. Doubters could
be portrayed as immoral, incapable of taking binding oaths, or
respecting the conventions of marriage. The issue of religious doubt
in Britain became especially heated in 1880, when the Liberal
reformer and professed atheist, Charles Bradlaugh, was elected to

Parliament for Northampton, but was not allowed either to swear loyalty 'on the true faith of a Christian' or to affirm loyalty as permitted for Quakers and Jews. This led to a prolonged controversy over whether atheists should sit in Parliament or hold positions of public trust; only after six years, was Bradlaugh finally allowed to 'affirm' his loyalty and take his seat in Parliament. Through his friendship with Morley, Stead had learned how a person without belief in God or hope for eternal reward could behave unselfishly and strive for human progress. But Stead could not abide Bradlaugh's aggressive atheism. Stead and Morley had only one serious clash over religion, when during the Bradlaugh controversy Morley proposed an article promoting agnosticism and Stead feared Morley intended to make the *Pall Mall* an avowedly pro-Bradlaugh, secularist paper. Stead threatened resignation, and Morley did not publish the article.[12]

As editor, Morley kept a firm controlling hand over Stead, restraining his exuberance, obsessions, passions, and claims to divine inspiration, and forcing him to concentrate on the work of editing a quality newspaper. Stead deferred to Morley on most matters, but did not think him a natural journalist. 'He is in intellect an aristocrat,' Stead later noted. 'No power on earth could command Mr. Morley's interest in three-fourths of the matter that fills the papers.' 'Mr Morley,' Stead confided to his journal, 'is so much superior to me in so many things', but 'I have more go, more drive, more journalistic capacity in fact than Mr. Morley, who is primarily a man of letters.' By 1883, Stead was impatient with being 'a very secondary personage' in the office, and dreamt of having sole control over running the newspaper. 'Then,' he wrote in his journal 'I will revolutionise everything... I shall in after years be the most powerful man in England. My great newspaper will seize me and I shall have a power for good which no one at present possesses.' He would make his newspaper 'the rescuer of the society of God, the director of the steps of His people ... the great tribune of the poor, the conscience of the rich, the brooding influence which will quicken into activity all good aspirations and spin into unrest all lethargic souls'. In short, he concluded, he would 'make my paper like Longfellow's universal Church:

> As lofty as the love of God
> And wide as are the wants of man.[13]

Early in 1883, Stead had a 'curious presentiment' that his period as Morley's apprentice was nearly over. And so it proved. In the summer of 1883, Morley entered Parliament for Newcastle in a by-election, resigning his editorship. The proprietor, Henry Yates Thompson, became nominal editor of the *Pall Mall*, but gave Stead effective editorial control. 'I am riding on the crest of the wave,' Stead wrote to Wemyss Reid, and Reid recalled that Stead now 'revelled in his power with all the zest of a schoolboy'.[14]

On assuming editorial control, Stead produced a thirty-page pamphlet, 'The Gospel According to the *Pall Mall Gazette*', which he had printed for internal circulation. It laid out newspaper policy, including equal rights for women, imperial federation, arbitration of all Anglo-American disputes, home rule for Ireland, justice and respect for all 'subject races', the promotion of friendship with Russia, and the ideal of a United States of Europe. The policy also included a practical, tolerant Christianity, including respect for other faiths as different ways of relating to God. 'A new catholicity,' Stead insisted, 'has dawned upon the world. All religions are now recognized as essentially Divine. They represent the different angles at which Man looks at God.' His practical Christianity meant following the example of Christ and being willing to sacrifice for others. 'To lay down one's life for the brethren—which is sometimes literally the duty of the citizen who is called to die for his fellows—is the constant and daily duty demanded by all the thousand-and-one practical sacrifices which duty and affection call upon us to make for men.'[15] Stead insisted that the *Pall Mall Gazette* now give increased attention to religion. He published a series of articles between November 1883 and November 1884 on 'Centres of Spiritual Activity', with diverse religious leaders invited to describe their spiritual centres in London. The list reflected a rich diversity of religious life, and included St. Paul's Cathedral, the Positivist Society at Newton Hall, Westminster Abbey, the Regent Square Presbyterian Church, the London Synagogues, Charles Haddon Spurgeon's Metropolitan Tabernacle, the Unitarian chapels, Charles Voysey's Theistic Church, the Primitive Methodist churches, the Theosophical Society, the Swedenborgian New Jerusalem Church, and the Salvation Army headquarters.[16] Stead also conducted and published personal interviews with prominent religious figures, including the American evangelist, Dwight L. Moody, the new Archbishop of

Canterbury, Edward White Benson, and the Baptist preacher, Charles Haddon Spurgeon.[17]

## The Salvation Army

Stead's arrival in London in 1880 coincided with the rapid expansion of a new evangelistic movement, the Salvation Army founded by William and Catherine Booth. The Booths were revivalists who from 1865 had conducted an evangelistic mission among the poor in East London. In 1878, they began dressing their evangelists in military uniforms, giving them military titles, and using brass bands to gather crowds for open-air meetings on the London streets. Exploiting the popular fervour for imperialism and military adventures, they christened their organization the Salvation Army, declaring 'war' on irreligion in the urban slums. Women were prominent as preachers and evangelists in the new movement. Their military-style uniforms, brass bands, processions, and denunciations of alcohol often met with violence, as local thugs, sometimes encouraged by pub owners, viciously attacked Salvation Army gatherings, assaulting men and women alike. In 1882 alone, 'General' William Booth claimed that 669 evangelists (including 251 women) were seriously injured in such attacks. But the movement grew: there were 440 Salvation Army corps and 1,019 officers by 1882, and this number more than doubled by 1884.[18]

Stead first encountered the Salvation Army in 1879, when still editor of the *Northern Echo*. Two young female evangelists, known as 'Hallelujah Lasses', arrived in Darlington to organize and lead a revival campaign, hiring the largest hall in town, collecting donations to rent and light the hall, posting notices, speaking on the streets, and conducting nightly meetings, Stead recalled, 'with hearty responses, lively singing, and simple gospel addresses, brief and to the point'. The two women arrived with no friends or supporters in the town, but soon they were packing the hall nightly with crowds of 2,000 to 2,500, reportedly converting some of the town's roughest characters. Stead attended the meetings to observe, and was 'amazed' by what he witnessed. 'I found two delicate girls—one hardly able to write a letter; the other not yet nineteen—ministering to a crowded congregation which they had themselves collected out of the street, and building up an aggressive church-militant out of the human refuse which other churches regarded with blank despair.' But while impressed by their dedication, he was concerned about the effects of the work on the women's health, especially as one, Captain Rose Clapham, appeared to be consumptive. He took it upon himself to write to 'General' Booth to say he was acting irresponsibly, and that if the woman should die, he would 'deserve to be indicted for man-slaughter'. Stead was taken aback by Booth's response.[19] The Salva-tion Army, Booth explained, was in a desperate struggle to save souls from eternal damnation and neither woman could be relieved from her posting. Captain Rose might die; it was war and it was 'inevitable' that some would fall. 'We should be compelled to abandon the work altogether,' Booth maintained, 'if we had not men & women perfectly prepared to face the utmost risk with a changeless resolution & a calm confidence in God.'[20] This willingness to sacrifice lives in its mission to the poor deeply moved Stead. In the emotive months following the end of his affair with Novikoff, the practical faith and spirit of self-sacrifice exhibited by the two women helped him. 'The Hallelujah Lasses,' he confided to his journal in January 1880, 'have done me a great deal of good, renewed my faith in the simple gospel and in the power of the preached word.'[21]

On arriving in London, he sought out the Salvation Army, fre-quently attending their meetings. He was impressed by their willing-ness to minister to the poorest and most desperate, and by the relative equality of women and men within the movement. The Salvation Army, he became convinced, was 'a miracle of our time', and 'no religious organisation born in these late years can show anything approaching to such material results within so short a space of time'. Even the agnostic Morley was impressed with their achievement, telling Stead that Booth had 'produced more direct effect upon this generation than all of us put together'.[22] Stead was 'often tempted very strongly ... to leave my appointed work and join the Army'.[23] After he gained editorial control of the *Pall Mall*, he gave considerable coverage to the Salvation Army and its work. On 13 December 1883, he published an article by William Booth on Salvation Army's inter-national expansion, on 31 January 1884, an article by Catherine Booth on 'Women as Preachers', and on 2 May 1884, an article on the 'Hallelujah Lasses', in which he argued that these women, now numbering more than 900 and mainly working-class, were demonstrating not only courage in the face of street violence and physical assaults, but also the capacity of women in the 'management of all affairs'.[24] In his report of 16 May 1884 on a great meeting for 'reclaimed drunkards' in Exeter Hall, Stead noted that while 'the Salvation Army was laughed at and looked down upon for the want of intellect among its members', they unquestionably improved lives.[25] Attending Salvation Army meetings in Whitechapel, meanwhile, exposed Stead to the real misery of the 'submerged tenth' in London.

### *The Bitter Cry of Outcast London*

In October 1883, a short, anonymous penny pamphlet was published in London, under the title, *The Bitter Cry of Outcast London: An Inquiry into the Condition of the Abject Poor*, providing graphic depictions of life among the extreme London poor. The authors were two Congregational ministers, Andrew Mearns and W. C. Preston, and they drew their evidence from reports by agents of the London City Mission. The pamphlet described a dark underworld of overcrowding, dilapidated housing, filth, accumulating sewage, rotting food, disease, starvation wages, overwork, sexual abuse, incest, prostitution, alcohol abuse, and casual crime. People wore rags, children died young, corpses often lay unburied for days in crowded rooms. 'Whilst we have been building our churches and solacing ourselves with our religion,' the authors observed, ' . . . the poor have been growing poorer, the wretched more miserable, and the immoral more corrupt; the gulf has been daily widening which separates the lowest classes of the community from our churches and chapels, and from all decency and civilization.'[26]

The pamphlet led to Stead's first major journalistic crusade as editor of the *Pall Mall*. *The Bitter Cry* was not the first denunciation of the horrendous conditions of the urban poor, nor apart from its vivid prose, was it exceptional. It would likely have been ignored, had not Stead used it to fire a protest campaign, similar in moral outrage to his *Northern Echo* campaign against the Bulgarian atrocities. On 16 October 1883, the *Pall Mall* published a summary of *The Bitter Cry*, including extensive abstracts. In the accompanying editorial,

Stead directed his readers to the intolerable human suffering the pamphlet revealed. The pamphlet's harrowing scenes could well have been drawn from Dante's *Inferno*—though with additional horror: 'For in [Dante's] Inferno the damned at least did not breed. With us they do. Every year sees an addition to the long roll of the new born lost.' He was most distressed over the children born and then destroyed in the slums. 'Born in the fetid atmosphere of a crowded cellar, suckled on gin, and cradled in the gutter, they never have a chance.'[27] The lucky ones died soon.

This did not have to be. Such conditions existed because society allowed people to inhabit 'pestilential rookeries' where it was simply impossible 'to live a human life'. The slum conditions revealed the failure of the churches, obsessed with theological 'wranglings' and ecclesiastical in-fighting, while largely ignoring the misery of the 'people of the abyss'. 'Why all this apparatus of temples and meeting houses to save men from perdition in the world which is to come, while never a helping hand is stretched out to save them from the Inferno of their present life?'[28] Yet, it was not only the churches but the whole of society that bore the blame. He declared it a cruel 'satire . . . upon our Christianity and our civilization that the existence of these colonies of heathens and savages in the heart of our capital should attract so little attention'.[29] There must now be practical action to clean up the slums and provide decent housing for the poor. Stead focused most particularly on housing, rather than on the low wages, widespread unemployment, and gross inequalities that were also indicted in *The Bitter Cry*. Housing could be addressed by government subsidies and there already were calls for parliamentary action to provide better housing for the poor. In singling out working-class housing, Stead defined a feasible object for his press campaign.

Over the coming months, the *Pall Mall* sought to rouse public opinion in demanding parliamentary action to improve the housing for the poor. There were editorials calling for cross-party parliamentary action, articles on the evil of slum conditions, digests of related articles from London and provincial newspapers and journals, and signed articles by prominent public figures or those experienced with urban poverty. Along with a long article by William Booth of the Salvation Army, there was one on 'Revolutionary Socialism', by the leading Marxist H. M. Hyndman, and one on 'Labourers' Dwellings in London' by Octavia Hill, who described her plan for renovating existing housing.[30] In this campaign, Stead worked closely with a young member of his staff, Alfred Milner, an Oxford graduate recruited by Morley. In January 1884, Stead and Milner conducted their own investigation of working-class housing for the *Pall Mall*. They mapped out a working-class district, and their investigators visited each home with a printed questionnaire, which they completed with help from the inhabitants. The investigators also inspected the condition of the buildings, and the results were published in four issues of the newspaper. They deliberately selected an average working-class district, rather than a slum, to show how most working families lived.

The campaign over *The Bitter Cry* represented what Stead later called 'the first great *coup* of the *Pall Mall Gazette* after Mr. Morley left it', and he insisted it 'caused the appointment of the Royal Commission on the Housing of the Poor, from which modern social legislation may almost be said to date'.[31] Stead exaggerated his newspaper's impact, but the public indignation it aroused did contribute to Parliament's appointment of the Commission in late February 1884. Stead's ability to gauge and respond to the public mood was impressive. As Kenneth Inglis has observed, Stead 'took up *The Bitter Cry* at a moment when the condition of the poor, and especially their housing, was being discussed in the monthly reviews, and threw the subject to the middle-class public at large, among whom many were prepared to feel uneasy about the plight of the outcast'.[32]

Stead's campaign also promoted a new social commitment within the English Churches. In April 1884, the main Nonconformist denominations held a two-day conference in London on the condition of the poor, culminating on the evening of the second day with a well-attended public meeting at Exeter Hall chaired by the veteran Evangelical politician, Lord Shaftesbury. An impassioned plea for a Christian socialism by the Wesleyan Methodist minister, Hugh Price Hughes, fired debate. In 1885, the president focused on *The Bitter Cry* in his address to the Wesleyan Methodist Conference.[33] In Oxford, *The Bitter Cry* as publicized by Stead galvanized dons and students. Montagu Butler, headmaster of Harrow, held up a copy of *The Bitter Cry* in a sermon at the University church of St Mary's on 31 October 1883, calling on Oxford for 'enlightened action' in response to the pamphlet, and praying 'that year by year her choicest sons may be

arrested by it'. In February 1884, a general meeting at Oxford agreed
to found and maintain a 'University Settlement in East London'
under the leadership of Samuel Barnett, Church of England vicar of
St Jude's in Whitechapel. Under this plan, Oxford students would
reside for a time in London's deprived East End, serving its people
through teaching, legal aid clinics, youth work, and social work. The
promoters named the settlement Toynbee Hall, in honour of a well-
loved Christian socialist tutor at Balliol College, Arnold Toynbee,
who had died in March 1883 at the age of 31.[34] Toynbee had been a
close friend of Alfred Milner, Stead's assistant in the *Bitter Cry* press
campaign, and Milner was active in the Toynbee Hall Settlement
from the beginning.[35] Toynbee Hall became the first of scores of
settlements established in cities across Britain. In the Roman Catholic
Church, the archbishop of Westminster and primate, Cardinal Henry
Manning, was appointed to the Royal Commission on the Housing of
the Poor and largely wrote the Commission's first report, becoming a
leading figure in the national movement for improved working-class
housing.[36] Stead welcomed this commitment to social reform within
the Churches. For him, children 'born in the fetid atmosphere of a
crowded cellar, suckled on gin, and cradled in the gutter' were largely
lost to Christian influence, and the churches must focus, not simply on
evangelistic work in the urban slums, but on political action and social
reform to improve the social environment.

### Gordon for the Sudan

In November 1883, Britain faced a crisis in the Sudan, a crisis that
Stead's *Pall Mall* elevated to epic proportions, involving Christian
heroism, martyrdom, and the moral and religious nature of the British
Empire. In 1881, there was a popular rising in Egypt, then part of the
Ottoman Empire. The causes of the rising included years of misgovernment by the Egyptian Khedive (or Ottoman viceroy), crippling
taxes on an impoverished Egyptian population, and heavy debts to
European financial interests. The overthrow of the Khedive was
accompanied by the killing of Europeans by angry mobs and the
disorder threatened to close the Suez Canal and shut off Britain's
main route to India. In 1882, Gladstone's government responded by
sending a military force, which defeated the poorly trained Egyptian

national army, placed the Khedive back on the throne, and took effective control of the country. Britain's occupation of Egypt sent shock waves through the Islamic world. To the south of Egypt lay the vast territory of the Sudan, nominally under Ottoman-Egyptian control. In 1881, Mohammed Ahmed ibn Abdullah, the son of a Sudanese *sharif* (or descendent of the prophet) proclaimed himself the Mahdi, or expected one, who would defeat the unbelievers and usher in a new Islamist world order. He won support among the Sudanese Arab tribes, who hated both their Egyptian overlords and Britain's occupation of Egypt. In early November 1883, the Mahdists annihilated an Egyptian army of 10,000, commanded by the British Colonel William Hicks, and now controlled most of the Sudan, apart from several garrisoned towns, including the Sudanese provincial capital, Khartoum. Gladstone's government decided to evacuate the scattered garrisoned towns, but how could it safely evacuate thousands of Egyptian soldiers, civil servants, European merchants, and their families, through hundreds of miles of desert and an inflamed Sudanese population? By occupying Egypt, Britain had become responsible for their lives, but was unwilling to send a British military force into the Sudan to assist their evacuation.

Britain, Stead believed, must not leave these people to be massacred. His memories of the Bulgarian massacres, especially Batak, and what he believed had been Britain's complicity, were still raw. It must not happen again. Then on 6 January 1884, Stead learned that the Christian soldier-scholar, General Charles Gordon, was back in England after nearly a year of private biblical and archaeological research in Palestine. Gordon had served in the Sudan as the Khedive's provincial governor-general between 1874 and 1879, and was familiar with the region. A brilliant, if unconventional, military commander, he had served the Chinese Emperor in helping suppress the Taiping Rebellion between 1863 and 1865, and had led successful military actions in the 1870s against slave traders in the Sudan. Gordon was staying with his sister, Augusta, in her home in Southampton, but was expected soon to travel to the Congo in the service of King Leopold of Belgium. On 8 January 1884, Stead rushed by train to Southampton and interviewed Gordon on the Sudanese situation in his sister's sitting room. Stead had been pioneering the methods of the personal interview in the *Pall Mall* since November 1883, and the format was still relatively new to him. In securing the interview, Stead was quietly helped by a cabal in the War Office, including Reginald Brett and Captain John Brocklehurst, who opposed a British abandonment of the Sudan. Brocklehurst accompanied Stead to Southampton, and checked the accuracy of Stead's report of the interview before it was published.[37]

At their meeting, Stead felt an immediate affinity with Gordon. Stead was thirty-four years of age and Gordon a very youthful fifty, both short in stature and slight of build. Both had a childlike simplicity of manner and were unconventional, impulsive, and high-strung. Both were devout Christians, though somewhat unorthodox, and both felt a special calling from God. In the interview, Gordon informed Stead that the Egyptian garrisons and civilians could not be evacuated, as there was insufficient transport. The best hope, he maintained, would be to leave the garrisons where they were, seek to bring humane, honest, effective political leadership to the Sudan, and then negotiate a settlement with the Madhists, offering a full amnesty for any crimes during the rising. Gordon believed the Mahdist rising was less about religion than about an oppressed people struggling to secure human rights and dignity; the Sudanese, he maintained, were a good people who 'deserve the sincere compassion and sympathy of all civilized men'. When they parted, Gordon gave Stead an inscribed copy of his favourite book, *The Imitation of Christ*, a work of personal devotion by the fifteenth-century priest, Thomas à Kempis, which Stead would treasure for life. Although they never met again, Stead would always call Gordon his friend.

Stead published the full interview in the *Pall Mall* on 9 January, along with an editorial demanding that Gordon be sent to the Sudan. Gordon, he insisted, was in England at precisely the right moment, as though by divine plan. If Britain would not send an army to the Sudan, 'we can send a man who on more than one occasion has proved himself more valuable ... than an entire army'. Gordon should go to Khartoum with full powers to negotiate with the Mahdi and do what he felt necessary to bring peace to the Sudan. 'He may not be able single-handed to reduce that raging chaos to order,' Stead insisted, 'but the attempt is worth making.' The government must act immediately, as Gordon was to leave for the Congo within days. On the next day, other newspapers took up the call for Gordon. Some within Gladstone's government also wanted a Gordon mission, and on 18 January the government agreed to send Gordon to Khartoum to observe the situation and advise on what steps should be taken. Gordon agreed, postponing his appointment in the Congo. 'I think that is the biggest thing you have done yet,' Alfred Milner told Stead on learning the news.[38] The decision, Stead announced in his editorial on 21 January, was received with 'a universal outburst of approval'.[39] Stead told his father that he now felt 'almost the most influential man in England'.[40]

As Gordon travelled to Egypt, and thence south into the Sudan, the *Pall Mall* published almost daily articles on the mission, as well as 'Extras' (or special issues) which reprinted articles from the *Pall Mall* and other newspapers. In his editorials, Stead portrayed Gordon as a model Christian soldier, who had campaigned while governor of the Sudan to suppress slave raiding, and now returned to bring justice and peace. In describing Gordon's work in the Sudan from 1874 to 1879, Stead noted how 'his almost superhuman activity', 'wonder-working personality', and 'feats of alacrity, feats of daring, feats of mere physical endurance' had won the love and loyalty of the Sudanese people.[41] The secret of Gordon's strength, Stead insisted in his editorial on 22 January, lay in his absolute obedience to God's will. 'In Gordon,' he continued, 'the tenderness of a woman, the gentleness of a child, the ready sympathy with all the sorrows and sufferings of others, are combined with an iron will ... which is indispensable to a ruler of men.'[42]

Gordon reached Khartoum by river steamer on 18 February, and made a triumphal entrance into the beleaguered town. The *Pall Mall* described how on his arrival Gordon told the welcoming crowds, in Messianic tones, that 'I come without soldiers, but with God on my side, to redress the evils of the Soudan. I will not fight with any weapons but justice.' Gordon proceeded on that first day to burn publicly the taxation records (symbols of the oppression of the poor) and implements of torture, to go to the prison and release scores of captives, and to visit the sick in the hospital. In the evening the city was illuminated in celebration.[43] 'That vivid picture,' wrote Stead on 20 February, 'of a solitary Englishman acclaimed by the whole population of an illuminated city as a saviour and a deliverer will not

soon be effaced from the memory.' 'The hero of this episode,' Stead
added, 'is the spiritual descendant of the judges of Israel.'[44]

On 4 March, Stead published an article on 'General Gordon's
Religious Ideas', based on his interview of Gordon in Southampton
and his reading of Gordon's religious writings. Gordon, Stead maintained, was a religious mystic believing in the reincarnation of souls
and the predestination of all things by divine wisdom. Gordon was
also convinced that he received direct communications from God.
This confidence in God's order and guidance gave him strength and
calm amid the world's vicissitudes. 'It is a fever life I lead,' Gordon had
written in 1877. 'Were it not for the very great comfort I have in
communion with God, and the knowledge that He is Governor-
General, I could not get on at all.' For Gordon, Christianity meant
following Christ's example of forgetfulness of self and service to others,
in complete submission to God's will. He disdained conventional
Christianity and those he called the 'Christian Pharisees'—idolizing
respectability and their own wealth and comfort. Gordon's Christ was
'a workman of Bethlehem' who challenged teachers of the 'old religion, and 'was always in the slums with very dubious characters',
bringing His gospel to the 'sick at heart', for it was they who most
needed Him. Gordon also expressed admiration for Islam and insisted
that Muslims, like Christians, were heirs to God's kingdom. He
believed religion should be cheerful and he rejected any notion of
eternal punishment. Stead concluded that Gordon's 'religious creed is
not unlike that of Cromwell. In essentials it is the same, but the
humanitarianism and Catholicity of the nineteenth century have
tempered the severity of the Puritanism of the Commonwealth.'[45]

As the weeks passed, Gordon managed to evacuate some 2,500
civilians from Khartoum up the Nile in steamboats, but he could not
attempt a mass evacuation of all the garrison towns, as he lacked the
means of transport. His request to be allowed to meet the Mahdi to
discuss peace was vetoed by the British authorities in Cairo, who
suspected that he would either be held hostage or give assurances
the government could not honour. By May, Khartoum was besieged
by Mahdist forces and Gordon cut off. Stead's *Pall Mall* now
demanded a military expedition to rescue Gordon and Khartoum.
Gladstone's government, however, resisted such calls. Gladstone
believed that to 'crush the Mahdi' would mean British occupation of

the Sudan—which he opposed. 'These are people,' he told the House
of Commons in reference to the Mahdists on 12 May, 'struggling to be
free, and they are struggling rightly to be free.'[46] Stead was appalled
by the prospect of abandoning Gordon and Khartoum, denouncing
Gladstone's speech in an editorial as falling 'miserably short of the
gravity of the occasion'. The Mahdists, Stead insisted, would over-run
not only the Sudan but also Egypt unless stopped at Khartoum.[47]

Under a mounting public clamour roused by Stead's *Pall Mall*,
the government agreed in August to send a relief expedition to
Khartoum. But not until September did the expeditionary force
begin moving slowly up the Nile, struggling against both the desert
and Mahdist attacks. Early in October, the Mahdi took personal
command of the forces around Khartoum. Across Britain, churches
held special prayer services for Gordon's rescue. By December,
Khartoum's population was starving. Gordon got his last journals out
of Khartoum by a remaining steamer, but refused to desert the
besieged town. Then, on the night of 25 January 1885, the Mahdist
forces took advantage of a gap that appeared between the city's
defences and the Nile banks, as a result of the seasonal fall in the
river's level, and they rushed into Khartoum. Indiscriminate slaughter
followed, with Gordon killed at the governor's palace. On 28 January,
two gunboats sent in advance of the relief expedition came within
sight of Khartoum. But seeing smoke wafting from charred buildings
and the Egyptian flag no longer flying, the gunboats withdrew under
heavy fire. The expedition made no attempt to retake Khartoum and
returned to Egypt.

On 5 February 1885, Stead's *Pall Mall* ran a famous headline,
extending across two columns, 'TOO LATE!' Its special issue under
that title sold 50,000 copies.[48] Stead's editorial laid the blame for
Khartoum's fall and Gordon's death 'solely and entirely' on the
Gladstone government, which had 'refused to allow the [relief]
expedition to start, in spite of all warning and all entreaties, until it
was too late'. Many others, however, blamed Stead for the catastro-
phe. It was Stead's newspaper that had roused public pressure for
sending Gordon to Khartoum. Morley told Stead that he should not
be able to sleep at night 'for thinking of all the men who have lost their
lives over this business'.[49] But Stead insisted that it had all been part of
the divine plan. Gordon had sacrificed his life for others, and it was

through just such sacrifices that humanity was elevated and renewed. 'While all speak of failure,' he wrote to Gordon's sister, Augusta, on 6 February, 'I see only the success, the greatest, the most glorious that has been given to any Englishman of our generation to achieve.' 'If your brother is dead,' he continued, 'we who mourn by his sepulchre may lament that it should have been his lot to attain unto a success of Calvary—the highest of all successes.' But if we simply lament his loss without gratitude for his sacrifice, we should be 'reproached for unbelief, for think you not that his spirit will rise again and that something of the Gordon soul will thrill the hearts and improve the souls of thousands?'[50] Stead wrote in similar terms in his 'In Memoriam' for Gordon in the *Pall Mall* of 11 February. The 'splendour of that stainless life,' he noted, was 'now crowned with the aureole of martyrdom', and 'there is not one of his friends who for a moment regrets that General GORDON was sent to the Soudan to suffer and die'. Gordon, Stead insisted, had often prayed that God would place on him the burden of the sins of the Sudanese people, 'and crush me with it instead of these poor sheep'. Those who killed him in their 'blind fury' knew not what they had done, and there should be no attempt to wreak vengeance on them.[51]

There was a national wave of grief and anger over Gordon's death. The Queen sent Gladstone an unencrypted telegraph expressing her moral outrage over the relief expedition's delay and she created a small memorial for Gordon, including his personal Bible, at Windsor Castle. At the end of February, a motion in the House of Commons to censure the government was only narrowly defeated. The Church of England held Gordon memorial services on 13 March in its cathedrals and many parish churches. Numerous sermons, addresses, biographies, poems, and other appreciations of Gordon appeared over the coming months, many of them portraying Gordon as a martyr and saint. The preacher at the Gordon memorial service at St Paul's Cathedral was, significantly, Ernest Roland Wilberforce, bishop of Newcastle and grandson of the great anti-slavery campaigner, William Wilberforce. He spoke of how Gordon's sacrifice had brought a new national commitment to the spread of Christian civilization across the world.[52] The Gordon cult, which Stead had done so much to foment, contributed to a renewed dedication to the British Empire's moral mission.

Stead was himself becoming a more committed imperialist, and was distancing himself from his former Gladstonian Liberalism. Beginning in September 1884, Stead, covertly encouraged and assisted by committed imperialists within Gladstone's government, began a 'truth about the navy' campaign in the *Pall Mall*—arguing that the navy had become badly outdated, and demanding greatly increased expenditures for its enlargement and modernization. Britain, he insisted, needed a navy far superior to those of other powers, in order to maintain its 'dominion of the sea', and preserve and extend its imperial power. This was vital both to her survival as a trading nation, but also to her moral leadership in the world. 'England,' Stead insisted on 18 September, 'is not merely our country and the teeming mother of new Englands beyond the seas, she is the Power which with all her faults yet leads the progress of the world in civilization—pacific, industrial, and free.'[53] By December 1884, the campaign had pressured Gladstone's government into increasing naval funding. 'I became,' Stead later recalled of this time, 'enamoured of the idea that the British Imperial power was the instrument for maintaining peace among races which would otherwise have been cursed by internecine warfare, and of putting down the horrors of slavery and of other barbarous works in vast regions.' But although now 'an impassioned Imperialist,' he insisted that 'my Imperialism was always an Imperialism of Responsibility, or . . . an Imperialism plus common sense and the Ten Commandments.'[54]

### 'The Maiden Tribute of Modern Babylon'

In the spring of 1885, some four months after Gordon's martyrdom in Khartoum, Stead was drawn into his best-known social reform campaign, a campaign that would both bring him international prominence and also seriously damage his reputation. This was the 'Maiden Tribute' campaign directed against the sexual abuse and sex trafficking of children and young women in London. The campaign began amid fears that a Criminal Law Amendment Bill, intended to raise the age of consent for sexual intercourse from thirteen to sixteen, would fail a third time. The bill was a response to growing concerns about sex trafficking and child prostitution, concerns finding support in the investigations of a Parliamentary Select Committee in 1882. The bill had been passed twice by the House of Lords, in 1883 and 1884, but had failed in the Commons. Stead had taken an interest in the bill, publishing a supportive article by Josephine Butler in the *Pall Mall* in July 1884.[55] On 22 May 1885, the bill was again brought before the Commons, but was talked out in a thin house and no vote was taken. There were well-founded fears that Commons would not pass the bill before the summer recess and that it would again be dropped.

On 23 May 1885, the day after the bill was talked out in the Commons, Stead was approached by Benjamin Scott, the Chamberlain, or chief financial officer, of the City of London. Scott was a Nonconformist, a veteran temperance advocate and social reformer, whose philanthropic work in the London slums had shown him the extent of child prostitution and sex trafficking. Would Stead, he asked, use his newspaper to mobilize public opinion in support of the bill? Stead said he wanted to help, but was reluctant for reasons of 'self-preservation'. 'The subject,' he knew, 'was tabooed by the Press. The very horror of the crime was the chief secret of its persistence. The task was almost hopeless.'[56] On the following day, 24 May, Josephine Butler visited him to support Scott's request. Stead had long revered Butler's Christian feminism and heroic campaign against the Contagious Diseases Acts, which had inspired his late mother to political activism. He could not refuse her. Butler introduced him to a thirty-five-year-old former prostitute and brothel-keeper, Rebecca Jarrett, who in January 1885 had entered a Salvation Army rescue home.[57] Jarrett told him, with great personal difficulty, dark stories of her former life, including her methods of drawing young girls into prostitution. Stead was also pressed to act by Bramwell Booth, the eldest son of the Salvation Army founders, and himself the Army's 'Chief of Staff'. Bramwell shared with him harrowing accounts of child prostitution and abuse, including stories told to him by his wife, Florence, who was involved in Salvation Army 'rescue' work among prostitutes.[58]

Horrified by what he had heard, and also by what he discovered from further meetings, including a visit to Howard Vincent of the Metropolitan Criminal Investigation Department (who told him of the conspiracy of silence surrounding the sexual abuse of children), Stead decided he must act, even at the risk of his career. Had not all those he most admired—Cromwell, Lowell, Butler, Gordon—put their lives on the line for a righteous cause, and had he not been stirred by the courage of the city missionaries, whose reports in *The Bitter Cry of Outcast London* had inspired housing reform? He decided on a bold plan, though one with serious risks. He would emulate the Quaker moral reformer and journalist, Alfred Dyer, who, in order to expose the sex trafficking of young English and European girls, had disguised himself and infiltrated Belgian brothels. In 1880, Dyer's influential pamphlet, *The European Slave Trade in English Girls,* had exposed the methods of abduction, widespread police corruption, and the large amounts wealthy men would pay for sex with virgin girls.

Stead's plan involved forming a 'secret commission' of a handful of supporters who would join him in infiltrating London's sex trade. They disguised themselves as potential clients or as procurers of young girls, and sought to gain the confidence of brothel-keepers, prostitutes, and other clients, and thus acquire inside information on London's child prostitution. Stead knew that those involved in child prostitution would not be forthcoming with information, especially to outsiders who might be detectives or police informers. For his part, Stead adopted the guise of a wealthy, experienced client with a taste for young girls, especially virgins. He became a 'regular', visiting brothels nightly, drinking, smoking cigars, mouthing sexual banter and lurid stories. His plan included purchasing young virgins for sexual purposes, to show that it was possible. But for this, he had to gain the confidence of brothel-keepers and procurers. Time was of the essence, as Parliament would soon break for the summer recess, and it was expected that Parliament would then be dissolved and a general election called. Stead stayed in a small room near his newspaper office, working as editor by day and haunting brothels and chatting up streetwalkers in the evenings. He was normally teetotal, so drinking night after night exhausted him physically and emotionally. 'He got valuable introductions from good names to the fashionable brothels', according to his friend the Congregational minister Benjamin Waugh (co-founder and honorary secretary of the London Society for the Prevention of Cruelty to Children), 'he [im]personated a wealthy voluptuary; he won his way into the lady keeper's private rooms, and through the good names he had and the free spending of money, he heard confidential secrets. He made the acquaintance of procuresses, priced and bought their virgins; he entered the shuttered and cloth-curtained room, where shrieks were drowned of maddened girls . . . He walked streets and parks, and got close to the pitiable women and girls who there made their bread.' 'It was all a dream, a nightmare,' reflected Waugh, 'he became a madman.'[59] Josephine Butler and her son joined his 'secret commission' for about ten days; she took on the guise of a procuress of young girls for prostitution, while her son acted the part of a client.[60] Andrew Mearns and agents of the London City Mission also assisted Stead's investigation, which continued over six weeks.[61]

Before beginning his undercover investigation, Stead visited three Christian leaders, Edward White Benson, archbishop of Canterbury and primate of the Church of England, Frederick Temple, Anglican bishop of London, and Cardinal Manning, archbishop of Westminster and primate of the Catholic Church in England. He told them of his plans in advance, in order to gain their approval, and also no doubt to ensure that if things went wrong and he was arrested, he would have credible witnesses concerning his intentions. Benson sympathized with his motives, but advised against the undercover investigation, fearing it might end with Stead 'being killed in a brothel'. Temple and Manning, both of whom exercised episcopal authority in London and knew the human costs of prostitution and sexual abuse, gave him their 'hearty' support.[62]

The undercover investigation took a heavy toll on Stead. 'I am living in hell,' he wrote to Olga Novikoff on 10 June. 'Oh, it is awful this abode of the damned. I go to brothels every day & drink & swear & talk like a fiend from the bottomless hell. It is a great risk but who else will adventure into the abyss to pluck the terrible truth out of the jaws of danger and disgrace. I have not been home for a fortnight.' 'God help me. Pray for me,' he continued. 'It is the bravest riskiest work I ever undertook. But it is for you . . . for your sex, for your too wretched oppressed womanhood I do it. Bulgarian atrocities—ugh— they go on nightly in London. But thank God I will do something to deliver this new Khartoum.'[63] Both Butler and Bramwell Booth found Stead in his newspaper office sobbing over the sexual abuse of young girls he witnessed night after night; he was a father devoted to his own children. Stead prayed with Booth daily throughout the period.[64] 'I saw Mr. Stead frequently during the time of his "descent into hell",' Butler wrote later that year:

I say now, as I have said before, that that man combines the deepest tenderness of a compassionate woman with the manly indignation and wrath of a father—a father whose feelings are outraged by the crimes committed against innocent maidens, the helpless, and the young. At the time that he was making his investigations, those who saw him were sometimes afraid for his reason. He scarcely slept. We know what his nights were, when he, a pure-minded man, nurtured in the most refined and sternly Christian home, was going through the agony of visiting the infamous houses of the West End...At times he was tempted to give up all faith in God, in justice, in the atoning sacrifice, and the love of Christ.

'It is a sham,' he would cry, 'a horrible sham, the whole of our professed Christianity and civilization.'

He felt as a man walking on the thin crust of a volcano, which might at any moment break.[65]

She may have felt partly responsible for his mental state, having used his admiration for her to draw him into the investigation.

It was while in this highly emotive state of mind that Stead committed a serious error of judgement concerning Eliza Armstrong. He was desperate to find evidence that because the age of consent under the existing law was thirteen, girls of this age were lured or pressured into prostitution. But while he asked procurers to bring him a girl of thirteen or younger, the girls presented to him were too old or they took fright. He should have left it at that. But instead he met with the former procuress, Rebecca Jarrett, and pressed her hard to find him a mother prepared to sell her young daughter's virginity. Jarrett was very uncomfortable with this, and wanted to consult with Josephine Butler, who was then back at her home in Winchester. But Stead insisted that it could not wait, and that she must 'make amends' for her past sins by assisting his investigation.[66] Jarrett was an emotionally fragile woman, in poor health, with a damaged hip and a drink problem, who feared being abandoned by her new friends and forced back into her old life. She did what she could to meet Stead's demand. Aided by Nancy Broughton, a companion from her former life as prostitute and brothel-keeper, Jarrett found a Mrs Armstrong, who had a drink problem, was raising six children in a single room in a Marylebone slum with a physically abusive partner, and seemed prepared to have her thirteen-year old daughter, Eliza, taken off her hands. A bargain was struck on 3 June, and Jarrett used Stead's money to pay Broughton £2 and Mrs Armstrong £1. Jarrett took Eliza to a woman who certified the girl's virginity and sold Jarrett chloroform to drug the girl while she was sexually assaulted. Eliza was then taken to a room in a Soho brothel. After Jarrett put her to bed, Stead entered the room, according to plan, which woke the girl and terrified her (she had successfully resisted the chloroform). Stead left, and Eliza was taken to a physician, who confirmed that she remained a virgin. The girl was then taken by a member of the Salvation Army to the home of a Salvation Army family in France. Stead and the Salvation Army, believing her mother had sold the girl into prostitution, intended that Eliza would remain in France and have a new life. There was little thought of Eliza's discomfort during the virginity examinations, her terror at Stead's entry into her room, her confusion at being taken to another country, or that she might miss her family and friends. For Stead, these were minor matters when set against the greater good of providing necessary evidence against child prostitution, and, incidentally, of Eliza's rescue from a probable life of vice.

Stead's account of his undercover investigation, 'The Maiden Tribute of Modern Babylon', appeared in in the *Pall Mall* in four parts, on 6, 7, 8, and 10 July 1885. The articles included lurid sub-headings and illustrations. The title of the series derived from the ancient Greek myth that every nine years Athens paid a tribute of seven boys and seven maidens to Crete; there they were thrown into the Labyrinth where they wandered, lost and terrified, until devoured by the Minotaur, half-beast and half-man. This 'maiden tribute', Stead insisted, had been revived in London, where every night young virgins were taken from the poorest districts and offered up to the lusts of modern-day Minotaurs in the form of upper-class men. His reports conveyed, with vivid language and graphic depictions, the dark underworld of London prostitution. He discussed his secret commission, going in disguise into brothels and the haunts of streetwalkers, often at great personal risk, to gather inside information. He described young girls lured or forced into prostitution. He related how procuresses, paid a commission, groomed young girls from impoverished backgrounds for prostitution; he told of their methods to meet and entrap young servant girls in public parks or young single women arriving at ports or railway terminals, or how they lured young country women into the city with promises of employment as servants. It was, he insisted, a 'London slave market'. He discussed the premium placed on sex with young virgins, the so-called physicians who would examine and certify girls as virgins, and the going rates for virgins. He described how girls were drugged with chloroform or opium before being sexually assaulted. And he described padded rooms, with heavy carpeting and curtains, where young girls were raped, often strapped down, or where sadistic men whipped or beat girls, their screams unheard. He instanced a wealthy man in London, whom he dubbed the Minotaur, who boasted he had purchased sex with 2,000 virgins.[67] Stead noted how some members of the police colluded with brothel-keepers for a share of the profits, or would shake down prostitutes on the streets for payment of 'tips'. Stead declined to name individuals, but claimed that prominent public figures, including MPs and even government ministers, were involved in child prostitution, with one MP assuring Stead he could supply a hundred virgins at £25 each.[68] The first article of the series included the story of Eliza Armstrong, called 'Lily' in the story, a girl of thirteen sold by her drunken mother into prostitution. Stead described her as a 'warm-hearted little thing, a hardy English child, slightly coarse in texture, with dark black eyes, and short, sturdy figure' and he quoted from a letter she had written, including some simple verse, so as make the girl seem more real.[69] He left his readers with the impression that the girl had been raped in the brothel. The series, as Deborah Gorham noted, portrayed the girls and young women engaging in prostitution as 'passive, sexually innocent victims', with little recognition that some may have become prostitutes because of the limited opportunities for women in a 'exploitative economic structure'.[70]

The lurid articles aroused intense public interest, and also public rage. Never before had a newspaper treated sexual matters, including prostitution, child abuse, seduction, and sadism, so openly. There was a rush for copies of *Pall Mall*, with thousands of additional copies printed; its circulation during the Maiden Tribute period soared to over 100,000 (it had been about 15,000).[71] Reprints appeared on the Continent and in the United States; an estimated one and a half million copies of the Maiden Tribute would be sold, in authorized and unauthorized editions.[72] Many were shocked over depictions of seemingly respectable upper-class men sexually abusing women and children in the 'labyrinth' of London brothels and streets. But others denied the truth of the reporting, denouncing Stead and his newspaper. Nearly all the other London newspapers accused the *Pall Mall* of peddling pornography and corrupting minds in order to increase sales. The news vendor, W. H. Smith, who had a monopoly over sales in railway stations, refused to carry the *Pall Mall* while the series continued. On 8 July, a large crowd outside the newspaper's offices on Northumberland Street turned violent, windows were broken and forty policemen were required to restore order. There were calls in Parliament for the *Pall Mall* to be suppressed and Stead to be prosecuted for obscenity.[73] Many not only dismissed Stead's accounts as fictitious, but also denounced the campaign for vilifying the upper classes and fomenting class hatred.

But Stead also received many expressions of encouragement, especially from the clergy. These included letters from the celebrated Baptist preacher Charles Haddon Spurgeon, the Baptist Christian Socialist John Clifford, the Methodist preacher and journalist Hugh Price Hughes, the Salvation Army general William Booth, and the High Anglicans Henry Scott Holland and Malcolm MacColl.[74] Although weak with his final illness (he died in the early autumn), the evangelical social activist, Lord Shaftesbury, pushed himself to his physical limits to support the campaign. On 10 July, in his last public speech, Shaftesbury spoke on the Maiden Tribute exposures before the Society for the Prevention of Cruelty to Children at the Mansion House, and later in July, he dragged himself to Parliament to meet with the home secretary, Richard Cross, and the new prime minister, Lord Salisbury, concerning Stead's revelations.[75] On 14 July, Stead announced in a lead editorial that the archbishop of Canterbury, the bishop of London, and the Catholic archbishop of Westminster, along with Samuel Morley (Nonconformist businessman, philanthropist, and Liberal MP for Bristol) would serve as a committee to review all the confidential evidence gathered during the 'Maiden Tribute' investigation, assessing the accuracy of its reports.[76] This so-called Mansion House Committee (from its place of meeting) issued its report on 29 July, confirming, after sifting through the evidence, that the 'Maiden Tribute' reports were 'substantially true'.[77]

On 30 July, the House of Commons again considered the Criminal Law Amendment Bill for raising the age of consent for sex. The country was now inflamed, and public meetings demanding its passage were held across the country; Stead compared this to Bulgarian atrocities campaign.[78] The Salvation Army alone gathered nearly 400,000 signatures for a petition in support of the bill.[79] While some MPs denounced the *Pall Mall* during the debates, there was no question that the bill could again be dropped. The bill, already passed by the Lords, was passed by the Commons on 10 August, receiving the Royal Assent on 14 August. It raised the age of consent from thirteen to sixteen, allowed the police to search brothels if there was evidence of child prostitution, empowered the authorities to remove young girls from immoral parents, and outlawed solicitation of girls under sixteen. It included an additional clause, introduced by the Liberal MP, Henry Labouchere, criminalizing sexual relations between men. The new act became popularly known as 'Stead's law'.

Stead's *Pall Mall* now called for a national movement to ensure enforcement of the Act, and to carry further the campaign against sexual abuse and the sex trade more generally. The 'New Crusade', as Stead termed it, began on 21 August with a national conference at St James's Hall, London, inaugurating a National Vigilance Association for the Protection of Girls, which would 'assist in the enforcement of the Criminal Law Amendment Act and the suppression of vice'.[80] It was followed the next day by a demonstration for 'social purity' in Hyde Park, which gathered an estimated 100,000, including large numbers of working men and women. Stead termed it the 'first London Town's Meeting'. Ten processions converged on the park from different parts of London, carrying banners blazoned with 'Shame, Shame, Horror' or 'Protection of Young Girls', and including darkly dressed female veterans of the fight against the Contagious Diseases Acts and wagonloads of young girls dressed in white, their banners crying, 'Innocents will they be slaughtered' or 'Sir, Pity Us'. In Hyde Park, there were ten speakers' platforms, each with several speakers; Stead spoke at platform 6, proclaiming that 'if it had not been for a faith in God above I would never have dared to have gone through this.'[81] 'The women,' the *Pall Mall* reported, 'were numerically strong. Mothers had brought their daughters, shopgirls and milliners mustered in great strength . . . The men were well-to-do citizens, tradesmen, handicraftsmen, such as mechanics and carpenters—good men and true, with . . . determination on their jaws.'[82] The speeches

and banners, as Judith Walkowitz observed, reflected the melodramatic
aspects of the 'Maiden Tribute' campaign, including images of innocent working-class girls sacrificed to the unnatural lusts of upper-class
men, and of working-class parents standing up to defend their
daughters.[83] In the following days, the *Pall Mall* published accounts
of public meetings being held across the country in support of the
'New Crusade'. It was a form of participatory journalism, by which
the newspaper not only reported the news, but also mobilized the
new mass reading public for social action.[84] Bishop Temple of
London gave the campaign his weighty support with a pastoral letter
demanding action for social purity from the established Church,
including the formation of societies of men to promote 'purity of life
and conduct' and of vigilance committees to ensure enforcement of
the new law.[85]

Then in early September, the 'New Crusade' was dealt a blow,
when Stead was indicted, along with Rebecca Jarrett, Bramwell
Booth, and three others, for crimes relating to the abduction of
Eliza Armstrong. The first Maiden Tribute article on 6 July, it will
be recalled, had described the shocking purchase of the thirteen-year
old 'Lily' for sexual purposes from her drunken mother. Mrs Armstrong's
neighbours had recognized that 'Lily' was Eliza, who had been
missing for over a month. On 11 July, shamed and threatened by
communal rage, Mrs Armstrong reported her daughter missing to
the Marylebone police station. The police made enquiries, Eliza's
location was soon discovered, and the girl brought back from France
and returned to her mother in late August. Charges were then
brought against Stead and three co-defendants for having taken the
girl out of the country without her father's permission, and against
Stead and two co-defendants for indecent assault. Stead's supporters
raised a substantial defence fund and employed legal counsel for
the co-defendants, although Stead insisted on defending himself.
The trial was conducted in thirteen sessions between 23 October
and 10 November 1885, attracting enormous public attention.
Cardinal Manning, Bishop Temple of London, Archbishop Benson
of Canterbury, Josephine Butler, John Morley and others appeared as
character witnesses for the defence. Stead emphasized that Eliza had
not been harmed and that their purpose had been to offer proof
that girls were sold for sex. He admitted, however, that he lacked

experience in such matters and that during those weeks he was drinking heavily and his judgement may have been impaired. Mrs Armstrong, for her part, insisted that she had understood Eliza was to become a servant in a respectable home in the country. Rebecca Jarrett's testimony was contradictory, as she did not want to incriminate her former associate, Nancy Broughton, or Mrs Armstrong.[86] Thus, it was not clear what Mrs Armstrong had actually been told, and there was good reason to believe she had been misled. What was certain was that Eliza's father had not given permission for Eliza to be taken to France; he had beaten his wife on learning she had allowed the girl to be taken from the home, which for some gave credence to his testimony. While the judge acknowledged Stead's good intentions, the jury found him guilty of abduction and indecent assault, and he was sentenced to three months in prison with hard labour. Bramwell Booth and his Salvation Army associate were exonerated, but the others were found guilty on one or both charges, receiving sentences of one to six months. One of them, an older woman, died in prison.

The London press applauded the verdict, denouncing Stead, the *Pall Mall*, and the Maiden Tribute campaign. Stead's articles had antagonized many in London, including upper-class men accused of sexually abusing working-class girls, the police accused of collusion with brothel-keepers and sex-traffickers, and even working-class parents, some of them accused of selling their children for sex. Now, it seemed, Stead had been exposed as immoral and dishonest. His account of the 'purchase' of the thirteen-year-old girl had been shown in a court of law to be fraudulent; clearly most, if not all, of the Maiden Tribute 'revelations' must have been fictions as well. Rival London newspapers declared that Stead had betrayed the public trust by spreading 'filth' and manufacturing evidence. For some, his motives were simply greed, to increase sales of his newspaper. For others, his mind had been muddled by drink and late nights in the brothels; according to the *St James Gazette*, 'he was probably intoxicated' when he wrote his 'Lily' story. For *The Times*, he was a fanatic, manipulating evidence to further his cause, or a hypocrite, hiding his own vile lusts behind 'the mask of holy purpose'. Even if sincere about his moral cause, the *Observer* maintained, he should not distort evidence for his moral crusades, for 'journalism, after all, is not a mission, and editors are neither missionaries nor evangelists'.[87]

Some who had supported Stead's campaign now felt they had been duped. They included the playwright, George Bernard Shaw, who had written occasionally for Stead's *Pall Mall* and had believed the Maiden Tribute revelations. 'Nobody ever trusted him,' Shaw later wrote, 'after the discovery that the case of Eliza Armstrong in the Maiden Tribute was a put-up job, and that he himself had put it up.'[88] For the author and journalist, Hugh Kingsmill, the treatment of Mrs Armstrong was especially cruel, for it appeared that 'she was tricked into appearing before the world, and among her neighbours, as a mother who had sold her daughter into a brothel.'[89] Stead's former Anglican friend, Dean Church of St Paul's, was morally repulsed by Stead's Maiden Tribute articles and ended contact with him.[90] His assistant, Alfred Milner, resigned from the *Pall Mall*. Stead agonized over what his father, who had died in early 1884, would have thought. 'He was a good man,' Stead wrote his sister on Christmas Eve from prison, 'I am not, never was, and, I fear, never will be.'[91] Before the trial began, a secretary came upon Stead 'sobbing' over a letter from his wife. A 'friend' had written Emma to say that no man who was faithful to his wife could have engaged in this sort of investigative work, and Emma agreed that Stead 'had not been fair to her'.[92] In the event, Emma stood by him throughout the trial and his imprisonment.

Many others also continued to support him, and believed that despite serious errors of judgement, his motives had been noble. The minister of the Wimbledon Congregational Church and Stead's friend, Walter C. Talbot, helped ensure that the majority of the congregation stood by Stead; many were moved by Stead's emotive address 'as a penitent sinner' after the evening service on 8 October.[93] 'Whenever observations are made upon the mode of your operations, they only imply that you are liable to error like all your fellows,' Spurgeon wrote Stead on 24 December 1885, 'but when your self-sacrificing spirit is thought of, it is with glowing admiration. You cast yourself into the abyss to rescue & preserve innocent children, & you are held in honour among the honourable.'[94] On beginning his prison sentence, Stead was initially incarcerated in Coldbath-in-the-Fields prison, where the conditions were harsh, creating fears for his health. Josephine Butler and another prominent Christian feminist, Millicent Fawcett, organized a large public meeting at Exeter Hall, from which hundreds processed to the Home Office. Fawcett was especially warm in Stead's defence, viewing him as the type of 'the hero saint who in every age of the world's history has been picked out for special persecution & misrepresentation'.[95] Within a few days, they gathered over 100,000 signatures for a petition calling for Stead's release. The new Conservative prime minister, Lord Salisbury, had Stead moved to a comfortable furnished private room, with fireplace and bookshelves, at Holloway prison, where he could edit the *Pall Mall* and receive visitors. Many Christian leaders wrote to him or visited him, including the Baptist John Clifford, and the Methodist Hugh Price Hughes.

Of those who stood by him, Stead derived the greatest comfort from the friendship and spiritual guidance of Cardinal Manning. It was a curious relationship. Manning was nearly eighty years of age, Oxford-educated, cultivated, careful, and ascetic. As a young man, he had been an Anglican archdeacon and married to the beautiful Caroline Sargent. His wife had died childless of consumption in 1837, and Manning, troubled by state interference in the Church of England, entered the Catholic Church in 1851, rising through his considerable abilities to become by 1865 archbishop of Westminster and primate of England and Wales. He was a prince of the Church, an effective ecclesiastical politician, and a man of authority, responsibility, and sombre demeanour. Stead was forty years younger than Manning, raised within an anti-Catholic tradition, proud of his Puritan and Nonconformist background, brash, opinionated, and restless, a radical journalist, with little formal education and narrow culture.

When Stead was arrested, Manning became highly visible in Stead's defence, subscribing to the legal defence fund, writing an article in defence of Stead's Maiden Tribute campaign for the *North American Review* (reprinted in the *Pall Mall*), attending some sessions of the trial, and serving as a character witness.[96] Manning encountered considerable hostility from Catholics for supporting Stead's campaign.[97] 'In the uprising against the horrible depravity which destroys young girls,' Manning recalled, 'I was literally denounced by Catholics—not one came forward.' But he would not abandon Stead's crusade. 'Twelve tribes of Pharisees and scribes would not hinder me,' he wrote to the editor of the Roman Catholic newspaper *The Tablet*. 'What do they take me for?'[98] Although Manning was

unwell and could visit him only once in prison, he wrote to Stead
regularly. '"All things work together for good to them who love
God",' he assured Stead on 11 November 1885. 'You have served
Him with a single eye . . . You now have the crown upon your work.'
'Whatever it may be in my power to do,' he added, 'shall be done.'[99]
This was the first letter Stead received in prison, and it moved him
deeply. 'During the time of the agitation that led to the passing of the
Criminal Law Amendment Act in 1885,' Stead later wrote, 'the
Cardinal was my most effective ally. He was to me from first to last
as a tower of strength and unfailing help in every time of need.'[100]
Manning became in a sense the father that Stead had lost early in
1884. 'Since my father died,' Stead wrote in 1890, 'there has been no
man who has been so good to me, so helpful, so loving, and so true as
Cardinal Manning.'[101] After his release from prison, Stead became a
frequent visitor at Manning's home, remaining, at Manning's insistence, for hours of conversation. 'Over and over again,' Stead wrote of
these conversations, 'when, after talking for an hour or an hour and a
half I rose to go, he would insist upon my sitting down again . . . and so
the conversation would begin again.'[102] 'Cardinal Manning,' recalled
one of Stead's friends, 'when he was nearly eighty years of age, used to
climb up to Stead's office on the second floor . . . from time to time. He
was much attached to Stead.'[103]

### His 'Third Conversion'

While Stead was in a highly emotive state in Holloway prison,
he experienced what he called his 'third conversion'. He described
the experience five years later in an interview with the journalist,
Raymond Blathwayt. Stead's first conversion, he informed Blathwayt,
had occurred at Silcoates School in 1861, with the sudden realization
that he had been saved from his sins by Christ's sacrifice on the cross;
this conversion was later reconfirmed by attending the meetings of the
two Salvation Army 'Hallelujah Lasses' in Darlington. His second
conversion had come when his apparently failing eyesight had
ended hopes of writing a history of Puritanism. He believed his
threatened blindness was a call from God to devote his life to helping
others: 'I realised that what I had to do was to do good.' The third
conversion occurred at Holloway when, alone on New Year's Eve, he

received what he described as a 'direct sign and intimation from heaven'. He believed he heard a divine call to become a Christ-figure, and be an example of self-sacrificing love in the service of all who suffer in the world. He was no longer to be a Christian, in the sense of accepting Christ as his personal saviour and believing Christ atoned for his sins. He was to be a 'Christ' and be willing to be hated, even martyred, for humanity. 'In that jail,' he maintained, 'a voice came to me, "Be no longer a Christian, be a Christ." That voice was as distinct and clear as possible.' It was, he believed, God's peremptory call to him not only to adopt a selfless manner of living, but also to help form a new Church, a Church of the Future, to be made up of Christs willing to lay down their lives for others. 'That is the word by which I have to live, and by which I shall be judged. That is the message the Church of the Future must deliver to all her flock, "Be a Christ!"' For, Stead added, 'it is not Christians who will save the world, nor Churches—it is Christs.'[104]

While in prison on New Year's Eve, he described his new religious insights in a long private journal entry. He noted how Christ must be 'very grieved' over what Christianity had become. While respectable Christians worshipped and praised Him in their churches, very few would follow Him into the 'slums'—where overworked needlewomen slaved and starved, where dockyard labourers clamoured for work, and neglected street children grew up 'like little wolves'. He imagined Christ in London, walking through the 'loveless and joyless' slums into comfortable churches, where He would find Christians 'sitting there in their cushioned pews, praying their prayers and saying their creeds, and worshipping Christ'. 'And then,' Stead insisted, 'Christ would stand up in the midst of the whole congregation and He would say out quite loud in terrible tones "Damn Christ!"' Christ would be enraged because, while largely indifferent to the suffering in the slums, respect-able churchgoers had 'made an idol of Christ and debased his worship into a mere word-clicking and puppet-jiggling performance'. Stead was convinced that the divine call to 'Be a Christ' meant sacrificing personal ambitions and respectability and entering the slums to help the poor and suffering. Although he was by nature 'rather timid', the experiences of past months had strengthened him, and 'law courts and jails are no longer to me terrors'. His journal entry imagined himself being murdered by a 'mob thirsting for my blood' (a reflection, no doubt, on the abuse levelled against him by the newspapers and public). He concluded with some reflections on the future role of journalism. He had, he believed, 'grasped a great idea', which was 'to organise a secular Church' with the journalist as preacher, readers as the congregation, and a select body of readers as lay leaders. This secular Church would strive for the kingdom of God on earth by promoting the ideal of 'The Citizen Christ', who would approach broken society 'as a healer' and elevate the body politic with an ideal of 'self-sacrifice in politics instead of selfish scrambling for place and power'.[105]

And had not the heroic Gordon accepted the call to be a Christ in going to his death at Khartoum? Stead was hated by many for his role in sending Gordon to die, just as he was hated over the Maiden Tribute crusade. He now believed it all had a higher meaning. In prison on that New Year's Eve, Stead felt compelled to write to Augusta Gordon, and tell her of how he was now certain her brother's death had had a higher purpose. This had been 'to make Christ real to people' in a world where 'the key idea of the Christ was dying out in many hearts'. 'It needed,' he explained, 'that one man should die for the people, that Khartoum should remind men of Calvary, and that your brother should recall to the soul of man and woman everywhere the Divine call to each one of us to be another Christ, a living sacrifice for the feeblest and most forsaken of Christ's brethren.'[106] Stead shared his religious experience with Cardinal Manning, who directed Stead's attention to Scripture, noting how St Paul had said that 'With Christ I am nailed to the Cross' (Galatians 2.19).[107] John Morley visited Stead in prison on 8 January, and found him a 'strangely exalted mood', believing that he was 'the man of most importance now alive'.[108]

## 'Government by Journalism'

Stead was released from Holloway prison on 14 January 1886 (his three-month sentence was counted from the trial's opening). Over 3,000 attended a meeting at Exeter Hall to welcome his release, and on 18 January, Stead began a series of articles in the *Pall Mall* entitled 'My First Imprisonment'. Stead's position at the newspaper was no longer secure. The *Pall Mall*'s proprietor, Yates Thompson, agreed to retain him as editor, on condition there would be no more 'Maiden Tributing'. It was only with difficulty that the newspaper, as well as the Salvation Army and Stead personally, avoided paying legal damages over the Eliza Armstrong affair. Contrary to popular belief, the *Pall Mall* had suffered heavy financial losses as a result of the Maiden Tribute articles. Sales had briefly surged while the articles were being published, but then the newspaper's circulation fell. Advertisement revenues also fell, and Yates Thompson only managed to retain the remaining advertisers by promising that 'Maiden Tributing' would end. The newspaper had lost some £2,500 as a result of the affair, which Stead promised to repay over time.[109]

The Maiden Tribute investigations were finished, but not Stead's commitments to social reform. He had witnessed horrendous poverty, sexual abuse, ruined lives, and human suffering and would not now be silent. He believed his imprisonment was a martyrdom, a divine call to proclaim the ideal of the 'Citizen Christ'. His newspaper campaigns of the past two years—the 'Bitter Cry', 'Gordon for the Sudan', the 'Truth about the Navy', the 'Maiden Tribute'—had been contentious, but had also demonstrated how journalism could mobilize public opinion for real change. While in prison, he began drafting his views of journalism's future role, which he published as two articles in the *Contemporary Review* in May and November 1886.[110] British society, he argued, had grown increasingly fast-paced, under the influence of the telegraph and mass printing. Parliament was no longer effective in responding to the rapidly changing demands of a vast empire, or in representing the changing public mood; it was overburdened with business, had frequent recesses, and general elections at least every five years. Newspapers, and not Parliament, Stead insisted, had become the real expressions of democracy in the new era of mass literacy. Journalists were in tune with the changing public mood; if they were not, their newspapers' circulations would quickly fall. Journalists shaped public opinion, defined political agendas, and decided which politicians' speeches got press coverage and which not. Editors often served for many years, gathering experience and information. Journalists were the public educators; newspapers, he maintained, were the only reading matter for most of the British public. In a complex, increasingly interconnected world dependent on information, the press (the 'Fourth Estate') was 'becoming more powerful than all the other estates of the realm'. 'The wielders of real power will be those who are nearest the people' and journalists were far closer to the people than politicians or statesmen.[111]

The journalism of the new era had a religious aspect; journalists were becoming the main moral and spiritual guides of millions. 'In the midst of the whirl of politics and the crash of war', it was often the journalist, 'both missionary and apostle', who communicated higher, enduring truths. The journalist, Stead insisted, was analogous to 'those ancient prophets [who wrote] on the ... politics of Judea and Samaria three millenniums ago'. And now the journalists 'have to write afresh', he claimed, 'the only Bible which millions read'.[112] Journalists also gave a voice to the poor and the outcast, and offered them hope of a better future. Stead referred to the Jewish legend of how Sandalphon, the angel of prayer, stood at the gates of heaven listening to the prayers rising up from the world, turning those prayers into flowers which he placed before Jehovah's throne. 'The editor,' Stead continued, 'is the Sandalphon of humanity. Into his ear are poured the cries, the protests, the complaints of men who suffer wrong, and it is his mission to present them daily before the conscience of mankind.'[113] The newspaper had the potential to elevate society. In its ideal, the newspaper would 'be a great secular or civic church' and would 'come to be the very soul of our national unity'. 'And its great central idea would be that of the self-sacrifice of the individual for the salvation of the community, [as] the practical realisation of the religious idea in national politics and social reform.'[114]

Stead's religious views were growing loftier, and also broadening out from his Nonconformist background. In June 1886, he published a call for a new civic Church, as a *Pall Mall* 'Special'. This consisted of articles by various religious leaders (many of which had first appeared in the 'Centres of Spiritual Activity' series he had published in 1883–4).[115] In his preface, Stead argued that the diverse religious figures represented here were all 'members of the Church universal—each one representing some facet of the Divine truth'.[116] They all agreed that the essential purpose of religious faith was to strive for the kingdom of God on earth: 'To spend our little life so that we may leave the great world better than we found it, that is the chief end of all good men.' Those striving for the righteous social order, he maintained, were not all Christians; they included agnostics and even atheists. But if they were 'Christs', prepared to sacrifice themselves for the good of others, they too were part of the universal Church. Indeed, many so-called Christians should be ashamed in the 'presence of some of these agnostic Christs', who, 'orphaned castaways in a world without God, nevertheless dedicate themselves with all sincerity to lifelong devotion to the service of the suffering, the sinful, the lost'. What was needed, he insisted, was a gathering in of all good people, 'a widening of the portals of the Church to include all who can minister to the service of humanity'.[117]

## Ireland, Evictions, and the Catholic Church

Stead's release from prison coincided with the political convulsions over the first Irish Home Rule bill. During the general election of late 1885, Gladstone let it be known that if called to form another government, he would introduce a Home Rule bill to create an elected parliament in Dublin to legislate on Irish internal matters. Following their narrow victory, Gladstone's Liberal party formed a government on 1 February 1886 and Gladstone introduced the Home Rule bill in April 1886. The British public was deeply divided over Home Rule, many fearing the break-up of the United Kingdom and a Catholic theocracy in Ireland, and the Protestant majority in Ulster rioted against it. Stead was a long-time supporter of Irish home rule, believing that Ireland had been misgoverned for generations and that Home Rule would bring Ireland better government and a brighter future. However, he was also committed to keeping Ireland within the British imperial state, and he had serious difficulties with Gladstone's specific Home Rule bill, which would remove all Irish MPs from the Imperial Parliament in Westminster.[118] This, Stead believed, would fatally weaken the Union of Great Britain and Ireland, and diminish the British Empire as a force for good in the world.[119] It would reduce Ireland to a 'tributary dependency', paying taxes levied by an Imperial Parliament in which it no representation.[120] Stead's own hope was that the British Empire would develop into an imperial federation of dominions, each with its parliament (including separate home rule parliaments for Ireland, England, and Scotland), and with an Imperial Council or Parliament in London. But for such a future imperial federation, it was imperative that Ireland have representatives in the Imperial Parliament.[121] In the event, the *Pall Mall* rather inconsistently gave conditional support to Gladstone's Home Rule bill, while insisting that the only lasting solution was imperial federation.[122]

Gladstone's Home Rule bill was defeated on 8 June 1886, and Gladstone called a general election. The Liberal Party now split, with a substantial body of Liberal Unionists breaking from the main Liberal Party. The general election gave the Conservatives and Liberal Unionists a large majority and they would govern Britain (with one brief interlude) for the next twenty years. As prospects for Home Rule receded, the Irish national movement focused on the land agitation, which had begun in 1870 to secure improved rights and conditions for Irish tenant farmers. From the later 1870s, there was a prolonged agricultural depression in Ireland, aggravated by growing imports of cheap American and Australian foodstuffs into Britain. With falling agricultural prices, large numbers of Irish farmers were unable to pay their rents. Irish landlords evicted thousands of families from their farms each year; those evicted were thrown into dire poverty, often left on the roadsides with their meagre possessions. Rural communities were being devastated.

In late October 1886 Irish nationalists and agrarian reformers renewed the land agitation with the 'Plan of Campaign', which was formally launched at a meeting in Woodford, a West of Ireland village suffering intensely from evictions. By the Plan, the tenant farmers on each estate would band together and offer the landlord what they determined to be a fair and affordable rent, taking into account the falling agricultural prices. If the landlord refused their offer, the tenants would not pay rent to the landlord, but would instead pay the 'fair' rent into an 'estate fund', which would be used to assist families evicted from their farms. Many Irish nationalists, including the leader of the Irish Parliamentary Party, Charles Stewart Parnell, had misgivings about the Plan of Campaign, fearing it would antagonize British public opinion and damage future Home Rule prospects. Their misgivings proved well founded, and the British press denounced the Plan as a form of revolutionary socialism.

Beginning in early October 1886, Stead made his first trip to Ireland. His aim was to investigate the evictions and social unrest, and he spent two months living in the countryside, meeting Irish farmers and parish priests. His visit was encouraged, and probably arranged, by Cardinal Manning, who empathized with the suffering Irish peasantry, and supplied Stead with introductions to prominent Irish Catholics, including the nationalist bishops, Thomas Croke, archbishop of Cashel, and William Walsh, recently consecrated archbishop of Dublin. Stead witnessed the launch of the Plan of Campaign at Woodford, and during the autumn he sent reports to the *Pall Mall* on Irish landlordism, the land war, the plight of the tenant farmers, and Irish parish priests. These included a long, five-part article on 'The Story of the Woodford Evictions', with vivid portrayals of the community and its personalities, bringing to life the human costs of evictions. Stead was appalled by the suffering, and his condemnation of the evicting landlords was uncompromising: 'Landlordism,' he wrote, 'is dead, but the stench of its decaying remains still pollutes the air', while its 'vampire' corpse continued to destroy lives.[123] He liked the Catholic parish priests he met, sorrowing for their flocks, identifying with the poor, restraining popular violence against the landlords, and keeping their sense of humour. The high point of his Irish investigation was his interview with Archbishop Walsh in Dublin on 30 November 1886, when Walsh gave a reasoned defence of the Plan of Campaign. According to Walsh, prior land legislation in Ireland had recognized that tenant farmers had rights, and the tenants were within their rights to pay an affordable rent in view of the falling prices. It was, Stead insisted, 'one of the most important interviews which have been published in the English press since the interview which led to the despatch of General Gordon', and he hoped it would open the eyes of English readers to the real conditions in Ireland. The interview 'caused a sensation'; it was reproduced in the leading British newspapers, and Unionists were 'roused to fury'.[124] Stead returned to London 'full of admiration for the Irish priesthood'; Cardinal Manning, he later recalled, 'was very pleased.'[125]

The *Pall Mall Gazette* was almost the only major British newspaper to support the Plan of Campaign. Catholic nationalists, as Archbishop Walsh observed, now viewed Stead as a great friend to Ireland.[126] Early in 1887, the Conservative government moved against the Plan of Campaign, securing coercive legislation to suppress the tenant associations and arresting many Irish activists and priests. Stead returned to Ireland in early April and interviewed Walsh a second time. He also interviewed two priests, Fathers Ryan and Keller, who were in Kilmainham prison indefinitely for refusing to give evidence against tenant farmers involved in the Plan of Campaign, as this would violate the confidentiality of the confessional. Stead felt a particular affinity for the imprisoned priests, and compared their cells to his at Holloway. He was enraged when later in April 1887 the British government successfully used its influence in the Vatican to secure a Papal condemnation of the Plan of Campaign. The Irish Catholics, he believed, were a highly devout people, who deserved better from the papacy. In Ireland, he insisted, 'the people and their priests are as one. The priest is the father, the leader, the tribune of his flock. Nowhere is there a population more devoted to the Catholic faith and to the discharge of their religious duties.' Priests and people were united in confronting 'the horrors of eviction and of starvation', and struggling for a better future.[127] Guided by Cardinal Manning, Stead found in Catholic Ireland a form of his Civic Church, and many parish priests were for him 'Christs', prepared to sacrifice themselves for their flocks. The popular Irish Catholic nationalist editor, MP, and promoter of the Plan of Campaign, William O'Brien, wrote Stead in the spring of 1887 to thank him: 'We all appreciate what an advantage your visits have conferred upon our cause, and we will not readily forget your courage and penetration.'[128] Then in September 1887 O'Brien was arrested and imprisoned for 'incitement' under the government's new coercion act.

### The Law and Liberty League

On 13 November 1887, some 10,000 demonstrators converged on Trafalgar Square to protest against O'Brien's imprisonment; they included Irish nationalists, socialists, trades unionists, radicals, and free speech activists. The London authorities had been seeking for months to end the use of Trafalgar Square for public protest meetings, and they prohibited the demonstration. As the demonstrators arrived, the London police, many on horseback and supported by soldiers, attacked them. In the violence of this 'Bloody Sunday', hundreds were injured and 400 were arrested. Stead witnessed the violence, writing to Gladstone on 14 November that the suppression of the demonstration 'was characterised by a brutality which I have never before seen in the whole of my life'.[129] The *Pall Mall* on 14 November devoted over eight and a half pages to 'Bloody Sunday', while Stead thundered forth with an editorial entitled 'At the Point of the Bayonet'. 'In order to prevent the holding of a lawful meeting,' he wrote, 'ruffians in uniform were despatched to ride down and bludgeon law-abiding citizens who were marching in procession towards the rendezvous. Scenes of savage brutality are reported from Westminster, from Shaftesbury-avenue, and from the Haymarket.'[130] The *Pall Mall* established a defence fund to provide legal assistance for those arrested.

On Stead's initiative, a diverse group, including the secularist, socialist, and feminist Annie Besant, the Gladstonian Liberal and feminist MP Jacob Bright, the radical Anglican priest Stewart Headlam, the socialist artist William Morris, and the labour politician John Burns (soon to be imprisoned for his part in the Trafalgar Square demonstration), met with Stead on 18 November to form the Law and Liberty League. The purpose of the League was to organize communities in defence of freedom of speech and assembly. The *Pall Mall* publicized the League and collected subscriptions, and Stead, together with Besant, Morris, and Headlam, served on the League's Executive Committee.[131] Another demonstration at Trafalgar Square on Sunday, 20 November, was attacked and broken up by mounted police, with one of those trampled by a police horse, a young clerk named Alfred Linnell, dying of his injuries. The League organized a funeral procession, which on Sunday, 18 December, moved through the London streets, watched by over 100,000 people, to a churchyard near St Paul's Cathedral. Stead and Morris led the procession, with Annie Besant, William O'Brien, MP (now released from prison), and R. B. Cunninghame Graham, MP, as pall-bearers. At the churchyard, Headlam read the funeral service and Morris gave an eloquent tribute.[132] There had not been such a public funeral, Stead maintained in the *Pall Mall*, since that of the Duke of Wellington in 1852.[133]

**Annie Besant**

Stead and Annie Besant were now working closely together. Stead had admired Besant for several years, but it was only amid the Trafalgar Square violence that they met. She was highly intelligent, well educated, attractive, a gifted orator, two years older than Stead, prominent in London socialist and radical circles, and Irish in background, with a devout Christian upbringing. In 1867, at the age of twenty, she had married an Anglican priest, Frank Besant, with whom she had a son and daughter. But she lost her Christian faith, the marriage broke down, and her husband received custody of their son. In 1873 she moved to London with her daughter, earning an income by journalism. She was drawn into the Secularist Society, collaborating with the prominent atheist, Charles Bradlaugh, writing for the Secularist *National Reformer*, and packing halls as a popular public lecturer. She was prosecuted in 1877 along with Bradlaugh under the Obscene Publications Act for reprinting a pamphlet promoting birth control. Although she was not imprisoned, her husband gained custody over their daughter in 1878 on the grounds that she was an unfit mother. In the mid-1880s, Besant was drawn to socialism, joining the Fabian Society.

Stead and Besant now founded and jointly edited a weekly newspaper to publicize the Law and Liberty League and promote networks of social activists and voluntary social workers. It was called *The Link: A Journal of the Servants of Man*; one editor described herself as 'an uncompromising and aggressive atheist' while the other claimed he had been called by God to 'be a Christ'. Their newspaper, which began on 4 February 1888, was to work 'simply and solely as the helper of the helpless, the friend of the oppressed, and the advocate and champion of the cause of the Disinherited of our race'.[134] The newspaper encouraged reader participation, including the sending of news items highlighting local social needs. 'Remember,' its readers were told, '*The Link* is your organ, dependent upon your co-operation, your information, and your support for its existence.'[135] For Stead, the Law and Liberty League and *The Link* were expressions of his Civic Church ideal, uniting people of different faiths and of no faith in shared work and sacrifice on behalf of those who suffered.

Besant relished their partnership, and felt attracted to Stead, a fellow-worker who truly 'cares for the salvation of the people'. She told him on 20 December 1887 that 'Like Diogenes, I have [been] looking for "a man" for some time, & you seem to me the very one who has head & heart enough for the work.'[136] A few days later, she acknowledged the 'very curious influence you have over me that

I should tell you of my troubles'.[137] She confided her longing to believe in his 'Church of the future' and recover faith in a divine presence. It was, she confessed, the misery of the world, and especially the suffering of the innocent, that had made her an atheist—she could not believe that a righteous God could permit so much evil: 'The horror & the hopelessness of it all nearly drove me mad, & then I won my way into the peace of Atheism which leaves man without an Almighty Torturer while it leaves him also without a Father.' But she found it difficult to live like an 'orphan' in a world bereft of spiritual meaning. Stead's Civic Church ideal offered her fresh hope, and she now longed 'for the realisation of your—or should I say our?—Church'.[138]

He became her 'dear Sir Galahad' and she tried to share his beliefs, reading, on his suggestion, Carlyle's *Cromwell* and one of Manning's works, and attending a sermon by Liddon at St Paul's Cathedral.[139] The Civic Church became for her their 'special movement', to be worked for, she hoped, through 'our political & spiritual marriage'.[140] She assured Stead on 26 March that 'in a very real sense you are a messenger of God to me for good'. Then on 17 April, she confessed that she loved him, and that she hoped he shared her feelings, and that despite his marriage he could tell her that 'you loved me best'.[141] But this was not what Stead intended for their partnership. He would not give up his wife and children for her. He now decided to go to Russia (and to Olga Novikoff) for a prolonged visit. She only learned of this from a second party. 'I was a little sorry,' she wrote to him curtly on 20 April, 'to have heard of your movements first from a stranger.'[142] But she had her answer. Their mutual projects, the Law and Liberty League and *The Link*, soon ended. While he was away, in the summer of 1888, Besant threw herself into organizing a strike of the London matchgirls, who worked fourteen-hour days, for low pay and in unhealthy conditions, producing matches. This marked a formative event in the 'new unionism', or the organization of semi-skilled and unskilled workers for industrial action. She reached out to Stead on his return from Russia. 'When, oh when,' she wrote on 23 July 1888, 'am I going to have one quiet hour with you my dear friend? I *do* so want it.'[143] They remained friends, though not in the way she had hoped.

Following his Russian trip of 1888, Stead's tenure as editor of the *Pall Mall Gazette* drew to a close. It had been a remarkable time, especially the years between 1883 and 1886, with his great campaigns over the 'Bitter Cry', 'Gordon for the Sudan', the 'Truth about the Navy', and the 'Maiden Tribute'. During those years, he profoundly influenced British journalism, effectively creating what Matthew Arnold, in an article in the *Nineteenth Century* of May 1887, dubbed the 'New Journalism'.[144] Stead had developed a distinctive style of journalism, emphasizing sensational, emotive stories to rouse public opinion for concerted action, subjective, often impassioned editorials to form an 'emotional bonding' between editor and readers, aggressive investigative reporting, interviews with prominent figures, and moral campaigns mobilizing reader participation and featuring public meetings, processions, and petitions. His New Journalism also changed the layout of the newspaper, with attention-seeking headlines, frequent and boldly phrased subheadings in articles, more maps and illustrations, and frequent 'extras' or special themed issues, reprinting related articles from previous issues.[145] It was 'journalism with a mission'.[146] 'The New Journalism,' Hugh Kingsmill observed, 'was for Stead predominantly a means to establishing an emotional bond between himself and the public. His stunts were never designed in order to make money.' Rather, 'they were essentially devices to kindle the passions of his readers.'[147] And underlying this journalism with a mission, these passionate appeals, were Stead's religious beliefs, his sense of the editor's desk as his pulpit, and of the editor as preacher and prophet, proclaiming the new spiritual truths of the Civic Church, the essential oneness of all true religions, and the divine call to 'be a Christ'.

## Notes

1. Private journal entry of 22 October 1880, cited in Robertson Scott, *Life and Death of a Newspaper*, p. 117.
2. Quoted in Raymond L. Schults, *Crusader in Babylon: W. T. Stead and the* Pall Mall Gazette (Lincoln, Nebraska, 1972), p. 21.
3. Edward E. Cleal, *The Story of Congregationalism in Surrey* (London, 1908), pp. 324–6.
4. Whyte, *Life of W. T. Stead*, vol. i, pp. 96–7; Stead, *My Father*, pp. 120–1.
5. W. T. Stead, 'Character Sketch: Two High Churchmen', *RoR* (January 1905), pp. 28–9, 34–5.
6. Schults, *Crusader in Babylon*, pp. xiv–xvi, 44; Robinson, *Muckraker*, p. 47.

7. Robertson Scott, *Life and Death of a Newspaper*, p. 79.

8. Private journal entry of July 1880, cited in Robertson Scott, *Life and Death of a Newspaper*, p. 114.

9. W. T. Stead, 'Character Sketch: October [John Morley]', *RoR*, 2 (November 1890), p. 424.

10. Basil Willey, *More Nineteenth Century Studies* (London, 1956), p. 250.

11. Stead, 'Character Sketch: October [John Morley]', p. 433.

12. Robertson Scott, *Life and Death of a Newspaper*, p. 119.

13. Undated private journal entry, probably 1883, cited in Robertson Scott, *Life and Death of a Newspaper*, p. 120.

14. Reid, *Memoirs*, pp. 345–6.

15. W. T. Stead, 'The Gospel According to the *Pall Mall Gazette*', Appendix 1, in Whyte, *Life of W. T. Stead*, vol. ii, pp. 321–7, quotations on pp. 321, 322.

16. 'Centres of Spiritual Activity', *PMG* (22, 29 November; 6, 13, 20, 27 December 1883; 4, 10, 17, 24 January; 7, 14, 21 February; 8, 21, 29 March; 19 April; 9 August; 10 September; 2, 20 October; 11 November 1884).

17. 'The Archbishop of Canterbury on Some Topics of the Day', *PMG* (25 March 1884); 'Mr Spurgeon at Home', *PMG* (18, 19 June 1884); 'Interview with Dwight L. Moody', *PMG* (12 July 1884).

18. Pamela J. Walker, *Pulling the Devil's Kingdom Down: The Salvation Army in Victorian Britain* (Berkeley, California, 2001), pp. 94–129, 206–34; Roy Hattersley, *Blood and Fire: William and Catherine Booth and their Salvation Army* (London, 1999), pp. 221–84.

19. W. T. Stead, 'In Darkest England and the Way Out', *RoR*, 2 (October 1890), pp. 386–8.

20. W. Booth to W. T. Stead, 19 July 1879, Stead Papers, Churchill College, Cambridge, STED 1/8.

21. Private journal entry of 11 January 1880, cited in Robertson Scott, *Life and Death of a Newspaper*, pp. 111–12.

22. Stead, 'In Darkest England and the Way Out', pp. 382, 384.

23. Ibid., pp. 390–92, 388.

24. William Booth, 'Centres of Spiritual Activity', *PMG* (13 December 1883); Catherine Booth, 'Women as Preachers', *PMG* (31 January 1884); [W. T. Stead]; 'Women who Work—Hallelujah Lasses', *PMG* (2 May 1885).

25. [W. T. Stead], 'The Latest Sensation of the Salvation Army', *PMG* (16 May 1884).

26. [A. Mearns and W. C. Preston], *The Bitter Cry of Outcast London* (London, 1883), p. 2.

27. [W. T. Stead], 'Is It Not Time?' *PMG* (16 October 1883).
28. Ibid.
29. Ibid.
30. H. M. Hyndman, 'Revolutionary Socialism', *PMG* (29 October 1883); Octavia Hill, 'Labourers' Dwellings in London', *PMG* (31 October 1883).
31. W. T. Stead, 'Character Sketch: Sir Alfred Milner', *RoR*, 20 (July 1899), p. 21.
32. K. S. Inglis, *Churches and the Working Classes in Victorian England* (London, 1963), p. 69.
33. 'The Condition of the Poor', *PMG* (3, 4 April 1884); Nigel Scotland, *Squires in the Slums: Settlements and Missions in Late Victorian London* (London, 2007), pp. 9–10.
34. J. A. R. Pimlott, *Toynbee Hall: Fifty Years of Social Progress 1884–1934* (London, 1935), pp. 25–36.
35. Stead, 'Character Sketch: Sir Alfred Milner', p. 20; Alfred Milner, *Arnold Toynbee: A Reminiscence* (London, 1901).
36. V. A. McClelland, *Cardinal Manning: His Public Life and Influence 1865–1892* (Oxford, 1962), pp. 129–39.
37. J. O. Baylen, 'Politics and the "New Journalism": Lord Esher's Use of the *Pall Mall Gazette*', *Victorian Periodicals Review*, 20 (1987), pp. 127–8.
38. Stead, 'Character Sketch: Sir Alfred Milner', p. 21.
39. [W. T. Stead], 'The Conditions of Success', *PMG* (21 January 1884).
40. Robertson Scott, *Life and Death of a Newspaper*, p. 97.
41. [W. T. Stead]. 'General Gordon as Governor in the Sudan, 1874–79', *PMG* (21 January 1884).
42. [W. T. Stead], 'Chinese Gordon's Policy for the Soudan', *PMG* (22 January 1884).
43. 'Who Is to Have the Soudan?' *PMG 'Extra'* (12 March 1884).
44. [W. T. Stead], 'General Gordon at Work', *PMG* (20 February 1884).
45. [W. T. Stead], 'General Gordon's Religious Ideas', *PMG* (4 March 1884) and *PMG 'Extra'* (12 March 1884).
46. Quoted in Richard Shannon, *Gladstone: Heroic Minister 1865–1898* (London, 1999), p. 332.
47. [W. T. Stead], 'A Plea for Mercy', *PMG* (13 May 1884).
48. James Mussell, '"Of the Making of Magazines There Is No End": W. T. Stead, Newness, and Archival Imagination', *English Studies in Canada*, 41 (2015), p. 77.
49. Reid, *Memoirs*, p. 346.
50. W. T. Stead to Augusta Gordon, 6 February 1885, BL, Moffitt Collection, Add. Mss. 51300, fol. 69.
51. [W. T. Stead], 'In Memoriam', *PMG* (11 February 1885).

52. 'The Gordon Memorial Services', *The Times* (14 March 1885).

53. [W. T. Stead], 'A Startling Revelation', *PMG* (18 September 1884).

54. W. T. Stead, 'The Great Pacifist', *RoR* (June 1912), p. 610.

55. Josephine Butler, 'Sir William Harcourt's Amended Bill', *PMG* (10 July 1884); Schults, *Crusader in Babylon*, p. 129.

56. Robertson Scott, *Life and Death of a Newspaper*, p. 126.

57. Pamela J. Walker, 'The Conversion of Rebecca Jarrett', *History Workshop Journal*, 58 (2004), 246–58; Jane Jordan, *Josephine Butler* (London, 2001), pp. 217–23.

58. Bramwell Booth, *Echoes and Memories* (1925) (London, 1977), pp. 124–30.

59. Waugh, *William T. Stead*, pp. 27–8.

60. Jordan, *Josephine Butler*, p. 223.

61. [W. T. Stead], 'The Truth about Our Secret Commission', *PMG* (9 July 1885).

62. Ibid.

63. W. T. Stead to Olga Novikoff, 10 June 1885, Bodleian Library, Oxford, MS.Eng.misc.d.182, fos. 204–5.

64. Booth, *Echoes and Memories*, pp. 131–2, 151.

65. Josephine Butler, *Rebecca Jarrett* (London, [1885]), p. 18.

66. Jordan, *Josephine Butler*, pp. 223–4.

67. [W. T. Stead]. 'The Maiden Tribute—III', *PMG* (8 July 1885).

68. [W. T. Stead], 'The Maiden Tribute—I', *PMG* (6 July 1885).

69. Ibid.

70. Deborah Gorham, 'The "Maiden Tribute of Modern Babylon" Re-examined: Child Prostitution and the Idea of Childhood in Late-Victorian England', *Victorian Studies*, 21 (1978), p. 355.

71. Baylen, 'The "New Journalism" in Late Victorian Britain', p. 382.

72. Walkowitz, *City of Dreadful Delight*, p. 82.

73. Schults, *Crusader in Babylon*, pp. 136, 140, 137.

74. Whyte, *Life of W. T. Stead*, vol. i, pp. 173–5.

75. [W. T. Stead], 'Letting Light into the Labyrinth', *PMG* (11 July 1885); Georgina Battiscombe, *Shaftesbury: A Biography of the Seventh Earl* (London, 1974), p. 331; Waugh, *William T. Stead*, pp. 39–40.

76. [W. T. Stead], 'Put to the Test', *PMG* (14 July 1885).

77. [W. T. Stead], 'True', *PMG* (30 July 1885).

78. Schults, *Crusader in Babylon*, pp. 161–2.

79. Grace Eckley, *Maiden Tribute: A Life of W. T. Stead* (Philadelphia, 2007), p. 63.

80. [W. T. Stead], 'The New Crusade', *PMG* (20 August 1885); 'The Protection of Girls: National Conference at St. James's Hall', *PMG* (21 August 1885).

81. Walkowitz, *City of Dreadful Delight*, pp. 104–5; Eckley, *Maiden Tribute*, p. 66.

82. 'The Hyde Park Demonstration', *PMG* (24 August 1885).

83. Walkowitz, *City of Dreadful Delight*, pp. 105.

84. Ann M. Hale, 'W. T. Stead and Participatory Reader Networks', *Victorian Periodicals Review*, 48 (2015), pp. 18–20.

85. [W. T. Stead], 'The New Factor in Politics', *PMG* (22 August 1885); E. G. Sandford (ed.), *Memoirs of Archbishop Temple*, 2 vols. (London, 1906), vol. ii, pp. 128–9.

86. Eckley, *Maiden Tribute,* pp. 80–3; Butler, *Rebecca Jarrett*, pp. 19–20; Walker, 'Conversion of Rebecca Jarrett', p. 249.

87. Schults, *Crusader in Babylon*, pp. 180–4; Walkowitz, *City of Dreadful Delight*, pp. 123–5.

88. Quoted in Whyte, *Life of Stead*, vol. i, p. 304.

89. Hugh Kingsmill, *After Puritanism 1850–1900* (London, 1929), p. 191.

90. W. T. Stead, 'Character Sketch: January [Dean Church], *RoR*, 3 (January 1891), p. 29.

91. Quoted in Stead, *My Father*, p. 141.

92. Robertson Scott, *The Life and Death of a Newspaper*, p. 133.

93. Whyte, *Life of W. T. Stead*, vol. i, pp. 211–13.

94. Charles Haddon Spurgeon to W. T. Stead, 24 December 1885, Stead Papers, STED 1/66.

95. Millicent Fawcett to Emma Stead, 11 November 1885, Stead Papers, STED 1/26.

96. Shane Leslie, *Henry Edward Manning: His Life and Labours* (London, 1921), pp. 459–69; Henry Manning, 'Inhuman Crimes in England', *North American Review* (October 1885) in *PMG* (1 October 1885); W. T. Stead, 'Character Sketch: Three of the Dead', *RoR*, 5 (February 1892), p. 131.

97. E. S. Purcell, *Life of Cardinal Manning*, 2 vols. (London, 1896), vol. ii, p. 653.

98. Leslie, *Henry Edward Manning*, p. 460.

99. W. T. Stead, 'Character Sketch: Cardinal Manning', *RoR*, 1 (June 1890), p. 481.

100. Stead, 'Character Sketch: Cardinal Manning', p. 480.

101. Stead, 'Character Sketch: Cardinal Manning', p. 481.

102. W. T. Stead, 'Character Sketch: Three of the Dead', p. 130.

103. H. S. Lunn, *Chapters from my Life with Special Reference to Reunion* (London, 1918), p. 132.

104. Raymond Blathwayt (ed.), *Interview of Mr. W. T. Stead on the Church of the Future* (London, 1891), pp. 14–15.

105. Private journal entry of 31 December 1885, cited in Robertson Scott, *Life and Death of a Newspaper*, pp. 137–42.

106. W. T. Stead to Augusta Gordon, 31 December 1885, BL, Moffitt Collection, Add. Mss. 51300, fos. 178–9.

107. Robertson Scott, *Life and Death of a Newspaper*, p. 135.

108. John Morley, *Recollections*, 2 vols. (London, 1917), vol. i, pp. 209–10.

109. Robertson Scott, *Life and Death of a Newspaper*, pp. 142–5; Schults, *Crusader in Babylon*, p. 191; Whyte, *Life of W. T. Stead*, vol. i, pp. 218–20.

110. W. T. Stead, 'Government by Journalism', *The Contemporary Review*, 49 (1886), pp. 653–74; W. T. Stead, 'The Future of Journalism', *The Contemporary Review*, 50 (1886), pp. 663–79.

111. Stead, 'Government by Journalism', p. 657.

112. Ibid., pp. 664, 663.

113. Stead, 'The Future of Journalism', p. 670.

114. Ibid., p. 678.

115. W. T. Stead, 'A Church "Exceeding Broad"', *PMG 'Extra'* (10 June 1886).

116. Ibid., p. 4.

117. Ibid., p. 5.

118. For their views and political actions over the Home Rule bill of 1886, see McClelland, *Cardinal Manning*, pp. 185–91; Whyte, *Life of W. T. Stead*, vol. i, pp. 221–9.

119. [W. T. Stead], 'This Won't Do', *PMG* (9 April 1886).

120. [W. T. Stead], 'Sine Quo Non', *PMG* (30 April 1886).

121. [W. T. Stead], 'Making Bad Worse', *PMG* (11 May 1886).

122. Whyte, *Life of W. T. Stead*, vol. i, p. 226.

123. [W. T. Stead], 'The Story of the Woodford Evictions—I', *PMG* (29 November 1886).

124. Patrick J. Walsh, *William J. Walsh: Archbishop of Dublin* (Dublin, 1923), p. 241.

125. Ibid., 235–6; Stead, 'Character Sketch: Three of the Dead', p. 132.

126. Emmet Larkin, *The Roman Catholic Church and the Plan of Campaign 1886–1888* (Cork, 1978), p. 75.

127. W. T. Stead, *The Pope and the New Era* (London, 1890), p. 149.

128. Quoted in Whyte, *Life of W. T. Stead*, vol. i, p. 236.

129. W. T. Stead to W. E. Gladstone, 14 November [1887], Gladstone Papers, BL, Add Mss 44303, fos. 378–9.

130. [W. T. Stead], 'At the Point of the Bayonet', *PMG* (14 November 1887).

131. Arthur H. Nethercot, *The First Five Lives of Annie Besant* (London, 1961), pp. 260–4.

132. 'Linnell's Funeral', *PMG* (19 December 1887).

133. [W. T. Stead], 'The Significance of Yesterday', *PMG* (19 December 1887).

134. Nethercot, *The First Five Lives of Annie Besant*, p. 263; Hale, 'W. T. Stead and Participatory Reader Networks', pp. 23–6.

135. Hale, 'W. T. Stead and Participatory Reader Networks', p. 25.

136. Annie Besant to W. T. Stead, 20 December 1887, Stead Papers, STED 1/6.

137. Annie Besant to W. T. Stead, 24 December 1887, Stead Papers, STED 1/6.

138. Annie Besant to W. T. Stead, 1 January 1888, Stead Papers, STED 1/6.

139. Annie Besant to W. T. Stead, 1 January, 14 January, 1 April 1888, Stead Papers, STED 1/6.

140. Annie Besant to W. T. Stead, 4 March 1888, Stead Papers, STED 1/6.

141. Annie Besant to W. T. Stead, 26 March, 17 April 1888, Stead Papers, STED 1/6.

142. Annie Besant to W. T. Stead, 20 April 1888, Stead Papers, STED 1/6.

143. Annie Besant to W. T. Stead, 23 July 1888, Stead Papers, STED 1/6.

144. Matthew Arnold, 'Up to Easter', *Nineteenth Century*, 123 (1887), pp. 638–9.

145. On the New Journalism, see especially Baylen, 'The "New Journalism" in Late Victorian Britain' and Schults, *Crusader in Babylon*, pp. 29–65; Whyte, *Life of W. T. Stead*, vol. I, pp. 237–89.

146. By J. W. Robertson Scott, quoted in Schults, *Crusader in Babylon*, p. 31.

147. Kingsmill, *After Puritanism*, p. 182.

# 3

# The City of God and the Civic Church, 1888–94

'I see now,' Stead reflected in his private journal on his fortieth birthday (5 July 1889), 'that I am called to found for the Nineteenth Century a city of God which will be to the age of the printing press and the steam engine what the Catholic Church was to the Europe of the 10th century.' Through his journalism, he would help found a multi-faith Civic Church, which 'will embody and render accessible for the meanest the ripest wisdom of the world. It will be father confessor, spiritual director, moral teacher, political conscience. It will be the great social nexus. It will be the mother of mankind'.[1] The six years from 1888 to 1894 were for Stead an immensely creative period. Inspired by the potential for the new media of mass communication to unite and elevate humankind, his ideas became increasingly global. During these years, he wrote perhaps his three most important books, the *Truth about Russia* (1888), *The Pope and the New Era* (1890), and *If Christ Came to Chicago!* (1894). He ghost-wrote for William Booth of the Salvation Army much of the highly influential book on urban social Christianity, *In Darkest England and the Way Out* (1890). He also founded in late 1889 a new monthly journal, the *Review of Reviews*, which aimed at providing readers with digests of the best books and articles from around the world and which he viewed as the 'first step to a world-wide journalistic, civic church'.[2]

## The *Truth about Russia*

His sense of world mission found expression in April 1888, when, at the invitation of his friend and former lover, Olga Novikoff, Stead travelled to Russia in the cause of peace. It was, he later wrote, 'my first peace mission to the Continent'.[3] The European political situation was tense, with rising French popular support for the right-wing nationalist General Georges Boulanger and the very real threat of renewed war between France and Germany. Stead was convinced that Russia's position was crucial. If Russia allied with either France or Germany, there would be general European war, but if Russia exerted its influence for peace, in alliance with Britain, the crisis would ease and a new era of peaceful co-operation begin. Stead hoped that by reporting in the *Pall Mall* on the real political situation in Russia, he could lay the foundations for a future alliance between Britain and Russia. He appealed to Novikoff, to help him gain an interview with the Tsar. She promised to do so, though she noted that Stead's recent public involvement with radicals and socialists in the Trafalgar Square riots would make this difficult.[4] None the less, through her family connections, she arranged the interview and Stead made a hasty departure from London. Stead's editorship of the *Pall Mall* was precarious; the newspaper had not recovered financially from the Maiden Tribute campaign and his relations with the proprietor were tense. So at a more personal level he hoped for a major journalistic success in Russia that would secure his *Pall Mall* position. And there was also the entanglement with Annie Besant from which to escape.

The journey across Europe began badly, with a less than successful visit to Paris. A fellow journalist, Mrs Emily Crawford, had arranged a meeting for him with the French prime minister, Charles Floquet, but when Stead arrived at the gilded apartment for the meeting, she felt 'heartsick' over his appearance, with his 'worn-out sealskin cap . . . yellowish-brown tweed suit, ill-cut, ill-fitting, and untidy' and his smile, which revealed 'two rows of peculiarly set teeth'. He had, she noted, 'the air of a dog-stealer', and his meeting with Floquet soon ended. Stead was allowed to speak with the foreign minister, René Goblet, on the promise he would not publish any of their conversation, but Stead then ruffled feathers with an article in the *Pall Mall* that was clearly based on the interview.[5] Matters improved in Russia, where Stead was supervised, and no doubt guided in matters of dress, by Madame Novikoff. Stead was in Russia for nearly two months. Novikoff accompanied him around St Petersburg, introducing him as a leading British friend to Russia; her family embraced him and he was warmly received everywhere. 'Never since I was in gaol,' he wrote after his return, 'had I two months of such exalted enjoyment, such constant consciousness of being led [by God].'[6] He interviewed Tsar Alexander III for nearly two hours (although he promised not to publish the interview, a commitment he honoured). Unaccustomed to Court protocol, Stead, on being conducted to the Tsar at the imperial palace at Gatschina, stepped forward and shook the Tsar's hand, and when he had finished his questions, suggested that he had kept the Tsar from his lunch for too long, which had the appearance of dismissing the Tsar. But their discussion, conducted in English, was cordial and Alexander, probably warned about Stead's eccentricity, was amused rather than offended.[7] Stead also obtained interviews with other prominent figures, including the retired diplomat, Count Nicolai Ignatieff, and the chief procurator of the Holy Synod of the Russian Orthodox Church, Konstantin Pobedonostsev. He was also invited by the Russian novelist, Count Leo Tolstoy, to spend a week at his country home at Yasnaya Polyana, near Tula. Stead had begun a correspondence with Tolstoy while he was in Holloway prison, telling him of the divine call he had received to 'be a Christ'. One of the first British visitors to Yasnaya Polyana, Stead enjoyed lengthy walks and conversation with Tolstoy, who spoke English well.[8]

While he was away, Stead posted articles 'from the special correspondent' for publication in the *Pall Mall*. On his return, he was devastated to learn that Yates Thompson had arranged that his articles from Russia, which Stead believed were vital to Europe's future, were printed in small font at the bottom of pages and received little attention. Stead now gathered and expanded those articles into a substantial 457-page book, the *Truth about Russia*, which he completed in early October 1888 and published before the year's end. It was his first book, and although Stead knew no Russian and had been less than two months in the country, he provided a lively overview of Russian politics, economics, culture, and religion. Stead portrayed Russia as an autocratic regime, but where the Tsar was a 'tribune of his people', genuinely concerned for their welfare. The Russian state and society, he claimed, were gradually moving in more liberal directions. The book was not uncritical. The *zemstvo* reforms of the 1860s, setting up provincial representative assemblies, had not in

Stead's view been successful, and the central Tsarist government was ill informed about the country's real needs. The peasant villages, with their communal assemblies or *mir*, were stable but stagnant, with widespread illiteracy (the result of too few primary schools) and archaic farming methods. Stead was impressed with the expanding railway system and Russia's natural resources, arguing that there were great opportunities in Russia for British trade and investment. He also maintained that the Russian government was committed to peaceful relations with its neighbours.

He took a special interest in Russian religion. 'For many years,' Stead wrote in *Truth about Russia*, 'I have held that the next great wave of religious revival that would influence European development would take its rise in *Russia*.'[9] In 1875–8, Stead had been profoundly impressed by the readiness of the 'sainted' Nicolas Kirieff (Olga Novikoff's brother) and other Russian volunteers to die for the liberation of the Slavic peoples. For him, 'the heroic Christlike death of Nicolas Kirieff' exemplified sacrifice, and being a 'Christ', and he had idealized a Russian Orthodox Church that could inspire such devotion. Coming to Russia in 1888, he now wanted to explore its religious life in light of his religious experience in Holloway prison. He was, however, disappointed by the Russian Orthodox Church. In part, this resulted from his Protestant Nonconformity, which led him to see Russian Orthodoxy as exemplifying the worst aspects of a state Church. Its hierarchy of bishops, he believed, chiefly relished exercising authority and social control, while its lower clergy seemed more concerned with chanting the liturgy or administering the sacraments than teaching the people a vital Scriptural Christianity.

He was highly critical of how Konstantin Pobedonostsev, the urbane chief procurator of the Holy Synod (who Stead dubbed 'Archbishop Laud redivivus' and the 'supreme State Churchman of our epoch') used the power of the Tsarist state to suppress evangelistic activity by dissenting churches.[10] Dissenting denominations were officially tolerated, but not allowed to proselytize, which meant their membership was restricted to those born within their communion. And despite the official toleration, dissenting prayer meetings were broken up by police, their leaders imprisoned or exiled, and dissenting magazines closed. This 'monopoly' on the part of the Orthodox Church, Stead believed, ensured that the great majority of Russian people, especially the peasantry, lived in lamentable ignorance of biblical teachings and saving truths. Stead acknowledged that there was much beauty in Orthodox devotion and liturgy, and he was moved by pious expressions in Orthodox worship. The 'look on the upturned face of a peasant girl [in worship],' he wrote, 'was one of the most beautiful things I saw in all Russia. Yes, I may say the most beautiful.'[11] But for Stead, radiant church interiors and luminous Russian icons mattered less than preaching and teaching God's word in Scripture. He had hoped to find in Russian Orthodoxy a missionary Church prepared to convey Christian truths to the world, but he found it merely an expression of 'Holy Russia', symbolizing Russian national identity.

Stead devoted over sixty pages of the book to his talks with Tolstoy. He liked the religious views of Tolstoy, but was not uncritical. Stead had not read the recent English translations of Tolstoy's *War and Peace* and *Anna Karenina*; the taste for Russian novels, he observed, was 'quite of recent growth in England'.[12] Rather, he knew Tolstoy as a religious writer—presumably through three translated texts published under the title *Christ's Christianity* in 1885.[13] These works formed the basis of their discussions during Stead's week at Yasnaya Polyana. What most impressed Stead was Tolstoy's devotion to Christ's ethical teachings and his effort to apply those teachings, without compromise, to social life. Stead respected Tolstoy's commitment to living in community, his insistence on the equality of all people before God, his simple manner of living, his manual labour, his generosity towards the poor, his refusal to take oaths, his rejection of aggressive nationalism, and his recognition of the essential unity of humankind. In Tolstoy's simple, communal manner of living and his effort to follow Jesus's example, Stead saw a striving to sacrifice self-interest and 'be a Christ'. He could not, however, accept Tolstoy's absolute pacifism, or his rejection of centralized governments, and he debated these points with his host. But above all, he could not accept Tolstoy's rejection of the doctrines of Christ's atonement for the sins of humankind and the resurrection from the dead. Stead believed that for Tolstoy Christ was divine only in the sense that He 'spoke the will of God' and had, like all humans, 'a spark of God in our breast'. But otherwise 'Christ was only a man like other men. The story of His birth and of His resurrection seem to Count Tolstoi purely mythical.'[14] For his part, Tolstoy was less than impressed by their conversations. Writing to a Russian friend in 1905, he recalled that Stead was 'a cunning fellow, I didn't like him'.[15]

Stead's book on Russia received mixed responses. The historian James Anthony Froude thought well of it. 'I have been reading Stead's book with real pleasure,' he informed Novikoff in March 1889. 'He is a far abler man than I supposed him to be, and with his political judgment generally I entirely agree.'[16] The reviewer in the radical *Westminster Review*, on the other hand, was disappointed that Stead, a radical journalist, flattered the Russian Tsar and his autocratic regime. It noted that he was willing to criticize the persecution of dissenting Christians, but not the far more brutal persecution of Russian Jews, the suppression of a free press, and the imprisonment and exile of political dissenters. Stead's 'plea that Alexander is the Tribune of his people', the reviewer concluded, 'is one of the ghastliest fictions ever invented to bolster despotism'.[17] The lapsed English Catholic and long-term resident in Russia, E. J. Dillon, writing in the Liberal *Fortnightly Review*, thought Stead presented a romanticized, superficial view of Russia, including 'an overmastering tendency to idealise Russian autocracy'. Viewing Russia through 'the rose-coloured spectacles of a Carlylean hero-worshipper', he failed to see the widespread suffering.[18] Olga Novikoff, for her part, thought the book highly unfavourable to Russia; she was enraged by Stead's criticisms of her country, and especially of the Russian Orthodox Church, which she viewed as monstrous ingratitude. After all, she and her family had arranged his Russian visit, introducing him to Pobedonostsev, who Stead denounced in the book as a religious persecutor. Stead's friendship with Novikoff would recover, but she had been hurt.[19] 'I am afraid,' Stead informed Gladstone on 18 December 1888, 'that by delivering my soul on this subject [of religious persecution] from the standpoint of an English Nonconformist, I have excited profound indignation in Orthodox circles, indignation which I fear will render it impossible for me to return to Russia so long as M. Pobedonestzeff remains in favour.'[20]

Stead's account of Russia was intellectually respectable, but not the journalistic triumph for which he had hoped. Neither his reports from Russia nor his book had restored his damaged relations with the *Pall Mall* proprietor. On 19 September 1888, Stead had a 'brutal' meeting with Yates Thompson, who reduced his salary and clearly wanted his resignation, but with a wife and six children, and a large house in Wimbledon, Stead was not in a financial position to resign. And despite this humiliation, Stead still believed in his prophetic mission as a journalist. 'When I left [St Petersburg],' he confided to his diary on 25 September 1888, 'I felt more confirmed in my ideas that I had been led and helped and was to be used of God. My great ideal of journalism seemed to come nearer realisation.'[21] But it was also clear to him that 'the next great wave of religious revival' affecting the world would probably not come from Russia.

## The Pope and the New Era

In the spring of 1887, Stead had conceived the idea of travelling to Rome and interviewing Vatican dignitaries about the Irish land question. This was shortly after his two visits to Ireland, and interviews with Archbishop Walsh of Dublin. Stead wanted to find out why there was so little sympathy in Rome for the suffering Irish tenant farmers. When he mentioned the idea to Cardinal Manning, he was taken aback by his fervent response. 'Go to Rome!' Manning told him, 'I think it will be good for the Holy Father to see you.' 'It will be good for them,' he continued with reference to the Pope's advisors, 'to hear from the lips of an Englishman what you have seen with your own eyes and heard with your own ears in Ireland.'[22] 'Cardinal Manning,' Stead wrote Gladstone on 26 March 1887, 'has advised me that he thinks it would be useful for the Holy Father to see me and hear what I have to say as an Englishman and an independent journalist, on the condition of Ireland.'[23] But then the Irish agitation against the Unionist government's coercive policies grew more heated, and Stead decided he must remain at his editor's desk in London.

Under Manning's influence, Stead was becoming warmer to the Roman Catholic Church and its potential for promoting social good in the modern world. His friendship with Manning steadily dissolved the anti-Catholic prejudices in which he had been raised. They enjoyed friendly banter about Stead's Nonconformity and love for Cromwell, Manning warning him in January 1889 that despite all this he might yet become a 'Papist': 'None are so near,' he joked, 'as those who think themselves safest.'[24] In December 1888, Stead published a long essay on 'The Progress of Man' in the *Universal Review*, a new London-based periodical.[25] Here Stead outlined what he viewed as evidence of a divinely ordained human progress towards ever-greater individual freedom, increasing democracy in politics, and greater catholicity in religion. By catholicity, he meant a recognition that all the great world religions contained elements of divine truth and had the potential to elevate human nature. Within Christianity, he argued, growing catholicity was enhancing the ecumenical ideal of the 'essential unity of the faith of the Church Universal', and this was leading ever more people to the Roman Catholic Church, 'the great organisation which has its seat, its centre, and its capital in the Eternal City... its princes in every capital and its priests in every village'.[26] The Catholic Church, Stead maintained, had an immense opportunity to exercise unrivalled spiritual and moral leadership in the world—if only it would adapt itself to the new 'Age of Democracy'.

Stead saw evidence of such a Catholic adaptation to democracy in Archbishop Walsh's support for Irish home rule and the rights of Irish tenant farmers. In the summer of 1889 there came still further evidence in the role played by Cardinal Manning in mediating the London dockers' strike. The union of dockworkers, struggling for better wages and conditions, went on strike and closed the port of London for several weeks. The striking dockers and their families were soon suffering greatly, and tensions mounted. In the fourth week of the strike, the employers planned to import foreign workers as strike breakers, which threatened to bring violent clashes and loss of life. Although eighty-one years of age and physically frail, Manning now personally intervened. With patience, hard work, and perseverance, moving continually between employers and union representatives, and earning respect from all parties, he mediated a settlement and brought the strike to a peaceful end. Stead described the settlement in the *Pall Mall* as 'The Cardinal's Peace'. 'The assistance which the Cardinal has rendered in adjusting this strike,' Stead enthused in his editorial of 13 September 1889, 'recalls those great acts of secular service by which alone his Church acquired that hold upon the world which long centuries have failed entirely to destroy.'[27]

In October 1889, Stead travelled to Rome for a three-week visit. His aim, he told Lord Carnavon on 7 October, was 'to ascertain whether the Holy Father is an effective moral force available for the solution of the social problems of the modern world'.[28] It was an auspicious time to visit Rome. Along with the land agitation in Ireland and the dockers' strike in London, the year 1889 saw social and political unrest across Europe. Events of that year included the defeat of a threatened coup by General Boulanger and his right-wing nationalist supporters in France, commemorations of the centenary of the French Revolution, the formation of the Second International (an alliance of socialist parties and societies) in Paris, widespread industrial strikes in France and Germany, and a pilgrimage of French workers to Rome, calling on Pope Leo XIII for leadership in the social crisis. In Rome, the dedication on 9 June 1889 of a memorial to Giordano Bruno, a philosopher burned for heresy in 1600, attracted a crowd of over six thousand in what became a demonstration of popular hostility to the papacy. Fearing mob attacks, Pope Leo XIII seriously contemplated moving permanently from Rome.[29]

Manning gave Stead introductions to high officials in Rome, including Monsignor Domenico Jacobini, secretary of propaganda, Monsignor Tobias Kirby, rector of the Irish College, and Cardinal Mariano Rampolla, papal secretary of state. 'Thanks to the kindness of Cardinal Manning,' Stead later wrote, 'I was received everywhere with the utmost cordiality.'[30] Stead also corresponded regularly with Manning throughout his time in Rome.[31] On 22 October, Stead met with Monsignor Mario Mocenni, deputy papal secretary of state, telling him, 'I wanted to see the Pope, to have a good square talk with him as I had with the Tsar.'[32] Monsignor Kirby, now in his eighties and 'one of the dearest and kindest of friends', helped Stead prepare a list of points for possible discussion with the Pope.[33] Stead wanted to impress upon the Vatican the serious damage done to the Catholic Church in Ireland by the Papal condemnation of the Plan of Campaign in April 1888. 'I told him very plainly,' he wrote Manning on 23 October 1889 regarding a conversation with Jacobini, 'how the Pope had made Archbishop Walsh eat dirt before all the Irish race by the rescript condemning the plan of campaign [and] that this kind of thing was dangerous.'[34] Unsurprisingly, Stead was not granted an interview with the Pope. He found Rome disappointing, 'about as hopeless a sink of idolatry and atheism as you could find anywhere'.[35]

While in Rome, Stead wrote eleven 'Letters from the Vatican', which Manning edited for him; they were published in the *Pall Mall* between 31 October and 16 December 1889. On returning to London, Stead revised and expanded these letters into a book of 256 pages, published in February 1890 under the title *The Pope and the New Era: Letters from the Vatican in 1889*. The book appealed to the Catholic Church to embrace the spirit of the modern world, and for the Pope to become the 'international Director-General of the Humanitarian forces of the world'. Stead saw a compelling need for such leadership. 'Humanity,' he asserted, 'wandering forlorn in the Wilderness of Sin, cries aloud for a new Moses to lead it across the desert to the Promised Land of the new social order. It is not for the Vicar of Christ to shrink back dismayed from the responsibility of answering to this call.'[36] The present situation of the papacy suggested the fifth-century fall of the Western Roman Empire, a period when a number of 'great Popes' extended authority over 'the fierce warriors from the fastnesses and forests of the North' and 'created Europe out of the chaos of barbarian invasion'.[37] Now the Pope must exercise spiritual influence over the new forces of industrialism, imperialism, democracy, and socialism.

For the Catholic Church to reassert its world leadership, Stead argued, it needed to adapt to the 'threefold Revolution' now reshaping the world order. First, it must embrace the world dominance of the English-speaking peoples, represented by the British Empire and the United States. Already the planet's *lingua franca* was English. The Catholic Church must drop Latin in religious services and ecclesiastical communications, and accept that 'the common speech of the New Era will be the tongue which Milton spoke and Shakespeare wrote'.[38] And the papacy must recognize that as the centre of world culture had now shifted from the Mediterranean to the North Atlantic, it was time for the papacy to leave Rome and move to London. 'Rome,' he insisted, 'is of the old world, archaic, moribund, and passing away. The centre, the capital, and the mother city of the new world, which Catholicism must conquer or perish, is not to be found on the banks of the Tiber, but on the Thames.'[39] Second, the Church needed to reorient its social teachings, and embrace the rise of the socialist movement. 'The world,' Stead insisted, 'is becoming

Socialist. Everywhere power is passing into the hand of the workman, who . . . demands to be allowed to live a human life.' The papacy should follow the example of Manning's role in mediating the London dockers' strike, which 'attracted the admiration of the world'.[40] It should develop new Christian social teachings, supporting the struggle of working people for decent living standards, and considering political action for the redistribution of wealth. Third, the Church needed to support the emerging struggle to elevate the status of women and achieve equal civil rights for women, including the right to vote. The women's movement, he maintained, was bringing a great moral revolution, to which the Church must adapt.

To exercise moral leadership in the new era, Stead argued, the Pope must cease longing to restore his temporal power over central Italy. The papacy had still not accepted the Italian unification of 1861 and the loss of the papal states; it still lamented the loss of its temporal power over Rome in 1870. But in truth, Stead argued, the Pope's loss of temporal power had liberated the Church, enabling papal concentration on the Church's world mission, which was based on spiritual and moral, not political, authority. The Pope must look beyond the grandeur that had been Rome, including its magnificent churches. Stead personally viewed the Roman churches largely as expressions of the old temporal power; his book offered no descriptions of church architecture, beautiful church interiors, or works of religious art. 'I have not felt in the least the fascination of Rome,' he wrote. 'Never was I less inclined to join the Papal Church than when I stood beneath the dome of St. Peter's.'[41] The one Roman ecclesiastical building that impressed him was the plain, modest building in the Piazza di Spagna housing the College of the Propaganda, where he was given a tour by its head, Monsignor Jacobini. Here he saw the records (many mouldering and illegible) of the Catholic missionaries sent out by the College since its formation in 1622. For Stead, the real power of the Catholic Church was in these missionary priests and their lives of selfless sacrifice in distant fields. He discerned a spiritual power in their archived letters sent to Rome over the course of centuries. 'Their handwriting is faint and faded now,' he observed:

> but with how fiery a zeal were the pens guided which traced these characters! What innumerable dramas, full of the noblest human heroism, enacted not in full amphitheatre before an applauding or

even a hostile throng, but lived out day by day in obscurity, in disease, in neglect, without hope of praise or of earthly reward! They wrote their epistles with their blood, and sealed their testimony with their lives.[42]

These missionaries exemplified sacrifice and devotion, often amidst the poorest peoples of the world, where they had lived and died as 'Christs'.

Stead gave Manning a copy of the book in February 1890, insisting that the prospect of a new, more positive relation between the papacy and the modern world 'would never have gained possession of the popular mind but for your life work'.[43] Stead's book received considerable attention, with rumours that he would soon convert to Catholicism, although the Catholic press 'saw no symptoms in him of conversion'.[44] The assessments of the book were mixed. Some found his perceptions of Rome, as a radical journalist and Protestant Nonconformist, fresh and entertaining. The reviewer in *The Speaker* liked his openness to 'what is truly great and noble in the Church of Rome' and his effort to 'enlist her marvellous organisation and spiritual forces into the service of the cause which he has so much at heart'.[45] Others, however, criticized his audacity in writing on the history and future prospects of a Catholic Church of which he knew so little. 'The strength of his prejudices,' observed the reviewer in the *Saturday Review* of 19 April 1890, 'the fathomless depth of his self-conceit, the colossal scale of his accumulated ignorances, and the peculiar character of his breeding, make his opinions...valueless, except as a source of amusement.'[46] Stead, to be sure, was primarily interested in the Catholic Church in relation to his own developing vision of a future universal Church, uniting all people of good will in social service.

### The Review of Reviews

In December 1889, Stead finally resigned as editor of the *Pall* Mall and was succeeded by his assistant, E. T. Cook. In partnership with George Newnes, a friend from Silcoates School and now a successful publisher, Stead began in January 1890 a new monthly journal, *The Review of Reviews*, conceived as an expression of 'a world-wide journalistic, civic church'.[47] The aim of *The Review of Reviews* was to provide short, engaging summaries of the best articles and books from the world press. Each issue opened with an article entitled 'The Progress of the World', in which Stead offered critical commentary on the main events of the past month. Each issue also featured a 'Character Sketch' of a major world figure, reflecting Stead's Carlylean belief that it was heroic figures who shaped the world. The journal's guiding principle was to promote the union of all English-speaking peoples for their divinely ordained mission of world leadership.[48]

The first issue began a lengthy mission statement, 'To all English-Speaking Folk', in which Stead outlined his prophetic purpose. 'There exists at this moment,' he declared, 'no institution which even aspires to be to the English-speaking world what the Catholic Church in its prime was to the intelligence of Christendom.' The journal would 'call attention to the need for such an institution, adjusted, of course, to the altered circumstances of the New Era' and would seek 'to enlist the co-operation of all those who will work towards [its] creation'. By bringing together the insights from the best of world literature, Stead's journal would help to discern God's ongoing revelation to the world. '"God is not dumb that He should speak no more",' he observed, 'and we have to seek for the gradual unfolding of His message to His creatures in the highest and ripest thought of our time.' God, he further maintained, continued to communicate His revelation first and foremost to a particular race, a chosen people; in ancient times this had been the Hebrew people and now it was the 'English-speaking race': 'We believe in God, in England, and in Humanity. The English-speaking race is one of the chief of God's chosen agents for executing coming improvements in the lot of mankind.'[49] What was needed was a new order of faithful activists, who would embrace the missionary zeal, discipline, and commitment of the Jesuit order or the Salvation Army, and infuse the English-speaking world with ideals of sacrifice in the service of humanity.[50] Specific editorial positions of his journal included support for a British 'imperialism within limits defined by common sense and the Ten Commandments', the goal of 'fraternal union with the American Republic', social reforms aimed at improving conditions for working people and a 'levelling up of social inequalities', equal rights and the vote for women, and the transformation of the Concert of Europe into a 'United States of Europe'.[51] The journal gave special attention to women's issues, becoming a major voice for late Victorian feminism. As Alexis Easley has noted, 'Stead provided a popular platform for the middle-class women's movement, in the years leading to enfranchisement. Working closely with women authors and activists, Stead succeeded in popularising the feminist cause, making it accessible to a broad audience.'[52] He meant for people to read his *Review of Reviews* 'as men used to read their Bibles, not to waste an idle hour, but to discover the will of God and their duty to man'.[53]

The first issue included a call for reader participation, asking readers around the world to send Stead appropriate extracts from their local press and suggestions for articles. He aimed to establish a formal network of readers who would work for the journal's ideals 'as zealously as hundreds of thousands are working for the ideals of churches'.[54] This resembled the short-lived magazine, *Link*, which he and Besant had established in 1888, only now he expanded such work from England to the wider English-speaking world. In March 1890, he founded the 'Association of Helpers' in connection with *The Review of Reviews*; it was to promote local efforts for various causes, including communal care for the elderly and dying; meals for school children from deprived families; country excursions for poor urban children, access to parks and recreational facilities, or better housing for working people. For Stead, the major Association ideal was 'the reunion of all religions into a federation of service on behalf of those who suffer'. Stead regularly issued specific directions in the journal on how local activists could help promote specific causes.[55] He made special efforts to recruit women and defined one of the goals as the 'recognition of the Humanity and Citizenship of Woman'.[56] By January 1893, the Association of Helpers had several hundred members, whose addresses Stead published in the journal so they could communicate with each other; they were based mainly in Britain, but with representation in the colonies, the United States, and the European Continent.[57] In 1891, Stead produced another monthly journal, *Help*, as a voice for his Association of Helpers, but this proved short-lived, closing in 1892.

In the first issue of the *Review of Reviews*, Stead invited all readers 'who feel the craving for counsel, for sympathy, and for the consolation of pouring out their soul's grief' to write with their concerns. His plan was to gather a group of 'competent and skilful advisers . . . from amongst the best men and women in the English-speaking world' who would respond to these readers' letters.[58] Critics mocked his efforts to become the 'Father Confessor to the Universe'. Stead's soaring ambitions for the journal soon brought a break with his partner Newnes, and in April 1890 Stead had to buy out Newnes' interest in the journal, borrowing the money, at 5 per cent interest, from the Salvation Army, on condition that the loan remain secret.[59] He was now both proprietor and editor of the journal, with a level of control he had never previously known.

*The Review of Reviews* was an immediate success, its first issue of eighty-four pages selling 60,000 copies on the first day of publication.[60] The circulation stabilized at about 100,000 within a few years. He employed several gifted women authors to write for the journal, including Flora Shaw and Marie Belloc Lowndes, and the office staff were largely female. While it was said he had a 'preference for pretty women', they were efficient and professional. In February 1891, he recruited the capable Edwin H. Stout, a former assistant editor at the *Methodist Times,* as business manager; Stout continued in this capacity until 1913, keeping the journal on a sound financial footing, despite Stead's extravagant schemes and inability to manage money. Stead also employed his younger brother, the Christian Socialist Francis Herbert Stead, who in 1889 resigned his ministry at a Congregational church in Leicester and later moved to London with his family. Herbert became effectively assistant editor, taking charge of the journal when Stead travelled. In December 1894, Herbert became the first warden of the Browning Settlement in Walworth, Southwark, London, but continued to work part-time at the journal, which helped support the Settlement's work. Stead took the work of the journal seriously, his business manager estimating that Stead personally wrote or dictated over 80,000 letters between 1890 and 1912.[61] In addition to 'The Progress of the World', he wrote the monthly 'Character Sketches', which proved one of the journal's most popular features; a number of the Character Sketches were also published separately as pamphlets. In 1891, he began publishing Christmas *Annuals,* substantial books for holiday reading, which also proved popular. He spent long hours at the office, sprawled over the furniture or sitting on the floor, amidst piles of books and papers. *The Review of Reviews*, with its short, lively summaries of books and articles from around the world, its 'Progress of the World', 'Character Sketches', featured 'Book of the Month', extensive illustrations, and pious tone appealed to clerks and office workers, products of the system of national education, who were committed to self-improvement and expanding their intellectual horizons. The circulation of *The Review of Reviews* remained at a high level, and it spawned successful subsidiary publications—*The American Review of Reviews* and *The Australian Review of Reviews*. *The American Review of Reviews* began in April 1891, under the editorship of the able Albert Shaw, and within two years it had a circulation of 85,000.[62] Stead became one of the most recognized journalists in the world.

Stead's views of a world dominated by the 'English-speaking race', as proclaimed by *The Review of Reviews*, were shared by the English imperialist, mining entrepreneur, and colonial official, Cecil Rhodes, and the two became friends. Stead first met Rhodes at a private lunch hosted by Sir Charles Mills, then agent-general of the Cape Colony, on 4 April 1889, during one of Rhodes' visits to England. They talked for three hours. Rhodes spoke of how he admired Stead's work at the *Pall Mall*, including the 'Maiden Tribute' campaign, while Stead told Rhodes of his support for expanding British imperial control in Africa. Both were sons of clergymen, were of a similar age (Rhodes four years younger), felt themselves outsiders, and had grandiose visions for the British Empire. 'Here is a strong man, an able man,' Stead enthused in Carlylean tones to his wife after their lunch, 'and I talked to him much about God and guidance.' 'I think,' he added, 'that I shall be God's instrument in doing him good.'[63] Stead enthused over Rhodes's friendship with the late General Gordon, who 'knew him well and trusted him absolutely'.[64] Stead and Rhodes met again when Rhodes next visited England (February 1891), discussing the idea of a 'Secret Society', to be called the 'Society of the Elect' and modelled on the Jesuit Order.[65] It would be made up of able, idealistic men of strong imperialist convictions, who 'would do for the unity of the English-speaking race what the Society of Jesus did for the Catholic Church immediately after the Reformation'. Rhodes admired *The Review of Reviews*, especially the Association of Helpers; he applauded the journal 'as a practical step towards the realization of his great idea, the reunion of the English-speaking world'. Although Rhodes was a professed agnostic, Stead convinced himself that there was a 'higher mystic side' to his character, which rested 'upon a foundation as distinctly ethical and theist as that of the old Puritans'.[66] In 1891, Rhodes designated Stead in his will as a trustee of his estate. Stead relished their friendship, lauded Rhodes's imperialism in *The Review of Reviews*, and seemed blind to Rhodes's British South African Company's brutal maltreatment of the Matabeleland peoples in its search for minerals.

## Stead's Nonconformist Conscience, Dilke, and the Fall of Parnell

Stead's Puritanism and his belief that he was God's vehicle led him to seek to impose high moral standards in political life, and this could take the form of persecution through journalism. Sir Charles Dilke was a Liberal politician, author, and imperialist, whose *Greater Britain* (1868) was a best-selling account of the expansion of the English-speaking peoples. Wealthy and well connected, he entered Parliament in 1868 and the Cabinet in 1882. His first wife died in childbirth in 1874, and he was rumoured to have extra-marital affairs. In 1885, Virginia Crawford, twenty-two years old, attractive, vivacious, and wanting out of a love-less marriage to a much older man, confessed to her husband that she had had an intermittent affair with Dilke for over two years, adding many salacious, but dubious details, including an account of a threesome with Dilke's maid, Fanny Gray. The matter was complicated by rumours (probably true) that Dilke had had an affair with Virginia's mother. At the subsequent divorce trial, in February 1886, Dilke, on legal advice, did not give evidence, and the divorce was granted. Dilke then brought a further legal action to clear his name, but he proved a poor witness at the second trial, in April 1886, and the jury found against him. His public reputation was now shattered and he lost his parliamentary seat at the general election of 1886.[67]

Stead had taken a close interest in the case from the beginning. While he did not know Dilke well, they shared friendships with Manning and Morley. The *Pall Mall* gave extensive coverage to the trials and initially Stead tried to be even-handed. But after the second trial, he became convinced that Dilke was a monster, abusing his wealth and power to ruin young women, in the manner of the 'minotaurs' in his Maiden Tribute articles. Manning introduced Stead to Virginia Crawford after the divorce, when 'with shattered health and a blasted name ... she experienced to the full the bitterness of social excommunication'. Stead employed her at the *Pall Mall*, and introduced her to H. P. Liddon and Catherine Booth, under whose influence she left the 'atheism in which she had been reared' and embraced Christianity, engaging in voluntary visiting of the sick with the West London Mission. Then, under Manning's spiritual direction, she was in 1889 received into the Catholic Church, becoming a prolific author, and a selfless Catholic social worker and reformer. Convinced she had been shamed on 'the pillory of the world' for Dilke's 'amusement', Stead conducted what he admitted was a 'relentless persecution' of Dilke, determined to ensure that his immorality was exposed, and that unless he sincerely and publicly confessed his sins, he would never return to public life.[68] This campaign of 'self-righteous vindictiveness' continued for years.[69]

In December 1890, Stead joined with fellow Nonconformists in condemning the immorality of another prominent politician involved in divorce proceedings—the Irish Home Rule leader, Charles Stewart Parnell. Captain William O'Shea, a former member of the Home Rule party, had filed for divorce from his English Protestant wife, Katherine, naming Parnell as co-respondent. The unmarried Parnell had been Mrs O'Shea's lover for several years, fathering at least two of her children. At the divorce trial in November 1890, he was portrayed as morally corrupt, abusing the friendship and trust of a political supporter in order to seduce his wife and use her for his sexual gratification. While Irish nationalists initially remained loyal to their chief, British Nonconformist journalists, led by Stead at *The Review of Reviews* and Hugh Price Hughes of the *Methodist Times*, were swift to demand Parnell's removal. Stead insisted it was not Parnell's adultery so much as his dishonesty that rendered him unfit to lead; 'the damning thing was the deliberate perfidy with which he had deceived.'[70] The Catholic hierarchy in Ireland now also turned against Parnell, the Irish bishops calling as a body for his resignation. The majority of the Irish Parliamentary Party then rejected Parnell as leader, and Ireland's 'uncrowned king' was effectively destroyed. Stead rejoiced at how Christian moral opinion in both Britain and

Ireland had brought Parnell down. 'It was worth the sacrifice of Mr. Parnell ten times over,' he boasted in *The Review of Reviews* of January 1891, 'to bring the Catholic clergy of Ireland into line with the militant Nonconformists of England.' In this, the Catholic priests of Ireland were acting as 'the nineteenth century counterparts of the Puritan preachers and Covenanting confessors of the reigns of the Stuarts'.[71] Parnell died of rheumatic fever, aged only forty-five, in October 1891.

In 1892, Dilke was elected to Parliament by the coal miners of the Forest of Dean constituency. On learning of the candidacy of the 'Standard Bearer of the Debauchees of the World', Stead was furious, campaigned against him and tried to organize a national conference of protest.[72] Stead was also cruel in his personal attacks on Dilke's second wife, the widow of the respected Oxford scholar, Mark Pattison.[73] But by now the public was weary of Stead's hounding of Dilke. 'Mr Stead,' asserted Cyril Waters in *The Westminster Review* of January 1892, 'is...fanatical in his religion. He is filled with the zeal of the Puritans of old, and, if he could, would, like them, wield the sword of the Lord and of Gideon, and purify as by fire the field of public life and private morals, reckless of all consequences in his thirst for righteousness. He has, indeed, all the pitiless cruelty of the bigot of virtue.'[74] Dilke would prove a very good constituency MP for almost twenty years, working hard on behalf of the miners and of workers generally, and showing great compassion for them.

## The Salvation Army in 'Darkest England'

Early in 1888, Catherine Booth, the co-founder of the Salvation Army, was diagnosed with breast cancer. An extraordinary woman, she was an equal partner with her husband, William, in urban mission work, preaching with great effect from 1860 (despite the widespread prejudice against women preachers), and becoming a formidable leader of the Salvation Army. Although never physically robust, she struggled against her cancer for over two years, continuing as best she could her work for the Salvation Army. In her final months she was bedridden. Stead had long held her in the highest esteem. 'My dear mother,' Bramwell Booth later recalled, 'was one of Stead's heroines'; he remembered Stead in those last months 'kneeling by the side of her

suffering bed and pouring out his soul to God'.[75] Stead thought her
the greatest English woman of her time, a figure of fearless resolve,
immense compassion, and uncompromising commitment to elevating
the lives and saving the souls of the poor and outcast, in urban Britain
and across the globe. He later wrote a biography of her. He had first
become close to her during the Maiden Tribute campaign of 1885,
when 'she was as kind, as sympathetic, as patient, and as helpful to
me, as if she had been my own mother'.[76] In their friendship,
she would argue with him, and seek to draw him back to more
orthodox Christian beliefs. 'She regarded me,' Stead recalled, 'as
latitudinarian, humanitarian, I know not what.' But she had also
supported him passionately in his struggle against child sex abuse
and trafficking, and was a 'splendid fighter'—'pre-eminently one of
those whom you would choose to have at your back in a fight'. 'There
was in her,' he added, 'a whole-hearted zeal, a thorough-going earn-
estness, a flaming passion of indignation, that cheered one like the
sound of a trumpet.'[77]

As Catherine lay dying, and in conformity with her wishes, her
husband began conceptualizing a new direction for the Salvation
Army. From its formation in 1878, the Salvation Army had concen-
trated on evangelism, with preaching, processions, meetings, and
literature directed to saving individual souls, especially among the
poor and marginalized. However, in the 1880s—Stead dated the
change from the Trafalgar Square riots of 1887—the Booths became
increasingly aware of the need to improve the material conditions of
the poor. This was based partly on a recognition that impoverished
people struggling for survival, and uncertain about their next meal or
having a roof over their heads, were not likely to take much interest in
the afterlife. More immediately, the Booths acknowledged that they
had a humanitarian duty to help the hungry, homeless, and suffering.
William envisioned a comprehensive plan for bettering the social
conditions for the 'submerged tenth', the poorest ten percentile in
society, and Stead volunteered to help him develop his ideas into a
book—drawing evidence from William Booth's 'field notes', writing
the book by dictation, and submitting chapters for Booth's approval.
Stead made regular visits to the Booth's small villa at Clacton-on-Sea
during 1890, sometimes bringing with him a couple of steno-
graphers.[78] He combined work on the book with visits to Catherine

at her bedside. She died on 4 October. On 20 October, the three-hundred-page book, *In Darkest England and the Way Out*, was published under General Booth's name and dedicated to Catherine.

*In Darkest England* was made up of two parts. The first part, entitled 'The Darkness', opened with an extended comparison of life in the central African jungles (from the explorer Henry Morton Stanley's *In Darkest Africa*) and life in England's urban slums. It provided vivid depictions of the social misery of England's 'submerged tenth', including widespread unemployment, homelessness, prostitution, starvation wages, malnutrition, drunkenness, and despair. Mostly written by Stead, it included passages lifted from his *Pall Mall* articles of 1883 on the 'Bitter Cry of Outcast London'. The second, and much longer part of the book, entitled 'Deliverance', described Booth's proposed programme for a new Salvation Army social outreach, including the establishment of hospitals, rescue homes for women wishing to leave prostitution, refuges for street children, day-care centres for single parents, enquiry offices for lost persons, industrial training schools, decent lodging houses, legal aid clinics, and savings banks. Most important were the proposals for a hierarchy of 'colonies' for people broken by long-term addiction to alcohol or drugs, or by chronic unemployment. These were the 'unworthy poor', who were shunned by most philanthropic and Christian aid associations; their 'low moral character' was seen by many as placing them beyond redemption. To help them, there were to be 'city colonies', homes providing basic accommodation in return for work within strictly regimented conditions, which would nurture sobriety and disciplined habits. Those who, over a period of time, demonstrated an improved moral character in the 'city colonies' would advance to a 'farm colony' in the countryside, where they would live in villages, grow their own food and be strengthened physically by outdoor labour. Finally, those reformed in the 'farm colonies' would emigrate to special Salvation Army 'overseas colonies' to be established within the British Empire.

'Today, to me, the horizon is radiant with a new hope,' Stead enthused of *In Darkest England* in *The Review of Reviews* (October 1890). 'Never since my life began, now more than forty years ago, have I seen as much cause to confront the future with such confidence.' 'No such book,' he continued, 'so comprehensive in its scope, so daring in its audacity, and yet so simple and practical in its proposals, has appeared in my time.'[79] He compared General Booth's book to Thomas Carlyle's works of social criticism, observing that while Carlyle's social commentaries had been mainly negative, Booth offered a programme for real social redemption. 'The Army,' Stead observed, 'now feels strong enough to attempt something more than the saving of the individual. It is entering upon a campaign for the salvation of society.'[80] 'You will be delighted,' Stead wrote to Alfred Milner on 23 October 1890, 'to see that we have got the Salvation Army solid not only for Social Reform but also for Imperial Unity. I have written to Rhodes about it and we stand on the eve of great things.'[81] Within weeks, 115,000 copies of the book were sold. Stead published a short, highly laudatory biography of William Booth in early 1891, describing him as the 'cosmopolitan man of our time' and leader of a great world religious movement. 'The Church of Rome and the Salvation Army,' Stead proclaimed, 'these are the only two organisations which operate directly and simultaneously in all the continents and among all the nations.'[82] Booth estimated that it would cost £100,000 to begin his programme and £30,000 per year to keep it going. Stead placed *The Review of Reviews* firmly behind Booth's fund-raising campaign, telling his readers how to contribute. He tried to unite all Christian denominations, including the Catholic Church, behind the campaign. By January 1891, he reported that Booth had nearly raised the initial £100,000.

Public opinion, however, was divided.[83] Many shared Stead's view that Booth's scheme could unite Christianity, common sense, and Socialism behind a great national and imperial campaign of social redemption. Others, however, were unimpressed, noting that there was little original in the book, and that the book had given little credit to social reform efforts already under way. There were serious doubts about how effective the city and farm colonies would be in the long term. Perhaps most important, many were critical of Booth as a person, viewing him as an autocratic leader of an organization of religious fanatics whose schemes, if successful, would threaten religious toleration and freedom of thought. The agnostic scientist, T. H. Huxley, in a series of letters against Booth's scheme in *The Times*, argued that prostitution, intemperance, and even starvation would be preferable to having the 'intellect of the nation' 'put down by organized fanaticism'.[84] Socialists dismissed Booth's programme, insisting that Britain needed far more fundamental reforms than those proposed *In Darkest England*. Other Christian organizations, including the Anglican Church Army (modelled on the Salvation Army), would not join Booth's programme.

Such opposition had its impact, and public contributions to Booth's social reform programme declined after January 1891. While £108,000 had been raised by January 1891, only £20,000 was raised between February 1891 and September 1892.[85] Some programmes, including a number of city and farm colonies, were set up, and the Salvation Army's overall commitment to social reform did prove permanent. But it did not become the great movement to unite and transform society that Stead had predicted. Stead ceased giving much attention to the *Darkest England* reform movement in *The Review of Reviews* after February 1891, and his relations with the Salvation Army, so strong when Catherine Booth was alive, now waned. As Bramwell Booth recalled, while Stead had been close to his mother, he had never got on well with the general and 'there was some reserve between the two'. The general, who insisted on exercising unquestioned leadership over the Salvation Army, may have been irritated by the public awareness that Stead had written most of *In Darkest England*. The devoutly evangelical Booth may also have suspected that Stead aimed to use the Salvation Army to advance his personal Civic Church agenda, based on his vague formula of 'being a Christ'. They continued an uneasy association, but after one of their last meetings, the general confided 'vehemently' to Bramwell that 'I cannot stand Stead!'[86]

The spring of 1891 saw Stead's attention shifting from the Salvation Army to the new social teachings of the Catholic Church. In May 1891, Pope Leo XIII issued his famous encyclical on the social question, *Rerum Novarum*, which Stead made his 'Book of the Month', reviewing it at length in *The Review of Reviews* of June 1891. Probably under the guidance of Manning, who warmly welcomed the encyclical, Stead expressed strong support for its main provisions, including its call for a minimum 'living' wage for all workers (sufficient to support a family in decent comfort), its acceptance of the need for trades unions, its call for state intervention in the economy to safeguard workers' rights, and its support for peasant proprietorship. For Stead, *Rerum Novarum* was a bold new commitment by the Church to improve lives in this world. It was part of a general shift in modern Christian civilization from a focus on personal salvation in the next life towards social salvation in this. 'What a change,' Stead enthused, 'has come over the whole aspect of Christendom since the century began!'

> This life is no longer merely the antechamber of eternity. We are no longer mere pilgrims through a wilderness to a heavenly city, which rises on the other side of the waters of the river of death. We have become, on the contrary, citizens of the kingdom of God on earth, charged with the duty of transforming the world and regenerating human society.[87]

In January 1892, Cardinal Manning died at the age of eighty-three. Tens of thousands, including large numbers of dockworkers, lined the London streets of London to witness the funeral procession. For Stead, it was the loss of a second father, who had loved him amidst all his weaknesses and failings. 'He was the only man in all London,' Stead believed, 'who cared enough for me to rap me across the knuckles if he thought I was doing wrong.'[88] For Stead, moreover, Manning had represented the prospect that the ancient Christian faith could again be a force for directing and elevating human affairs in the global context. Manning, for his part, evidently enjoyed Stead's boyish enthusiasms, energy, and continual scrapes; he would write to Stead playfully to 'come and be scolded' or 'come and be mended', as the case might be.[89] As Catherine Booth's death had loosened Stead's ties to the Salvation Army, so Manning's death now loosened his links to the Catholic Church. Another of Stead's close friends, the renowned Anglo-Catholic preacher and theologian, Canon Liddon of St Paul's Cathedral, had died in September 1890, removing yet another spiritual mentor. These three spiritual guides and authority figures had widened his religious perspectives and also reined in his more extravagant ideas and proposals.

### The Civic Church

Late in 1890, Stead gave an interview to the journalist, actor, and playwright, Raymond Blathwayt, which first appeared in the London journal *Great Thoughts* on 3 January 1891, and then in a 110-page booklet, which included critical commentaries on Stead's ideas by a number of religious leaders and Stead's response to these critics. Here, Stead outlined his ideas concerning what he called the 'Church of the Future', the 'Church of the New Era', or simply the 'Civic Church'. This Church would be 'a community of living men who are associated together with a distinct altruistic purpose', inclusive of all, prepared to unite in the work of helping others. It would embrace atheists as well as theists, reflecting Stead's belief that some who have 'most nearly approximated to the life of Christ', such as John Stuart Mill or Annie Besant, were atheists. Moreover, these unbelievers might find their way to faith, because 'men's definitions of themselves are not free from the blunder of self-deception, and many professing Atheists are unconscious Christians'.[90] Within the 'Church of the New Era', there would be no distinctions based on gender or race. The sole criteria for membership would be a willingness to work and sacrifice for the betterment of humanity, or in Stead's phrase, to 'be a Christ'.[91] 'The Universal Church, according to [the poet] Longfellow, is to be as "lofty as the love of God, and wide as are the wants of man."' The 'true note' of the Church of the Future, he insisted, must be 'the wants of man' and it must 'include all who can minister to the service of Humanity'. In the last fifty years, Stead continued, social theologians had recovered a sense of the 'Fatherhood of God'. Now it was time to embrace the equally important 'Motherhood of the Church'.[92]

For some years, Stead had been promoting through his journalism the vision—which he believed had been given him by God in Holloway prison—of a Church of the Future or a Civic Church, to unite all people of good will in serving all who were in need. He had shared this Civic Church idea with Annie Besant in 1888–9, and she had for a time viewed it as their special joint project. In 1889, he had hoped to discuss the plan with the Pope Leo XIII, but was not invited to meet him. In 1890, he conceived *The Review of Reviews* as a means of communicating this vision to the English-speaking world. For a period in 1890 and early 1891, he had believed that the Salvation Army social reform programme might unite much of Britain behind a religiously motivated social ideal, but he had been disappointed. Now in late 1891 he began a movement through *The Review of Reviews* to establish branches, or congregations, of the Civic Church in towns and cities throughout Britain.[93] His Civic Church would revive national religion and reunite communities around a common set of moral values. The Civic Church, he explained in a public address at Cardiff in February 1892, 'is really the recognition of the essence of a National Church; it is a recognition of the relation of the conscience of the community to its secular affairs'.[94] It was to be, he wrote in *The Review of Reviews* of August 1892, 'a real Church, a working Church, a Church co-extensive with the community in which it exists...a Church which embraces the whole range of human life and which influences all the affairs of life, alike in personal conduct and in affairs of municipal and national government'. In rekindling the ideal of national religion in Britain's diverse society, his Civic Church would play a role similar to that of the Catholic Church in medieval England, with responsibility for promoting education, literature, the arts, family life, charitable giving, festivals, and holidays.[95]

By March 1893, Stead's *Review of Reviews* reported that local efforts were well underway to form Civic Churches in Brighton, Bradford, Birmingham, Cardiff, Edinburgh, Glasgow, Liverpool, Manchester, Maidenhead, Rochdale, and Swansea. There were also local plans for Civic Churches in Adelaide and Melbourne, reflecting Stead's larger goal of uniting all English-speaking peoples. In some cities, such as Brighton, the Civic Church took the form of a civic centre, bringing together various churches, trades unions, temperance societies, and school boards and poor law guardians in support of community building and social improvement. In other cities, including Birmingham, the movement took the form of a federal council of churches.[96] Stead took a particular interest in Edinburgh, speaking at a conference in the Free Church Assembly Hall on the Mound, and calling on the city's 148 churches and philanthropic associations to unite as a Civic Church, and embrace a 'new social edition of the "Westminster Confession of Faith", applied to...the actual needs of human beings living in modern society'.[97]

In April 1893, Stead sent around a circular appealing for support in preparing a 'Bible Book of the English-Speaking Race', which would give expression to the 'the religious side of imperial patriotism' and serve as a sacred text for the Civic Church in its mission to the English-speaking peoples. His plan was to gather extracts from the greatest English language works in poetry, fiction, philosophy, and theology, and combine them with a historical narrative, so that the ordinary person would find inspiration from the 'England as she looms through the mists of history as well as the England of to-day and the England that shall be tomorrow'. The Old Testament, he explained, 'is a kind of REVIEW OF REVIEWS edition of a great mass of writings which have been lost, but from which the editors of the SACRED CANON extracted that which now forms the collection of Booklets bound together, and labelled the Old Testament. I want to do for English literature and History what the editors of the Sacred Canon did for the Hebrew literature and History.'[98]

Stead developed his ideas further in a paper on 'The Civic Church' that he prepared for the first World's Parliament of Religions. The Parliament met in September 1893 in Chicago in association with the World's Fair; its aim was to promote co-operation and unity among the world religions.[99] Stead did not attend the Parliament, but his paper was read for him and later published in the proceedings.[100] His paper maintained that the Civic Church 'is concerned not simply with the salvation of the individual man, but with the regeneration of the whole community. The work of the Civic Church is to establish the kingdom of heaven here among men—in other words to reconstitute human society, to regenerate the state, and inspire it with an aspiration after a divine ideal.'[101] There should be one Civic Church in each town and city, to unite, co-ordinate and energize the efforts of the various religious and social bodies. 'One town, one church,' he observed, 'is as old as the days of the apostles.'[102] The difference between the municipal government and the Civic Church was that the one enforced the law, while the other sought 'to secure conformity, not to the clauses of a law, but to the higher standard which is fixed by the realizable aspirations of mankind for a higher life and a more human, not to say divine, existence'.[103] The Civic Church would inspire and inform, with higher spiritual ideals, the future municipal democracies in towns and cities across the world: 'The duty of the church is ever to be the pioneer of social progress, to be the educator of moral sentiment.'[104] The Civic Church would not replace Christian churches, nor would it be exclusively Christian. Rather, he hoped it would become a worldwide, inter-religious movement, uniting Christians, Hindus, Muslims, and Buddhists in every urban centre for shared service to humanity. Indeed, he suggested that 'if this Parliament of Religions is to found the church of the future', it should proceed on the basis of the Civic Church.[105] Stead's paper was, according to Dennis Downey, 'perhaps the clearest evocation of the churches' role in a program of social renewal' presented at the Parliament and it received a warm reception.[106]

In September 1893, Stead attended the Church Reunion Conference at Lucerne, Switzerland, where he presented his Civic Church as a programme for Christian reunion. The Lucerne Conference was part of the Grindelwald series of Church Union Conferences, held between 1892 and 1895, and forming a significant contribution to the modern ecumenical movement.[107] In an article in *The Review of Reviews* prior to the conference, Stead argued that his Civic Church ideal offered a new beginning for the ecumenical movement.[108] For too long, he maintained, ecumenical efforts had centred on negotiations between denominations aimed at securing a 'uniform creed, uniform ritual or uniform church government'. All these efforts had failed. A more promising way forward, he insisted, was to begin with co-operation among the different denominational churches in locally based, practical social work: 'Instead of seeking to get the churches to unite and form one church the true plan is to form a civic or municipal or national union, comprising all existing churches and all who will co-operate with them in any geographical or social unit.'[109] Stead had hoped the Lucerne Conference would embrace his Civic Church as a practical path to Christian reunion through shared social service at the municipal level, but he was disappointed. Although the Conference devoted a full day to discussing his Civic Church, it rejected his proposals. His friend, the London-based Methodist preacher, journalist, and social activist, Hugh Price Hughes, led the opposition, insisting that 'he could not accept Mr. Stead's Civic Church, as it was not based on any recognition of Christianity.'[110]

During the summer of 1893, Stead had become absorbed with plans to establish a new London newspaper, *The Daily Paper*, which would help promote his socio-religious mission and have for its motto: 'For the Union of All who Love in the Service of All who Suffer'. A sample number of the newspaper was issued on 4 October 1893; among its editorial principles, it included a call for a socially active, 'revived and militant' Church.[111] Late in October, with *The Daily Paper*'s future uncertain (it would fail to secure sufficient financial backing), Stead made his first visit to the United States—a country which, alongside Russia, he had idealized since childhood. He placed his brother, Herbert, in charge of *The Review of Reviews,* and travelled with his eldest son, Willie, to see the Chicago World's Fair before it closed and to promote his Civic Church programme in the New World.

### If Christ Came to Chicago!

Stead was in Chicago from 31 October 1893 to 2 March 1894 (apart from a couple weeks in Toronto and shorter visits to Grinnell, Iowa, and Detroit).[112] Before he arrived, he was already well known in the city for his 'Maiden Tribute' campaign of 1885 and the successful *American Review of Reviews.*[113] Shortly after arriving in Chicago, on the afternoon and evening of 12 November, he conducted, at his own expense, two large public meetings in the Central Music Hall to introduce his Civic Church ideal to the people of Chicago; these meetings were lauded in the Chicago press as among the most remarkable ever held in the city. They would lead in February 1894 to the formation of the Civic Federation of Chicago, a non-profit organization promoting and co-ordinating the charitable activities of the churches and other philanthropic associations; it was, Stead maintained, 'the . . . most complete realization of the Civic Church'.[114] He was surprised and moved by his reception: 'It is curious to see how I became the centre and leader of the whole [progressive] movement in Chicago,' he wrote his friend, the Liberal politician and senior civil servant, Reginald Brett, on 22 November 1893. 'Chicago is said to be the most energetic city in America. I don't think there is any one in it today who does not admit that I went one better all round, & woke them up in a way that startled them not a little.'[115] Alongside his activities in Chicago, Stead made connections with the 'Kingdom Movement'—a Christian movement working for the Kingdom of God on earth through political and social action, and associated with the Congregational minister and radical social gospeller, George D. Herron, professor of applied Christianity at Iowa College, Grinnell (where Stead gave three lectures in January 1894). For Stead, Herron was 'the American Prophet of the Social Revolution'.[116] Stead felt very much at home in the United States, and he briefly contemplated turning the editorship of *The Review of Reviews* over to his brother

Herbert, establishing a Chicago weekly newspaper, and moving there permanently with his family.[117] During the winter, he conducted an investigation of social, political, and religious conditions in Chicago, visiting lodging houses, bars, jails, brothels, law courts, churches, missions, and interviewing scores of ordinary people. He rapidly wrote a book, intended as a major statement of his religious-social ideal, and then returned to England, arriving back in London in mid-March 1894. *If Christ Came to Chicago! A Plea for the Union of All Who Love in the Service of All Who Suffer* was published in both the United States and Britain in April. A substantial book of some 460 pages, it would eventually sell some 300,000 copies on both sides of the Atlantic, and be translated into German and Swedish. Stead considered it his best work, and it was an extraordinary piece of social investigation.[118]

The title was inspired by James Russell Lowell's poem, 'A Parable', one of Stead's childhood favourites, in which Lowell imagined Christ returning to earth and seeing his image, not in grand churches or respectable church goers, but in the faces of a haggard, over-worked artisan and a half-starved, orphan girl. As the subtitle indicated, the book was also a manifesto for his Civic Church. For Stead, Chicago was fast becoming the greatest city in the world, the major industrial and commercial powerhouse of the American republic, and a place of immense private wealth and dynamism. And yet it was also deeply flawed, and Stead's book explored the city's failings, including the suffering of the poor and homeless, dominance of wealthy business interests, widespread bribery of public officials, corruption in public finances, election fraud, tax evasion by the rich, exploitation of women through low wages and prostitution, indifference to public safety by the railways, gross inequalities in income, alcohol and opium abuse, and gun violence. Stead provided vivid first-hand accounts of conditions in the slums, brothels, and jails (where the homeless were allowed to huddle in passages between the cells on bitterly cold nights). Chicago was suffering from the severe economic crisis gripping the United States in 1893, with large numbers out of work, many homeless, and many making their way from rural districts to Chicago in a desperate search for employment—struggling to survive the bitterly cold winter of 1893–4. For Stead, the conditions he witnessed were not simply the result of a temporary crisis, but rather showed Chicago, for all its impressive growth and industrial might, to be a fallen city, in need of redemption. He contrasted the destitution of the poor with the huge wealth of such millionaires as Marshall Field in retail sales, Philip D. Armour in meatpacking, and George M. Pullman in the manufacture of railway carriages; these men were the 'deities of modern Chicago' and the 'idols of the market-place'.[119] But these commercial 'deities', Stead argued, and indeed all the middle and upper classes, were doing precious little to alleviate the social misery around them. Stead insisted that his book was not 'an attack upon Chicago', whose appalling conditions mirrored those in cities throughout the Western world. What these conditions revealed was the loss of faith in the essential Christian message of selfless service to others. 'How we believe in Christ,' Stead insisted in the preface to the British edition, 'is shown not by what we say about Him, not by the temples which we build in His honour, nor by the hymns which we sing in His praise, but by the extent to which we succeed in restoring in man the lost image of God.'[120]

If Christ came to Chicago, Stead maintained, He would not look to the city's churches for the work of social redemption. Chicago's churches, Stead argued, were well meaning, but weak and ineffective in their responses to social suffering and injustice. They had become 'whited sepulchres', places for weekly Sunday gatherings to hear comforting sermons and soothing music. They provided no united front against the social and political evils of the modern city. Divided by sectarian animosities and 'tethered' by wealthy trustees or major donors, they had lost the respect of the working classes. Were Christ to come to Chicago, Stead maintained, He would go not to the churches, but rather to the city hall, for it was here that He would find real prospects for combating endemic social evils and achieving social righteousness. 'If Christ came to Chicago, the city and county admin-istration would seem to Him to be more like the Church which He founded nineteen hundred years ago than any other organisation lay or ecclesiastical which exists in Chicago at this moment.'[121] Christ in Chicago would draw together all those working for social improve-ment, in the police, fire service, newspapers, ward politics, labour unions, and churches, and form them into a progressive Civic Church. The Civic Church was destined to be the new Church Universal for 'saving the world by self-sacrificing love'.[122] It would elevate the new democracy with spiritual values and unite men and women of all religious persuasions. 'A new Catholicity,' he maintained, 'has dawned upon the world. All religions are now recognized as essentially Divine. All have something to teach us—how to make the common man more like God. The true religion is that which makes men most like Christ.'[123]

In the penultimate chapter, Stead directed attention to the institution in Chicago best exemplifying his ideal of the Civic Church. This was Hull House, on the city's West Side, a secular settlement established five years earlier by Jane Addams and eighteen residents. Hull House was, he maintained, superior to the settlements in England, including Toynbee Hall. It was far more inclusive, zealous, and humane in its 'multifarious activities'—in part because it was headed by a gifted woman who insisted upon being independent from the churches. 'Hull House has been enthusiastic without being intolerant, and broad without losing the fervour of its humanitarian zeal.'[124] It hosted women's clubs, men's clubs, ethnic clubs, boys' clubs, girls' clubs, cooking clubs, nature excursions, playgrounds, crèches, gymnasium, games room, reading room, dispensary, doctor's surgery, nurse home visits, library, literary clubs, dramatic groups, musical groups, university extension courses, and choral societies. This approached Stead's ideal of the Civic Church: what Chicago needed was 'a multiplication of Hull Houses all over the city'.[125] His final chapter portrayed Chicago as it might be if redeemed by the Civic Church—an attractive, dynamic and caring modern city of God, elevated and transformed through the union of religion and progressive politics. He closed with a plea for his new civic religion, which would bring the 'New Redemption' through a spiritualized democracy.[126]

## If Christ Came to the British City

On its publication, Stead sent copies of *If Christ Came to Chicago!* to a number of political leaders in Britain, including Lord Rosebery, who recently succeeded Gladstone as the Liberal prime minister, and Lord Salisbury, the Conservative leader. While Salisbury simply acknowledged receipt, Rosebery told Stead he had read it with special interest.[127] In sending a copy to his friend, John Burns, socialist labour leader and comrade from the Trafalgar Square protests, Stead wrote,

'I want you particularly to read it, because I think there are many things in it which will enable you to feel more at one with me than I think you have done in the past.'[128] In Britain, Stead continued campaigning for the development of Civic Churches.[129] Speaking in April 1894 in Edinburgh's Grassmarket, at that time a notorious slum, he announced what he called the 'new incarnation' of 'God made manifest once more in the Christ of the Slums, of the Shelter and of the Gaol'.[130]

In the autumn of 1894, Stead attempted to repeat his achievement of initiating the Civic Federation of Chicago—now by creating a new national, London-based umbrella organization to promote and coordinate the formation of Civic Churches in towns and cities across the United Kingdom. He named this the 'National Social Union', and described it at length in *The Review of Reviews* for September 1894.[131] It was to be a federation of Churches and voluntary associations, under the general direction of what he termed an 'ecumenical council' comprising leading representatives from all the 'political, social, religious, moral, philanthropic, educational, administrative and recreational' areas of national life. The Union would 'establish among all who love their fellow-men such a sense of the unity of their aspirations, and of the need for concerted effort, as in the earlier years the Catholic Church supplied to an undivided Christendom'.[132] *The Review of Reviews* would be its main voice. As well as restoring the sense of national religion, the National Social Union would seek to promote and direct the new initiatives in local democracy under the Local Government Act of 1894 (which established elected councils in rural and urban districts). The Union would also organize local social work, striving to reconcile labour and capital through arbitration boards.

Adopting the model of the successful launch of the Civic Federation of Chicago the previous year, Stead inaugurated his National Social Union with afternoon and evening public meetings on 28 October 1894 in London's Queen's Hall.[133] The meetings were very much Stead-centred events. To chair the afternoon meeting, Stead rather dramatically recruited James Branch, a member of the London County Council, who had been the chairman of the jury that had found Stead guilty in the Eliza Armstrong case in 1885. Stead convinced some leading social activists (including the socialist John Burns, the temperance campaigner Mrs Ormiston Chant, and the Baptist

Christian socialist pastor Dr John Clifford) to join him on the platform. After opening the meeting with prayer, Stead spoke for an hour, focusing on issues of child poverty and child welfare. He then moved a resolution, seconded by Clifford, 'that in order to promote the union of all who love for the service of all who suffer, this meeting proposes to form a National Social Union, with affiliated unions in every constituency, to act as a common centre of all the moral, social, industrial and philanthropic forces of the community'. At the evening meeting Stead's address was entitled 'If Christ Came to London', and he directed particular attention to the growing public role of women as poor law guardians and members of district and county councils, and the potential of women to lead the way to large-scale improvements in social welfare.

Stead became secretary and the driving force of the new organization. According to the London *Liberty Review* of 24 November 1894, the whole movement 'has sprung, Minerva-like, from the vast brain of Mr. Stead'.[134] During the London school board elections of November 1894, the National Social Union devised, with the assistance of John Clifford and Sidney Webb, a set of questions for candidates. It also issued a national address, signed by leaders of several Christian denominations, demanding a 'new regime' in social welfare at the elections of poor law guardians and parish councils on 4 December.[135] In Newcastle-upon-Tyne, near his childhood home of Howdon, on 10 December 1894, Stead held afternoon and evening public meetings on 'If Christ Came to Newcastle' and inaugurated a Newcastle branch of the National Social Union. 'There was,' he proclaimed, 'no better way of serving God than by getting Christian men and women to occupy places in their municipal bodies.'[136] In mid-December, Stead and the National Social Union called for a national census of the unemployed, and over the following months they developed an eclectic set of proposals for Church reunion, labour bureaus, free school meals, hospices for the terminally ill, holidays for urban children, and a statistical mapping of drunkenness and crime.[137]

But despite this promising start, Stead's Civic Church movement failed to gain broad public support, and he met opposition from influential figures in the Churches. On 10 May 1894, a highly critical editorial, 'If Christ Came—', appeared in the leading Nonconformist newspaper, the *British Weekly*. The article was written by the editor, the prominent London-based, liberal Scottish Presbyterian journalist, William Robertson Nicoll. For Nicoll, Stead's *If Christ Came to Chicago!* was a dangerous work, which condemned 'existing churches' and called 'for a new organisation of religion based on a new creed'. This Civic Church was to control municipal governments and manage political, social, economic, and cultural life. Nicoll insisted that Stead's proposals amounted to a system of social engineering—all the more ominous because it claimed the sanction of Christ. For Nicoll, Stead's Civic Church recalled the 'imperial aspirations' of the medieval papacy—bolstered by the efficiency of the modern bureaucratic state. Such an authoritarian, interventionist, theocratic government would undermine the human freedom that was, for Nicoll, essential to Christianity. A society based on Stead's Civic Church, if ever actually imposed on the world, would 'pass quickly into the real Sodom'.[138]

Stead replied with an indignant letter to the editor published in Nicoll's *British Weekly* on 24 May, and also with a lengthy signed article in the *Methodist Times* on the same day (although the *Methodist Times* did not give any editorial support to Stead's movement).[139] Stead said he had read Nicoll's article with 'amazement': he could not see how Nicoll's position could be called Christian. Do not Christians, he asked, pray 'Thy kingdom come', as instructed by Jesus? Was not the Church founded for the great work of achieving the Kingdom of God on earth? Now, with the real possibility of uniting modern social democracy and religious faith, was it not a Christian duty to make full use of this opportunity? Nicoll, in Stead's view, endeavoured to set Christianity against the rise of the working class. It was, Stead insisted, not his vision of the Civic Church, but rather Nicoll's narrow notion of individual freedom, that threatened to degrade working people to the 'level of beasts'. The present capitalist system, Stead explained, meant for most working people 'a constant preoccupation with the question, Shall I get enough to eat to keep my body and soul together'. And this in turn left most of the working class with 'lack of opportunities of enjoying books, society, music, and most of the things that constitute the culture of the mind'.[140]

On 31 May, Nicoll fired back another lengthy editorial in his *British Weekly*, entitled 'If Chicago Came to Christ', denouncing what he viewed as the fundamental weakness of Stead's approach—that is,

Stead's use of Christ to further his own social agenda. 'To be a Christian,' he reminded Stead, 'is not to vaguely admire the character of CHRIST; not to take some of His sayings as stones to fling at capitalists.' Rather, Nicoll proclaimed, 'To be a Christian means to be in contact with the living centre of force—to be alive in the Spirit.'[141]

Other Christian public intellectuals echoed Nicoll's criticisms. In *The Contemporary Review* of September 1894, the liberal journalist and historian Goldwin Smith derided Stead's plan 'to bring back the Churches to real Christianity by turning them into fraternities for the relief of the poor'. He could not 'agree with Mr. Stead that the Church would improve by identification with the trade-union'.[142] The Church of England clergyman and historian, Frederic Relton, denounced Stead's Civic Church in October 1894 in the *Economic Review*—an organ of the Christian Social Union (a highly influential Anglican association for social investigation and reform).[143] While supporting many of the social reforms advocated in *If Christ Came to Chicago!* he rejected Stead's claim that Christ 'would have regarded the City Council as the proper centre for His Operations'.[144] He compared Stead's call for Christians to support his Civic Church to Satan's temptation of Christ in the wilderness. Were Christ to return to the world, His response to 'Mr. Stead's proposed Collectivist machinery of reform' would be 'Get thee hence, Satan!'[145] For the Anglican *Church Quarterly Review* of October 1894, Stead's *If Christ Came to Chicago!* contained 'phrases about sacred matters, and even about sacred Persons, which shock our sense of reverence'.[146]

Encountering such blistering opposition from Christian journalists—including the prominent voice of the Nonconformist Conscience, Robertson Nicoll—Stead's National Social Union, and indeed his larger Civic Church movement, soon came to an end. During the summer of 1895, the National Social Union collapsed. The various Civic Churches across Britain largely ended as well. What he had thought his special revelation, his clear call from God in Holloway prison in 1885–6, had not led to a great religious movement of sacrifice and service. Stead continued his interests in urban social and political reform, and in 1898, he returned to the theme of the American city, visiting New York City and publishing a book-length critique of its municipal corruption, entitled *Satan's Invisible World Displayed or, Despairing Democracy*. Significantly, this work focused exclusively on political and social criticism, with no references to Christ's social ideal, to the work of the Churches, or to the Civic Church.[147] Stead by now felt unable to pursue his campaign to shape cities of God through a new Church of the Future.

Stead's Civic Church had represented an innovative programme aimed at uniting religious bodies, labour organizations, voluntary charities, and secular agencies for social improvement at the local level. He believed that he had been called by God to work for a Civic Church, a Church of the Future, that would rebuild communities in an era that was seeing the global spread of capitalism, that would help restore faith in God, and that would help 'unite all who loved in the service of all who suffered'. Stead's Civic Church had been a serious effort to make the historic Christian Church again a powerful force for social cohesion in an increasingly complex urban-industrial world. His appeals to the English-speaking peoples as God's new chosen people, including his call for a new 'Bible Book of the English-Speaking Race', while unsavoury in cultural arrogance, did seek to elevate British imperialism with a higher moral and spiritual purpose. None the less, despite the success of his *Review of Reviews*, despite the immense sales of *If Christ Came to Chicago!* the large attendances at his public meetings, and the initial activism of the National Social Union, Stead's Civic Church failed to gain sustained public support. Nor had his earlier efforts succeeded in influencing the world mission of the Roman Catholic Church or transforming society through the Salvation Army. For many, Stead discarded too much Christian doctrine in trying to reduce Christianity to an essential message of love and service; his Civic Church was overly based on what he thought his personal revelation, the call to 'be a Christ' which he had heard so distinctly at Holloway prison.

Stead was an able, experienced journalist, whose journalism was infused by his religious faith. His three major books of 1888–94—on Russia, the papacy, and Chicago—while flawed in some of their analysis, had contained valuable insights concerning society, human nature, progress, and the challenges of the modern world. He saw himself as a prophet, called to interpret the designs of providence for an increasingly secular world, and as a judge, pronouncing God's judgement on such 'immoral' politicians as Dilke and Parnell. And he perceived himself a preacher, whose editor's desk was a pulpit from which to proclaim God's will for society and a social gospel of love, sacrifice, and service. In all of this, the influence of Carlyle, Lowell, and Cromwell, and what he viewed as their Puritan cause of social righteousness, provided the background. As Hugh Kingsmill observed, Stead's 'impressionable nature responded to every aspect of the multifarious modern world, while at the same time his inherited Puritanism sought incessantly for some formula which should unify the age without impairing its heterogeneity'.[148] But Stead was neither a theologian nor a constructive politician: he lacked the temperament or ability to organize and lead a socio-religious movement, especially such a grandiose movement as he envisaged for his Civic Church. He was feeling more isolated after the deaths of Catherine Booth and Cardinal Manning. His failure by the mid-1890s to promote a new, uniting Church of the Future through his journalism was hard for him. But by now his religious beliefs were moving in new directions.

## Notes

1. Quoted in Robertson Scott, *Life and Death of a Newspaper*, p. 152.
2. Ibid., p. 155.
3. Stead, *The M.P. for Russia*, vol. ii, p. 236; Stead, 'The Great Pacifist', p. 612.
4. Stead, *The M.P. for Russia*, vol. ii, pp. 237–9.
5. Whyte, *Life of W. T. Stead*, vol. i, pp. 255–9.
6. Quoted in Robertson Scott, *Life and Death of a Newspaper*, p. 147.
7. For Stead's two separate accounts of the interview, see Whyte, *Life of W. T. Stead*, vol. i, pp. 259–65; Stead, *The M.P. for Russia*, vol. ii, pp. 243–9.
8. W. T. Stead, *Truth about Russia* (London, 1888), p. 451; R. F. Christian, 'The Road to Yashnaya Polyana: Some Pilgrims from Britain and their Reminiscences', *Slavonic and East European Review*, 66 (1988), pp. 526–52, at 529–33.
9. Stead, *Truth about Russia*, p. 405.
10. Ibid., pp. 322–9, quotation on p. 325.
11. Ibid., p. 448.
12. Ibid., p. 404.
13. Leo Tolstoi, *Christ's Christianity*, ed. H. F. Battesby (London, 1885).
14. Stead, *Truth about Russia*, p. 434.
15. Christian, 'The Road to Yashnaya Polyana', p. 533.
16. Stead, *The M.P. for Russia*, vol. ii, p. 249.

17. Sheridan Ford, 'Tzar-Tyrant of Tzar-Tribune?', *Westminster Review*, 132 (July 1889), pp. 204–12, quotation on p. 212.

18. E. J. Dillon, 'Some Truths about Russia', *Fortnightly Review*, 46 (August 1889), pp. 274–92, quotations on p. 281.

19. Stead, *The M.P. for Russia*, vol. ii, pp. 249–51, quotation on p. 250.

20. W. T. Stead to W. E. Gladstone, BL, Gladstone Papers, Add Mss 44303, fos. 391–2.

21. Quoted in Robertson Scott, *Life and Death of a Newspaper*, p. 148.

22. Stead, 'Character Sketch: Three of the Dead', p. 132.

23. W. T. Stead to W. E. Gladstone, 26 March 1887, BL, Gladstone Papers, Add Mss 44303, fos. 367–8.

24. Stead, 'Character Sketch: Three of the Dead', p. 135.

25. W. T. Stead, 'The Progress of Man', *Universal Review*, 2 (December 1888), pp. 449–68.

26. Ibid., pp. 454, 453.

27. [W. T. Stead], 'The Cardinal's Peace', *PMG* (13 September 1889).

28. W. T. Stead to Lord Carnavon, 7 October 1889, Carnavon Papers, BL, Add Mss 60777, fos. 132–3.

29. Owen Chadwick, *A History of the Popes 1830–1914* (Oxford, 1998), pp. 302–3.

30. W. T. Stead, *The Pope and the New Era, being Letters from the Vatican in 1889* (London, 1890), p. 17.

31. Whyte, *Life of W. T. Stead*, vol. i, p. 284.

32. W. T. Stead to H. E. Manning, 22 October 1889, Stead Papers, STED 1/51.

33. W. T. Stead to H. E. Manning, 24 October 1889, Stead Papers, STED 1/51.

34. W. T. Stead to H. E. Manning, 23 October 1889, Stead Papers, STED 1/51.

35. W. T. Stead to H. E. Manning, 5 November 1889, Stead Papers, STED 1/51.

36. Stead, *The Pope and the New Era*, p. 145, 146.

37. Ibid., pp. 25, 27.

38. Ibid., p. 204.

39. Ibid., p. 28.

40. Ibid., pp. 28–9, 30.

41. Ibid., p. 250.

42. Ibid., p. 94.

43. W. T. Stead to H. E. Manning, 21 February 1890, Stead Papers, STED 1/51.

44. Whyte, *Life of W. T. Stead*, vol. i, p. 286.

45. 'The Pope and the Journalist', *The Speaker*, 1 (April 1890), p. 462.
46. 'The Pope and the New Era', *Saturday Review*, 69 (April 1890), p. 481.
47. Robertson Scott, *Life and Death of a Newspaper*, p. 155.
48. Joseph O. Baylen, 'W. T. Stead as Publisher and Editor of the "Review of Reviews"', *Victorian Periodicals Review*, 12 (1979), pp. 70–84; Mussell, 'W. T. Stead, Newness, and the Archival Imagination', pp. 69–91.
49. [W. T. Stead], 'To All English-Speaking Folk', *RoR* (January 1890), pp. 15, 17.
50. Ibid., pp. 18–19.
51. Ibid., pp. 16–17.
52. Alexis Easley, 'W. T. Stead, Late Victorian Feminism, and the *Review of Reviews*', in Brake et al. (eds), *W. T. Stead: Newspaper Revolutionary*, pp. 37–8.
53. Ibid., p. 20.
54. W. T. Stead, 'A Word to Those Who Are Willing to Help', *RoR*, 1 (January 1890), p. 53.
55. Hale, 'W. T. Stead and Participatory Reader Networks', pp. 26–32, quotation on p. 31.
56. Easley, 'W. T. Stead, Late Victorian Feminism, and the *Review of Reviews*', p. 43.
57. 'List of Members of the Association of Helpers', *RoR* (January 1893), pp. 112–16; 'The Association of Helpers—Corrections', *RoR* (March 1893), p. 308.
58. W. T. Stead. 'A Practical Suggestion', *RoR*, 1 (January 1890), p. 76.
59. Baylen, 'W. T. Stead as Publisher and Editor of the "Review of Reviews"', pp. 71, 73–4.
60. Ibid., p. 71.
61. Ibid., p. 76.
62. Lloyd J. Graybar, *Albert Shaw of the Review of Reviews* (Lexington, 1974), pp. 44–54.
63. Whyte, *Life of W. T. Stead*, vol. i, pp. 269–71.
64. W. T. Stead, 'Cecil Rhodes of Africa', *RoR* (November 1899), pp. 552–3.
65. Whyte, *Life of W. T. Stead*, vol. ii, pp. 207–09.
66. W. T. Stead, *The Last Will and Testament of Cecil John Rhodes with Elucidatory Notes* (London, 1902), pp. 56, 62–3, 83, 99.
67. Roy Jenkins, *Sir Charles Dilke: A Victorian Tragedy*, 2nd edn. (London, 1965).
68. W. T. Stead, *Has Sir Charles Dilke Cleared his Character?* (London, [1891]), pp. 15–16.
69. Jenkins, *Dilke*, pp. 241–3.
70. [W. T. Stead]. 'The Fall of Mr Parnell', *RoR* (December 1890), p. 602.
71. [W. T. Stead]. 'Catholics and Nonconformists', *RoR* (January 1891), p. 59.

72. [W. T. Stead]. 'Character Sketch: Sir Charles Dilke', *RoR* (August 1892), p. 127; 'Private Morals and Public Life', *RoR* (April 1891), p. 336.
73. [Stead]. 'Character Sketch: Sir Charles Dilke', pp. 131–2.
74. Cyril Waters, '"Steadism" in Politics', *Westminster Review* 137 (1892), p. 620.
75. Booth, *Echoes and Memories*, p. 153.
76. W. T. Stead, *Life of Mrs Booth, the Founder of the Salvation Army* (New York, 1900), p. 209.
77. Ibid., pp. 210–11.
78. Elizabeth Tilley, 'Christianity, Journalism, and Popular Print: W. T. Stead and the Salvation Army' in Laurel Brake et al. (eds), *W. T. Stead: Newspaper Revolutionary* (London, 2012), p. 61.
79. W. T. Stead, 'In Darkest England and the Way Out', *RoR*, 2 (October 1890), p. 382.
80. Ibid., p. 394.
81. Quoted in Whyte, *Life of W. T. Stead*, vol. ii, p. 13.
82. W. T. Stead, *General Booth: A Biographical Sketch* (London, 1891), pp. 89, 91.
83. Inglis, *Churches and the Working Classes*, pp. 199–212; Herman Ausubel, 'General Booth's Scheme of Social Salvation', *American Historical Review*, 56 (1951), pp. 519–25.
84. Inglis, *Churches and the Working Classes*, p. 208.
85. Ibid., p. 210.
86. Booth, *Echoes and Memories*, pp. 153–4.
87. W. T. Stead, 'The Pope's Encyclical on the Condition of Labour', *RoR*, 3 (June 1891), pp. 620–6, quotation on p. 622.
88. Stead, 'Character Sketch: Three of the Dead', p. 130.
89. Ibid.
90. Blathwayt, *Interview with Mr. W. T. Stead on the Church of the Future*, p. 88.
91. Ibid., pp. 7–15, quotations on pp. 8, 9.
92. Ibid., pp. 91–2.
93. 'Mr Stead's Civic Church', *Bristol Mercury and Daily Post* (8 December 1891).
94. 'Mr W. T. Stead at Cardiff', *Western Mail*, Cardiff (8 February 1892).
95. 'The Civic Church: What It Was, and What It May Be', *RoR* (August 1892), p. 157.
96. 'Towards the Civic Church: A Report of Progress', *RoR* (March 1893), pp. 309–14.
97. Ibid., pp. 311–12.
98. W. T. Stead, 'Circular Letter', 14 April 1893, Bryce Papers, fos. 97–104.
99. D. B. Downey, *A Season of Renewal: The Columbia Exhibition and Victorian America* (Westport, Connecticut, 2002), pp. 148–60; R. H. Seager, *The World's Parliament of Religions* (Bloomington, Indiana, 1995).

100. W. T. Stead, 'The Civic Church' in *The World's Parliament of Religions*, ed. J. H. Barrows (London, 1893), vol. ii, pp. 1209–15.

101. Ibid., p. 1209.

102. Ibid., p. 1213.

103. Ibid., p. 1214.

104. Ibid., p. 1214.

105. Ibid., pp. 1212–13.

106. Downey, *A Season of Renewal*, p. 159.

107. C. Oldstone-Moore, 'The Forgotten Origins of the Ecumenical Movement in England: the Grindelwald Conferences, 1892–95', *Church History*, 70 (2001), pp. 73–97; R. Rouse and S. C. Neill (eds), *A History of the Ecumenical Movement 1517–1948* (London, 1954), pp. 338–41.

108. [W. T. Stead], 'The Chronicles of the Civic Church: The Forthcoming Conference at Lucerne', *RoR* (August 1893), pp. 186–9.

109. Ibid., p. 187.

110. H. S. Lunn, *Chapters from my Life with Special Reference to Reunion* (London, 1918), pp. 379–81, at p. 381; Eckley, *Maiden Tribute*, p. 201.

111. 'The Church Congress at Birmingham', *The Daily Paper* (4 October 1893), p. 6; for Stead's sense of religious purpose behind this venture, see Whyte, *Life of W. T. Stead*, ii, p. 58.

112. W. T. Stead, 'My First Visit to America', *RoR* (April 1894), p. 410.

113. Ibid., pp. 410–11.

114. D. B. Downey, 'William Stead and Chicago: A Victorian Jeremiah in the Windy City', *Mid-America*, 68 (1987), pp. 159–61; Joseph O. Baylen, 'A Victorian's "Crusade" in Chicago, 1893–1894', *Journal of American History*, 51 (1964), pp. 423–8.

115. W. T. Stead to Reginald Brett, 22 November 1893, Rosebery Papers, National Library of Scotland, MS 10006, fos. 157–8.

116. [W. T. Stead], 'What Would Jesus Do?' *RoR* (May 1899), pp. 488; Robert T. Handy, 'George D. Herron and the Kingdom Movement', *Church History*, 19 (1950), p. 104; Graybar, *Albert Shaw*, p. 76.

117. W. T. Stead to Reginald Brett, 25 December 1893, Rosebery Papers, National Library of Scotland, MS 10007, fol. 3.

118. Baylen, 'A Victorian's "Crusade" in Chicago, 1893–1894', p. 433; Gary Scott Smith, 'When Stead Came to Chicago: The "Social Gospel Novel" and the Chicago Civic Federation', *American Presbyterians*, 68 (1990), p. 199.

119. W. T. Stead, *If Christ Came to Chicago! A Plea for the Union of All Who Love in the Service of All Who Suffer* (London, 1894), pp. 59–60.

120. Ibid., p. xiii.

121. Ibid., p. 264.
122. Ibid., p. 335.
123. Ibid., p. 334.
124. Ibid., p. 401.
125. Ibid., p. 401.
126. Ibid., p. 434.
127. Lord Rosebery to W. T. Stead, 29 April 1894, W. T. Stead, 'Memo of conversation with Lord Rosebery over lunch on 21 May 1894', Stead Papers, STED 1/62; Lord Salisbury to W. T. Stead, 1 May 1894, Stead Papers, STED 1/63.
128. W. T. Stead to J. Burns, 24 April 1894, John Burns Papers, BL, Add Mss 46287, fol. 228.
129. 'Sunderland: Mr Stead's Civic Church', *Methodist Times* (19 April 1894); 'Mr W. T. Stead in Leeds: An Appeal for a More Practical Christianity', *Leed's Mercury* (9 July 1894).
130. [W. T. Stead], 'The Chronicles of the Civic Church: Is There a Remedy for the Miseries of the World?' *RoR* (May 1894), p. 505.
131. [W. T. Stead], 'The National Social Union: Statement of its Aims, Methods, and Organisation', *RoR* (September, 1894), pp. 286–96.
132. Ibid., p. 286.
133. 'The National Social Union', *RoR* (November 1894), pp. 496–500; 'If Christ Came to London: Mr Stead at Queen's Hall', *The Woman's Signal* (1 November 1894); 'W. T. Stead's Two Conferences at Queen's Hall', *British Weekly* (1 November 1894); 'Mr Stead's Purity Crusade', *Reynold's Newspaper*, London (4 November 1894); W. T. Stead to John Burns, 19 October 1894, BL, Add Mss 46287, fol. 232.
134. *The Liberty Review*, London (24 November 1894).
135. *Daily News*, London (19 November 1894); *Leed's Mercury* (23 November 1894); *Bristol Mercury* (27 November 1894).
136. *Newcastle Weekly Courant* (15 December 1894).
137. *Reynold's Newspaper*, London (23 December 1894); W. T. Stead to Lord Rosebery, 19 December 1894, Rosebery Papers, National Library of Scotland, MS 10100, fol. 130; 'The National Social Union', *RoR* (January 1895), pp. 66–9; (June 1895), pp. 557–60.
138. [W. Robertson Nicoll, 'If Christ Came—', *British Weekly* (10 May 1894).
139. W. T. Stead, 'If Christ Came. To the Editor', *British Weekly* (24 May 1894); W. T. Stead. '"If Christ Came": A Reply to the *British Weekly*', *Methodist Times* (24 May 1894).
140. Stead, '"If Christ Came": A Reply to the *British Weekly*'.
141. [W. Robertson Nicoll], 'If Chicago Came to Christ', *British Weekly* (31 May 1894).

142. G. Smith, 'If Christ Came to Chicago', *The Contemporary Review*, 66 (1894), pp. 380–9, at p. 386.

143. F. Relton, 'Is the Individualist or the Collectivist View of Social Progress More in Accordance with the Teaching of Christ?' *Economic Review*, iv (1894), 499–518.

144. Ibid., p. 510.

145. Ibid., 517–18.

146. 'If Christ Came to Chicago!' *Church Quarterly Review*, 39 (1894–5), pp. 253–4.

147. W. T. Stead, *Satan's Invisible World Displayed or, Despairing Democracy: A Study of Greater New York* (London, 1898).

148. Kingsmill, *After Puritanism*, p. 172.

# 4

# Spiritualism and the Other World, 1880–1912

In December 1891, Stead published a Christmas *Review of Reviews* annual under the title, *Real Ghost Stories*. Intended as an entertaining read for long winter nights, the issue comprised diverse accounts of supernatural phenomena which Stead had collected and edited, including premonitions, doppelgängers, multiple personalities, clair-voyance, and ghosts. Many of the accounts were drawn from evidence published by the Society for Psychical Research, an association which promoted scientific investigations into paranormal activity. The accounts included a number of incidents of telepathy, a term coined by the prominent essayist, psychical researcher, and public intellec-tual, Frederic Myers, to describe supernatural communications or relations between minds at a distance.[1] In the introduction Stead drew attention to the increasing public interest in paranormal forces, an interest linked to new developments in physics and electricity and the study of human psychology. Phenomena that a century earlier would have seemed beyond belief—including photography, the tele-graph, the telephone, and the phonograph—were now becoming commonplace, the pace of scientific investigation was ever quickening, and who knew what new natural forces were soon to be discovered? 'There is,' Stead maintained, 'a growing interest in all the occult phenomena to which this work is devoted . . . The topic is in the air, and will be discussed and is being discussed, whether we take notice of it or not.' Nor should the study of the paranormal be left solely to experts, such as the researchers of the Society for Psychical Research.

> We live in a democratic age and we democratise everything. It is too
> late in the day to propose to place the whole of this department under

the care of any Brahmin caste; the subject is one which every common man and woman can understand. It is one which comes home to every human being, for it adds a new interest to life, and vivifies the sombre but all-pervading problem of death.[2]

*Real Ghost Stories* was an immediate commercial success; Stead claimed that 100,000 copies of the Christmas annual were sold within two days.[3] The work established Stead in a new public role—as a leading advocate and popularizer of research into psychical and paranormal phenomena. Although attempting to present the stories in an object-ive, scientific manner, he made his personal belief in the occult phenomena clear. Indeed, he admitted that he had begun work on the volume 'somewhat lightly', but then came to a serious sense of the subject's importance. He sought to involve *The Review of Reviews* participatory readers' network in the subject. In each copy of the annual, Stead enclosed a notice, endorsed by the Cambridge moral philosopher and psychic researcher, Professor Henry Sidgwick, on behalf of the International Congress of Experimental Psychology, inviting readers to submit accounts of their own paranormal experiences.[4] In response to the success of the annual, Stead quickly wrote a second volume, *More Ghost Stories*, which appeared in February 1892. Stead soon became absorbed in matters of the occult. 'It was in the early nineties,' recalled his assistant and friend, Edith Harper, 'that Mr Stead's interest in matters psychic began rapidly to develop.'[5] This interest in the occult developed alongside his campaign for the Civic Church with its call to social service. Both reflected similar commitments to reviving faith in spiritual and transcendent values in an increasingly materialist and secular world.

## The *Fin de Siècle* and the 'Other World'

The last decades of the nineteenth century were a time of considerable unsettlement in the United Kingdom. There were new movements among hitherto oppressed or marginalized classes and groups—unskilled labourers, women, Irish and Jewish migrants, impoverished slum dwellers—who were now finding a political voice, challenging established institutions, values, and beliefs, embracing radical ideolo-gies, and sometimes dreaming of revolution to end long-endured injustices and inequalities. The growth of literacy through the expansion of public education, combined with the expanded franchise under the Third Reform Act of 1884, contributed to an increasingly democratic politics. The traditional authority of institutional Christianity, in both the established Churches and nonconformist Churches, was being openly rejected by a growing number of secularists, socialists, and reformers, with many portraying the Churches as bastions of privilege and hierarchy. Some findings of biblical scholarship and early Christian history undermined belief in the miraculous foundations of Christianity.

Science was transforming conceptions of the natural order. It was dissolving Newtonian conceptions of the universe, with their fixed natural laws, solid matter, and absolutes of time and space. Science was showing the atom to be divisible, and matter to consist of energy. The discovery of new forces—infrared and ultraviolet light, electromagnetic fields, radio waves, and X-rays—brought new opportunities, but also revealed levels of uncertainty and relativity in physics. Wireless telegraphy emerged in 1887 and by 1901 wireless messages were being sent across the Atlantic. New research in anthropology included studies of the gradual development of primitive social life, and of the early beliefs and myths that formed the foundations of later religions. J. G. Frazer's multi-volume *The Golden Bough*, which began appearing in 1890, argued that the origins of all religion would be found in the efforts of primitive peoples to propitiate unseen forces with sacrifices. The new science of psychology, including the work of French psychologists pioneering hypnotic therapies, portrayed individual personality as multi-layered, with some individuals exhibiting multiple personalities. During the 1880s and early 1890s, Frederic Myers developed his theory of the subliminal consciousness, with its premise that every individual consists of both a conscious self and an unconscious self, and that the unconscious, or subliminal self, formed the real foundation of personality.

Some viewed the approach of the *fin de siècle* as a time of decline and decadence. There was a sense that the United Kingdom had passed its height of power and influence, and that the glory of the British Empire was beginning to fade. Many artists and authors turned inward, became introspective, reflecting on how all greatness was fleeting. It was a time of evening shadows, eroticism, sensualist art, self-indulgence, 'madder music', and 'stronger wine'. For others, however, the *fin de siècle* was an exhilarating time of new beginnings. It was bringing the rise of democracy and the common people, of feminism and the 'new woman', of the beginnings of 'modernism' in the arts, of new technologies of communication, of the discovery of hitherto unknown forces in nature, and forces beyond nature.

There was an openness to new forms of religious belief. Many embraced the spiritualist movement, with its claims to communicate with the spirits of the dead through rappings, seances, and automatic writing. Spiritualism in its modern guise had arrived in Britain from the United States in the early 1850s and gained a broad following, with a number of celebrity mediums, including Florence Cook and Daniel Douglas Home, emerging to prominence in the 1870s. For many, spiritualism took on the form of a new religion, proclaiming the existence of an afterlife where the spirits of the dead continued to grow in wisdom and compassion, and from where they continued to take an interest in the living. The growing interest in alternative religious beliefs found expression in the Theosophical Society. Founded in 1875 in New York City by Helena Blavatsky and Henry Steele Olcott, it claimed knowledge of the ancient 'wisdom-religion' that formed the basis of all the major world religions—including belief in a creator deity infusing the whole universe, a universe that evolved through cycles of emanations of the deity, the reincarnation of the soul, and the existence of a higher self within each individual. The revival and spread of this 'original wisdom religion' now promised to draw the world religions together and usher in an era of peace and world unity. The *fin de siècle* in the United Kingdom also saw the emergence of the movement for psychic research, with its systematic efforts to apply the methods of modern science to the study of occult phenomena. The movement was represented in part by the Society for Psychical Research, founded in 1882 and including Henry Sidgwick, Frederic Myers, Edmund Gurney, and Arthur Balfour. An important early publication of the Society, the two-volume *Phantasms of the Living*, appeared in 1886, and included studies of telepathy, doppelgängers and apparitions.

## Automatic Writing and Julia Ames

Stead participated in his first seance in early 1881, shortly after arriving in London. He denied knowing anyone in the room or taking the experience very seriously, though he was struck by how his silent, mental questions to the medium seemed to evoke appropriate responses. As he was taking his leave (or so he later told his daughter, Estelle), the medium stood and said, 'Young man, you are going to be the St. Paul of Spiritualism.'[6] Over the next several years, Stead gave sporadic attention to spiritualism and theosophy in the *Pall Mall*, publishing, for example, accounts of the theosophist Helena Blavatsky (April 1884) and the spiritualist Stuart Cumberland (June 1884).[7] Early in February 1886, a few weeks after his release from Holloway Gaol, he attended another seance and was again impressed by a sense that he had psychic powers. 'It was most wonderful,' he informed Olga Novikoff, 'the answers that came from the medium to questions that were silently uttered in my own mind.' 'There is,' he added, 'something in this strange business & I want to get to the bottom of it.'[8]

In early 1888, Novikoff introduced Stead to her Russian friend, Helena Blavatsky, who had settled in London in September 1887. 'I hear from our mutual friend, Mme de Novetsky [sic],' Blavatsky wrote to Stead on 24 February 1888, 'that you do not hate me as I thought you did. She goes even so far as to tell me that if I write to you you will come to see me. I hope it is so.'[9] Stead called on her at her home and was both 'delighted with' and also 'somewhat repelled' by her. 'Power was there,' he later recalled, 'rude and massive, but she had the manners of a man, and a very unconventional man.' Although she told him 'that she knew I was a good theosophist', Stead did not embrace belief in the movement.[10] He did, however, admire her for bringing others to believe in spiritual matters. 'Madame Blavatsky,' he wrote in 1891, 'in the midst of a generation that is materialist and mechanical ... did at least succeed in compelling a race of scientists and economists to realise the existence of a conception that all material things are but a passing illusion, and that the spiritual alone is.'[11] One of those Blavatsky brought to faith in the spiritual life was Stead's friend, the atheist and socialist, Annie Besant. When Stead had received Blavatsky's massive two-volume work, *The Secret Doctrine*, to review in the *Pall Mall*, he had given the assignment to Besant, who occasionally wrote for the newspaper. Her review appeared in April 1889.[12] Captivated by the book, Besant asked Stead to introduce her to Blavatsky. She soon became a disciple of Blavatsky, embraced a spiritual faith, and following Blavatsky's death in 1891, became one of the leaders of the Theosophical Society, residing primarily in India from 1893. 'To me,' Stead wrote in October 1891, Blavatsky's great 'miracle is the conversion of Mrs Besant from Materialism to a firmly based belief in the reality of the spiritual world.'[13]

From 1890, Stead expressed a growing interest in psychic research in *The Review of Reviews*.[14] The work of the Society for Psychical Research, he believed, was providing 'scientific' proof of the continuance of individual personality after death, whether revealed through apparitions or telepathic communications from spirits. This in turn was challenging the widespread materialism and scepticism of the times, and bringing many to recognize a higher spiritual dimension to existence. In September 1891, he appealed in *The Review of Reviews* to readers around the globe to send him accounts of ghosts and paranormal experiences, which he could then forward to the Society for Psychical Research.[15] The work of psychical research, he maintained, was of vital importance for the future of all religious faith. 'The evidence and experiments of the Physical Research Society have already shattered,' Stead observed in *The Review of Reviews* for December 1891, '... all purely materialistic hypotheses. If the testimony of many credible witnesses may be believed, there is no death.' 'It seems,' he added, 'as if Science were once again to vindicate her claim to be regarded as the handmaid of Religion.'[16]

Then in June 1892 Stead's life took a new direction when he received what for him was incontrovertible proof that he was one of the 'sensitives' who possessed telepathic powers and could connect the seen and unseen worlds. His telepathic powers found expression through the practice of automatic writing, a practice for which there was a long-established tradition. He was directed to automatic writing by a woman (the daughter of an Indian army officer) then working for him in *The Review of Reviews* office in Mowbray House. Claiming to possess the gift of automatic writing, she insisted that one of the spirits informed her that Stead also had the gift and must exercise it, as there were spirits wanting to communicate to him. Stead's initial attempt at automatic writing, sitting still with a pen in his hand over a blank sheet of paper, produced no results, but the next morning he tried again, and his hand began writing with, he insisted, no conscious effort on his part. 'Whether,' he maintained, 'my hand was directed by the intelligence of one deceased, or by a living person, or by my subjective self,

I did not control it; I rested the point of the pen on the paper, and the mysterious force did all the rest.'[17] He began devoting a half hour each morning to practicing automatic writing, believing that he received regular telepathic messages both from the spirits of the departed and also from the minds of living persons. Of these messages, the most important came from the spirit of a recently deceased American woman, who became his guide to the other world and his religious mentor.

Julia A. Ames (1861–91) was a Methodist feminist journalist and temperance reformer, who had been raised in a prosperous family in Streator, Illinois, attended Illinois Wesleyan University, and became active with the Women's Christian Temperance Union—settling in Chicago where she wrote articles promoting the work of the Union and became one of the editors of its principal publication, the *Union Signal*, in 1889. She was attractive, confident, and vivacious, with a love of literature and the arts, and a strong social conscience.[18] In the spring and summer of 1890, she travelled to Europe with a friend to see the passion play at Oberammergau and tour Britain and Western Europe. Introduced to Stead by their mutual friend, the Christian feminist temperance campaigner, Isabella, Lady Henry Somerset, Ames visited him on 27 May at his London office. 'He received me,' she wrote in her journal, 'as a sister beloved, is just what I expected him to be, warm and brotherly.' 'Not handsome,' she continued, 'rather gaunt, but so *good*-looking... He won my heart at once.'[19] Later, before returning to the States, she visited Stead again at his Wimbledon home, and they sat together in the garden. They had both attended the Oberammergau passion play that summer and both had found it a profoundly spiritual, even mystical experience, infusing their lives with renewed meaning.[20] Stead may have been sexually attracted to her, and they corresponded after her return. Little over a year later, while she was attending the Women's Christian Temperance Union conference in Boston, she fell ill and unexpectedly died, aged thirty, on 12 December 1891.

In the summer of 1892, soon after Stead had begun automatic writing, he and his wife were the guests of Lady Henry Somerset at Eastnor Castle. There he was approached by a fellow guest and close friend of Julia Ames, who claimed she had been receiving visions of Julia and asked if he could use his new gift to communicate with her spirit. He made the effort and on 9 August began receiving what he believed were messages from Julia through his handwriting. These messages included details of some private matters between Julia and her friend, which for both Stead and the friend were proof that the messages were indeed coming from Julia's spirit. Julia provided him with still further evidence, including a reasonably accurate prediction of the vote in John Morley's by-election as MP for Newcastle. Stead was convinced, and he and Julia began a regular 'correspondence', with Julia writing with his hand, while he put mental questions to her. She described for him her after-death experiences and the nature of the afterlife, and she gave him guidance on religion and morals. The author Hugh Kingsmill was permitted to view the original Julia letters for 1892 and 1893. 'The writing,' he observed, 'is Stead's, but slopes backward more than his usual handwriting, and sometimes becomes disordered and straggling, or degenerates into a formless scribble.'[21] For Stead, the letters from Julia provided empirical proof of the survival of personality after death, the existence of a heaven, and the truth of Christianity. Through these telepathic experiences, he insisted in *The Review of Reviews* of April 1893, 'many attributes which have hitherto been regarded as the exclusive possession of the Deity will be shared with His creatures. The past mingles with the present and the future unfolds its secrets. Death loses its sting, and parting its sorrow.' 'Spirit,' he added, 'is manifested through matter, and we enter into a new heaven and a new earth.'[22] He would later insist that 'if I am remembered at all a hundred years hence, it will be as Julia's amanuensis'.[23]

In his seminal book on telepathy, Roger Luckhurst has shown how Stead's interest in telepathy was linked to his fascination with modern communication technologies and also to his journalistic aims, especially in *The Review of Reviews*, of bringing the world more closely together. For Stead, telepathy was in one sense a natural force, with the potential of becoming another form of global communication, alongside the telegraph, telephone, and wireless.[24] At the same time, Stead also linked his commitment to the study of telepathy and psychical phenomena to his Christian faith. It is significant that his three principal Christian guides and mentors, Henry Parry Liddon, Catherine Booth, and Cardinal Manning, had all recently died; they might have discouraged his growing absorption with spirits and the occult. As it was, the spirit of Julia, with whom he communed almost daily through his automatic writing, now became his religious guide and, it seemed, also his closest friend. 'To me,' he wrote in July 1895, 'Miss Julia is as real an entity, as distinct a personality and as constant a friend as any of the men and women in my own family or in the circle of my acquaintance. The only difference is that she is more uniformly affectionate, hopeful and sympathetic.'[25] Some of his living friends were concerned. They included Frances Evelyn (Daisy) Greville, Countess of Warwick, society beauty and mistress of the Prince of Wales. 'Don't commune *too* much with "Julia",' she wrote him in September 1893, 'but write occasionally to a "flesh & blood" friend! Do not forget us all—toiling to find our ideals, & to whom *your* encouragement means much—or forsake *us* for the world of "spirits", who have had their day on this earth, & who need your sympathy & friendship less than *we* do!'[26]

### Borderland

In July 1893, about a year after he began automatic writing, Stead launched a new quarterly journal, *Borderland*, dedicated to conveying the results of psychical research to a larger reading public.[27] According-ing to Stead's statement of purpose, 'How We Intend to Study Borderland', the journal would approach supernatural subjects with an open mind and rigorous scientific methodology. At the same time, however, the journal would be infused with religious purpose, show-ing how understanding of psychic phenomena would revive ancient Christian teachings. 'We seek,' he insisted, 'the scientific verification of that Life and Immortality which were brought to light nineteen hundred years ago.' 'Unless all religions are based upon a lie,' he observed, '... there is a world beyond the impalpable veil that shrouds it from our eyes, a world which is not empty but teeming with life.' His journal would bring 'to the study of these obscure phenomena the religious enthusiasm born of a great hope, wedded to the scientific spirit which accepts nothing on trust'.[28]

To help him with *Borderland*, Stead appointed an assistant editor, Ada Goodrich Freer, an attractive single woman in her mid-thirties. She had been writing reports for the Society for Psychical Research under the pseudonym 'Miss X', and had been recommended to Stead by Frederic Myers. The daughter of a Yorkshire veterinarian, Freer was less than honest about her background, claiming she came from the landed gentry and had connections to the Scottish Highlands. But she did have a broad knowledge of occult phenomena, including the Gaelic folklore of the Scottish Highlands. She continued to sign her *Borderland* articles as 'Miss X' and she carefully maintained her anonymity. Stead felt a close connection to her and claimed that he regularly communicated with her through automatic writing. 'Whenever I wish,' he explained to his readers, 'to know where she is, whether she can keep an appointment, or how she is progressing with her work, I simply ask the question, and my hand automatically writes out the answer.'[29] Stead was also assisted by Annie Besant, who wrote on theosophy for the journal. Each issue opened with a 'Chronique of the Quarter' (an overview of developments in psychical research over the past three months), and the rest of the issue consisted of articles on a wide range of occult topics, book reviews, and lists of recent publications in psychical studies. Later issues included lengthy character sketches of prominent spiritualists or psychical researchers. The early numbers of the journal coincided with Stead's visit to Chicago in 1893–4, and he published a number of reports on mediums, paranormal phenomena, and psychical research in the United States. The overall tone of the journal was serious, but the articles avoided jargon and were directed to a non-expert readership. A major aim of the publication was, as Stead put it, to 'democratise the study of the spook'.[30] A distinctive aspect of the journal was the promotion of readers' participation in psychical research through the formation of study circles in the fields of astrology, telepathy, spiritualism, hypnotism, clairvoyance, automatic writing, palmistry, crystal-gazing, and theosophy. These study groups were encouraged to gather and sift evidence, and send regular reports to Stead (he believed such reports would be of interest to the Society for Psychical Research). Membership of the study circles was open to all subscribers, and members' names were published near the end of each issue. Stead also created a Borderland Library, which was available to subscribers.

In an article on 'Borderlanders of the Bible', appearing in the second number, Stead addressed what had become a major obstacle to religious belief in the modern era—that is, the 'miraculous element in the sacred writings', including angels, demons, and other spirits. Many in the modern world could not accept the Bible as true, or see it having any relevance for their lives, because they could not believe in its miracles and spirits. For them, miracles and spirits introduced 'an element of unreality into the Bible which goes far to minimise its usefulness as a guide to life'. However, Stead believed, if it could be demonstrated that spirits, telepathic communications, and supernatural phenomena infused the modern world, many would accept the Bible as an accurate record of events, with continuing relevance for their lives. 'If it can be proved,' he insisted, 'beyond any cavil or gainsaying that the present world is quite as full of the miraculous element as the old world was ever believed to be, then the value of the Bible rises enormously.' With such 'inconvertible evidence...the corner-stone [would be] knocked out of the whole imposing edifice of modern unbelief' and many could be brought back to faith. For this purpose, Stead proposed in *Borderland* to treat the Bible 'as if it were a report of the proceedings of the Psychical Research Society'.[31] In subsequent articles, Stead provided lengthy lists of biblical references to paranormal and psychical events.[32]

In a lengthy article, 'The True Basis of the New Catholicism', in the October 1895 number, Stead argued that the new scientific understanding of psychical phenomena could not only revive Christianity in the modern world, but also unite the Churches and indeed the major world religions around a common understanding of their shared spiritual foundations. The article opened with a consideration of the attempts then under way to promote church union between the Roman Catholic and Anglican communions. This was a positive development, not least because the Catholic Church was, in Stead's view, the world's best expression of psychical truth. 'The Pope and the Church to which he belongs,' Stead insisted, 'are the most excellent witnesses the world can show to the truth of the phenomena of Borderland. The whole fabric of the Roman Creed is saturated through and through with a living faith in the truth of the psychic phenomena.'[33] But plans for religious reunion, Stead believed, must, in light of the new understanding of the spiritual foundations of the world, go further than a union of churches. 'What is wanted is not merely the reconciliation of Christian sects, but the reconciliation of Science and Religion, and the recognition of the underlying substantial unity of all the creeds . . . This is the new Catholicity that is dawning on the world.'[34]

Stead's article went on to consider the anthropological studies of early religion, including J. G. Frazer's *Golden Bough* and studies of ancient Semitic folklore. While some saw this scholarship as undermining Christian belief, Stead asserted the opposite. For, he insisted, 'it is in the study of folklore, legend, myth, dreams, and, in short, of the traditions and literature of the Borderland, [that] mankind will seek and find the key to a truer interpretation of Christianity'.[35] Christianity, the new scholarship showed, had only emerged through a slow process by which humankind sought to comprehend, through folklore and myths, the spiritual forces that were always present in the world. 'We can hold all the more firmly to the essential truth of the God-man, born of the Virgin, when we find in the long travail of the ages the same idea struggling to express itself in the myths and religious traditions of all peoples in all times.'[36] The study of psychical phenomena, he argued, confirmed spiritual truths that humankind had felt and sought throughout the millennia to express, in a faltering manner, through their varied religious conceptions, and this psychical research thus revealed the spiritual truths that formed the basis of all the world religions. Here, he insisted, was 'the essence of all creeds' and the promise of the new catholicity:

> The Fatherhood of God, the Brotherhood of Man, Redemption through Sacrifice, the Ministry of Unseen Intelligences, and a Future Life in which the soul will have to answer for the deeds done in the body—the key to these things is to be found in the Borderland across which we must venture boldly if we would re-establish the waning faith of men in the existence of the soul.[37]

Stead developed this theme of psychical research and the new catholicity in a follow-up article (July 1896), in which he drew upon the work of great scholar of the religions of the East, F. Max Müller, the writings of Annie Besant, and proceedings of the first Parliament of Religions held in 1893 in Chicago.[38]

Stead believed that his most important contributions in *Borderland* were the 'Letters from Julia', communicated to him, he claimed, by Julia Ames through automatic writing. 'Nothing that I have published in *Borderland*,' he claimed in 1897, 'has attracted so much attention as the Letters from "Julia".' 'The fact,' he added, 'that Julia's letters have commanded such sustained interest is more marvellous than their origin.'[39] Nearly every issue included one or more Julia letters—with the exception of a year between September 1895 and September 1896, when ill-health forced Stead to give up automatic writing for a time. Julia's letters provided descriptions of the afterlife, including such topics as the survival of individual personality, the reunions of the souls of family and friends, the nature of spiritual bodies, the hierarchy of social ranks in heaven, the reality of angels and demons, the astral travel around the universe enjoyed by spirits, the luminous presence of Christ, the lack of importance of former religious affiliations in the afterlife, and the passion of spirits to continue learning new things. Her observations confirmed traditional Christian views of the afterlife: she observed, for example, that angels had wings even though these wings were not needed for their astral travel; the wings were rather 'scenic illusions useful to convey ideas . . . of superiority to earth-bound conditions'.[40] Her most important lesson from the afterlife was the unifying power of disinterested, self-sacrificing love; it was this love that formed God's essence and bound the universe together. She insisted that, motivated by this love, many spirits longed to communicate with the living, just as she knew that many living people sought communication with the spirits of their loved ones. To facilitate this, she pressed Stead to establish a 'bureau of communication', an office staffed with trained mediums, who would help living persons to establish contact with the spirits of loved ones in the other world.

Late in 1897, Stead published the letters in a separate volume, *Letters from Julia; or Light from the Borderland*.[41] The work went through numerous editions, and was translated into French, German, Italian, Greek, Russian, Swedish, and Hindustani. Later entitled *After Death: A Personal Narrative*, it became perhaps the most popular of Stead's books. Stead insisted that he received numerous letters from people who had derived comfort from Julia's depictions of the afterlife, and he further claimed that people of all faiths assured him they could embrace Julia's teachings. The book included an appendix outlining the 'Companions of the Rosary', an attractive idea for 'modernizing' the Roman Catholic Rosary which Julia had first communicated to

Stead on 27 September 1896. Individuals were to make a list of all the people with whom they had a relationship and all the causes to which they were committed. Then each morning before they began their daily work, they were to meditate on the list, asking themselves what they could do for this person or that cause during the coming day. Julia told him that thinking in this way of their 'Companions of the Rosary' would be a form of prayer—'for a loving thought is a prayer'. What was important about the exercise, she assured him, was that it involved thinking of individuals and thus preserving a 'vital connection with them. For love dies when you never think of the person loved.' Stead claimed he kept such a personal 'Rosary list', opening each day by meditating on it.[42]

The famed author, Arthur Conan Doyle, who embraced spiritualism in 1916, read the Julia letters and was convinced that they came from a spirit. 'I differed from Stead in all things when he lived,' Conan Doyle wrote to his brother, Innes, then on the Western Front, in 1917, 'and now I find the book which came from his hand but never from his brain, called "After Death", to be absolutely the best religious book I have ever read.'[43] Others, however, were less impressed with Julia's letters. The novelist Walter Besant observed in the journal *Light* that Julia had nothing new to say, but simply repeated platitudes. A commentator in the *Illustrated London News* dismissed the letters as products of Stead's unconscious mind and as 'dreary, dreaming nonsense', while the reviewer in *The Times* thought that Julia spoke 'in catchphrases familiar to emotional journalism' and 'is somewhat of a bore'.[44]

It is difficult to assess the Julia letters. Stead clearly believed that these communications came from the spirit of his departed friend, and he would continue corresponding with Julia for the rest of his life. As his friend, the journalist A. G. Gardiner later wrote of Stead's spiritualism, 'he believed with all his heart and brain. He would have joyfully gone to the stake for his belief.'[45] She brought comforting messages, which he believed confirmed the Christian faith. Stead acknowledged that Julia tended to write in a 'Steadese' style, and that the messages he received through automatic writing may well have come from his subconscious mind—but then Stead also agreed with Frederic Myers that it was through the 'subliminal consciousness' that individuals received messages from the other world. Stead acknowledged, moreover, that Julia had nothing new to say in her letters, but he insisted this was because she confirmed the ancient revealed truths of Christianity and other world faiths. In an insightful analysis of Stead's Julia letters, Sarah Crofton has argued that Stead unconsciously created Julia's other-worldly persona from a patchwork of sources, including his memories of her before her death, Christian teachings and biblical passages, fragments of theosophy gleaned from Annie Besant, and even passages from the supernatural novel, *A Romance of Two Worlds* (1886), written by his friend, Marie Corelli. 'Julia was a literary creation,' Crofton observed, 'born of the diverse range of occultisms by which Stead was inspired, who became his personal avatar in the journalist's mission to democratise spooks.'[46] Or as Hugh Kingsmill maintained, Julia 'was really a synthesis, on a plane beyond the reach of disillusionment, of Stead's two chief preoccupations, God and woman'.[47] There was also, in Julia's character of the wiser and more experienced woman who guided Stead in the ways of the next world, something reminiscent of Olga Novikoff guiding the young, provincial Stead through the ways of London society some twenty years previously.

Stead brought *Borderland* to a close with the October 1897 issue; he suggested it would be only a temporary suspension, but it proved permanent. Stead was (as will be discussed in the next chapter) turning his attention increasingly to the peace movement and the growing threat of war in South Africa. Moreover, his relations with his assistant editor, Ada Goodrich-Freer, were becoming increasingly fraught. From mid-1894, she had been seeking to gain the patronage of Lord Bute, one of the wealthiest men in Britain, a Catholic convert, and a Vice-President of the Society for Psychical Research. Knowing that Bute despised Stead, she wrote to him of her contempt for Stead and his 'dissenting profanities', and told him that Stead published material in *Borderland* that he knew to be false. In a letter published in the *Oban Times* on 17 October 1896, she claimed that her interest in the paranormal phenomena had 'absolutely nothing to do with journalism as represented by Mr W. T. Stead'.[48] She levelled a parting shot at Stead in her closing statement in the last issue of *Borderland*, when she dismissed 'automatic writing' and those 'silly enough' to believe in it, noting that 'it is a subject which lends itself, above all others, to self-deception'.[49] It is not clear why their relations deteriorated so, as all their correspondence has disappeared.[50] Still another reason for bringing *Borderland* to an end was that it was not proving successful. 'Progress has been made,' he observed, 'but not so much as we hoped for. That fact, indeed, is the chief justification of the suspension for the present of BORDERLAND.'[51]

Over the next several years, Stead continued practicing automatic writing and studying psychical phenomena. He reviewed William James's University of Edinburgh Gifford Lectures, published in 1902 as *The Varieties of Religious Experience*, in *The Review of Reviews*, and was impressed by James's psychological approach to religious experience. He was particularly drawn to James's argument that religious experiences, including religious conversion experiences, originated in the subconscious (though Stead also wondered whether this could explain the mass conversions that accompanied religious revivals). Stead was still more impressed with the posthumous publication of Frederic Myers's great synthesis of his nearly thirty years of psychical research, *Human Personality and its Survival of Bodily Death*. Stead had long admired Myers, who had died in 1901. Both were sons of clergymen, and both were friends of Josephine Butler. Stead warmly embraced Myers's views of telepathy. 'What I am amazed at,' he had written Myers in October 1894, 'is that without any personal experience of the extraordinary subtlety and fascination of telepathic communication, you should have divined so marvelously its possibilities.'[52] Myers's two-volume work was *The Review of Reviews* Book of the Month in March 1903, but it was really, Stead insisted, 'the book of our time'.[53] Stead was attracted to Myers's arguments that individual personality was rooted in the 'subliminal consciousness', to his portrayal of love as a form of telepathy, and to his claims that a person's subliminal consciousness survived bodily death and could communicate telepathically with the living. For Stead, the growing public awareness of Myers's ideas—especially 'the possibility of communication with disembodied spirits'—promised to bring 'a day of hope, of exaltation' which the world had not known 'since the message of Pentecost'.[54]

## The Revival of 1904–5

Stead soon found further evidence of the coming of a new spiritual era for the world, with the extraordinary religious revival that spread across Wales in 1904 and 1905, claiming more than 100,000 Welsh converts. The revival was characterized by protracted prayer meetings, impassioned personal testimonies, vibrant communal singing, uncontrollable weeping, cries, and prostrations, and some electrifying preaching. It was a genuinely popular movement, which seemed to have emerged spontaneously; for believers, it was a singular downpouring of the Holy Spirit. The revival meetings had a democratic ethos, with people of all social ranks feeling called to speak, and women often taking a leading role. It was also very much a young people's revival, with children prominent at meetings and processions. As it spread, the movement found an emotive, charismatic leader— the young, Welsh-speaking former coal miner and candidate for the Calvinistic Methodist ministry, Evan Roberts. He proved a compelling preacher, proclaiming the presence of the Spirit and exercising an almost hypnotic effect on his hearers; observers spoke of his penetrating eyes and 'telepathic' ability to recognize, with uncanny accuracy, troubled enquirers in congregations. News of the revival attracted professional revivalists to Wales, including the English revivalist, Gypsy Smith, and the American revivalist team, Reuben Torrey and Charlie Alexander. After their meetings in Wales, Torrey and Alexander moved on to London in February 1905, holding revival meetings in the Albert Hall which claimed over a million attendances and 20,000 converts. The revival spread through Britain, to France, Scandinavia, the Netherlands, and Germany, and then, through Welsh missionaries, to Northeast India.

Stead travelled to Wales in December 1904 to report on the movement and soon became convinced that it was the work of the Holy Spirit. In the following months, he gave a number of newspaper interviews on the revival, and wrote three 'Revival pamphlets', which were subsequently published in February 1905 as a single volume, *The Revival of 1905*. The short work sold over 200,000 copies in Britain and some 500,000 copies in America, and Stead became the leading publicist of the Revival movement.[55] He told his readers that he himself was 'a child of the Revival of 1859 to 1861', and that he continued to be filled with the sense that 'this is God's world', infused with divinity.[56] In an interview published in the *Methodist Times* of 15 December, Stead testified that in Wales he felt himself in 'the presence of the unknown' and compared the atmosphere to a ghostly haunting. 'There is,' he wrote of the pervasive spiritual presence, 'something there from the Other World. You cannot say whence it came or whither it was going, but it moves and lives and reaches for you all the time.' At revival meetings, he felt 'the pull of that unseen hand'.[57] This same spiritual power, he maintained, had charged the atmosphere of the great revivals in the past. It was the 'strange, mysterious, invisible influence' which 'people of the olden-time religion called the Power of God', and it now permeated Wales.[58]

Stead was deeply impressed with Evan Roberts, tall, graceful, with a 'winsome smile', speaking 'simply, unaffectedly, earnestly', and accompanied by the five 'singing sisters'. At their meetings, Stead felt an 'all-pervading influence of some invisible reality'.[59] Stead was one of the few journalists to whom Roberts granted an interview. He described to Stead how, deeply troubled in the months before the revival over what he viewed as Christianity's failure, he began having mystical experiences. One night, he claimed, he was awakened about one in the morning, 'and I found myself, with unspeakable joy and awe, in the very presence of the Almighty God. And for the space of four hours I was privileged to speak face to face with Him as a man speaks face to face with a friend.' Stead asked Roberts if he might have been dreaming, but Roberts assured him that he was 'wide awake' and added that this 'wonderful communing with God' continued for four hours every night during the course of three or four months. In these 'conversations', Roberts observed, God had appeared to him not as Jesus Christ, but rather as the Holy Spirit. Stead was impressed with Roberts' mystical visions, which Stead attributed to paranormal powers. 'The truth about Evan Roberts,' he wrote, 'is that he is very psychic, with clairvoyance well developed and a strong visualising gift.' In highlighting Roberts' other-worldly presence, Stead noted how many believed of Roberts that no 'watch will keep time when it is carried in his pocket'.[60]

Stead was impressed with the spontaneous nature of the revival meetings, which seemed guided by the Spirit alone. 'The most extraordinary thing about the meetings which I attended,' he enthused, 'was the extent to which they were absolutely without any human direction of leadership. "We must obey the Spirit" is the watchword of Evan Roberts.'[61] Stead interviewed the professional revivalists who were drawn to Wales, including Reuben Torrey and Gypsy Smith, but insisted they were not directing the movement. Rather, something deeper was at work, the divine presence moving through the subliminal consciousness of numerous individuals, to use the language of the new psychological approaches to religion. Stead drew upon the recent work of William James and his own studies of the paranormal in interpreting the revival. In the revival meetings, the divine Spirit acted upon the minds of thousands so that all became 'intensely conscious of the all pervading influence of some invisible reality... moving palpable though not tangible in their midst'.[62] The prayer circles were a form of telepathic communication, bringing messages, as though by wireless communication, from those 'mysterious' powers of which 'the Scripture speaks'. The revival meetings were forms of direct democracy, in which all were equal under the Spirit's influence, women as well as men. 'Women,' Stead observed, 'pray, sing, testify, and speak as freely as men—no one daring to make them afraid.'[63] It was, Stead believed, a new beginning, linking Christianity, the paranormal, democracy, and feminism: 'We are at last on the eve of a great spiritual awakening among the masses of our people.' Stead hoped this would prove to be a 'world-wide Revival'.[64] He interviewed Annie Besant in July 1905, and she assured him that the Welsh revival was part of a 'great religious movement which is in evidence all over the world'. 'Yes,' he responded, 'I suppose that is so. The light is piercing through the veil in every direction.'[65] While Stead was speaking at a revival meeting in March 1905 in Manchester, he believed that his body was taken over by the Holy Spirit, while a friend in the audience recalled being 'transfixed by his face and words'.[66]

In late August 1905, Stead travelled to Russia to report on the revolutionary upheavals sweeping the country, and he remained in Russia until the end of October, promoting the cause of a representative Duma and constitutional monarchy.[67] He returned with an enhanced sense of new beginnings, believing that in Russia he had witnessed the 'birth throes of a mighty state' which made him 'full of radiant hope'.[68] By now, the British revival movement was drawing to a close, with excitement waning and attendance at revival meetings dwindling. In Wales, Evan Roberts experienced a physical and emotional collapse and permanently withdrew from public life in 1906. The revival movement had lasting effects. Church membership in

Wales was 10 per cent higher in 1912 than it had been in 1903. Most significantly, the revival of 1905, as Stead had hoped, contributed in part to a global movement of spiritual renewal, the Pentecostal movement, which proclaimed the return of the spirit gifts and which during the coming century became one of the world's largest Christian movements.

### 'Julia's Bureau'

On 14 December 1907, Stead's eldest son, William, died of blood poisoning, after a three-day illness, at the age of thirty-three. Stead was extremely close to his son, who had followed his father into journalism and 'whom I had trained in the fond hope that he would be my successor'.[69] Willie Stead, as he was known, had accompanied his father to Chicago in 1893–4, served as private secretary to E. T. Cook, editor of the *Daily News*, and then to Stead's friend, John Morley (to assist him in writing his *Life of Gladstone*), and he assisted Stead in editing *The Review of Reviews*. He had married Lottie Royce, the daughter of an American educator from upper New York State, in 1896. He volunteered for eight years at his uncle's Browning Settlement at Walworth, teaching adult education classes and embracing a commitment to Christian social work.[70] Stead, his wife, and Willie's wife were at the bedside and watched him die; the unexpected death of this 'most gentle of souls' left Stead devastated.

Shortly after his son's death, Stead began receiving messages from the spirit of his dead son, with the messages coming through two friends who claimed the gift of automatic writing. These messages became weekly occurrences. Stead was in no doubt that these messages came from his son. In an article, 'How I Know that the Dead Return', published in the *Fortnightly Review* of January 1909, he wrote of how during the past year, 'I have been cheered and comforted by messages from my boy, who is nearer and dearer to me than ever before.' These messages were profoundly comforting in themselves and they also provided Stead with absolute proof of the survival of personality after death: 'For me the problem is solved, the truth is established, and I am glad to have this opportunity of testifying publicly to all the world that, so far as I am concerned, doubt on this subject is henceforth impossible.'[71] Speaking of his son in

July 1909 at Halifax, Stead observed that 'one friend has seen him at least three times fully materialised, as was our Lord after His resurrection'. For Stead, these communications with his son opened new prospects for humankind. 'I can say,' he told the Halifax audience, that 'Spiritualism has made death other than death for me.'[72] He felt called to share this good news about life after death for the comfort of others.

Early in 1908, Stead began writing what would be his last major book, a biography of his former lover and long-time friend, Olga Novikoff, based on her extensive correspondence. The occasion for the book was the signing of the Anglo-Russian Entente in August 1907 and a major theme of the book was the importance of friendship and co-operation between the British and Russian empires. In his book project, he relived the episodes of his youth, the death of the 'saintly' Nicolas Kirieff, the 'Bulgarian atrocities' agitation, the struggle to avert war between Britain and Russia, Gladstone's prophetic denunciations of Beaconsfield's imperialism, and the friendship with Novikoff that had helped make him a national figure. Madame Novikoff was still very much alive, but she felt unable to write her memoirs and was content to leave the work to Stead. It was, he remarked, 'the story of two lives', the strangely intertwined lives of Novikoff and Stead.[73] To assist him in writing the book, he appointed Edith Harper, the daughter of a family friend from Newcastle. Harper claimed telepathic gifts and practiced automatic writing, including conveying messages from the deceased Willie; she would later write an affectionate memoir of Stead's final years.

In the late summer and autumn of 1908, while immersed in writing the Novikoff book, Stead experienced what Harper described as a period of 'unusual psychic activity'.[74] On 20 August 1908, Stead received what he believed were messages from the spirit of Frederic Myers through Harper's hand, which he then published in *The Review of Reviews*. Myers's spirit informed Stead that there was 'no limit to the possibilities of intercommunication' between spirits, whether living or dead, and that with this dawning truth, humankind would move beyond the credal orthodoxies in seeking union with the divine. 'The day has passed,' Myers observed, 'when mankind will seek salvation by means of the varied dogmas of the warring churches.'[75] Although Stead had only a slight personal acquaintance with Myers in life, he now felt a unique bond with Myers's spirit. Later in the summer, while immersed in writing his Novikoff biography, Stead believed that the spirit of the eighteenth-century Russian Empress, Catherine the Great, conveyed messages to him about the destiny of 'Holy Russia'. Indeed, he now became convinced that Catherine's spirit had for decades, from his first employment with the Russian Vice-Consul in Newcastle, been quietly directing his ardent advocacy of Russia and the Slavic peoples. Stead, according to Harper, was certain 'that there was some driving force, some unseen power at work which constantly energised his Russian sympathies. That power called itself Catherine II of Russia.' Catherine's spirit, Stead informed Novikoff in October 1908, was very pleased with the recent upheavals in the Balkans, which signified that 'the Slav . . . is coming into his Kingdom'.[76] Stead insisted that Catherine had dictated, through automatic writing, most of his article on 'The Arrival of the Slav', which appeared in the *Contemporary Review* of January 1909.[77] He completed his biography of Novikoff in late 1908, and *The M.P. for Russia: Reminiscences and Correspondence of Madame Olga Novikoff* was published in two volumes in early 1909.

With the book complete, Stead believed the time had come to establish the bureau to facilitate communications between the living and the dead for which Julia had long been pressing him. The necessary funds for the bureau came in December 1908 when the American publisher, William Randolph Hearst, offered Stead £500 a year to serve as a special correspondent for his newspapers. Stead asked for £1,000 a year, and in January 1909 Hearst agreed. With this money, Stead proceeded to form what he called 'Julia's Bureau'. He transformed part of his home in Wimbledon, Cambridge House, into the 'inner sanctum' of the bureau. He also moved the offices of *The Review of Reviews* from their long-term home in Mowbray House to a building on the Kingsway, and turned Mowbray House, which still housed the former *Borderland* library of psychical books, into the bureau's active hub, where mediums would engage with clients and research would be conducted. 'Cambridge House,' he observed, 'will be the Mecca, and Mowbray House the Medina, the sacred places of the New Revelation.' In addition to a permanent secretarial staff, including his daughter, Estelle, and Edith Harper, he hired 'sensitives'—one automatic writer based at Cambridge House and two 'trance mediums' based at Mowbray House—to provide consultations to applicants. 'I have opened,' he wrote, 'an office for the purpose of facilitating communications between those who love each other, but who are temporarily divided by the grave.' The Bureau would form 'a bridge between the living and the dead' and as such it had the potential to change the world.[78] The plan was for individuals wishing to be in touch with the departed to apply in writing to the governing committee, named 'Julia's Circle', which would assess the merits of each application. Successful applicants would be given private sessions with a medium. Julia, Stead insisted, was the 'Invisible Director' of the Bureau—a special empty chair was placed prominently for her at all meetings—and Julia had the final say, through automatic writing, on all applications as well as all decisions affecting the Bureau. In addition to Julia, Stead claimed that his son, Willie, and Frederic Myers promised their support for the project on the 'other side'.

'Julia's Bureau' was formally launched on 24 April 1909. Over the next three years, the bureau accepted over 600 applicants and arranged over 1,300 individual sittings with a medium, free of charge to the clients (though donations were welcomed). Among the clients was the Irish poet, W. B. Yeats, who attended the Bureau for sittings between 1909 and 1912.[79] During the first year, 'Julia's Circle' met for about an hour every morning, except Sundays, in Mowbray House, and unless he was away from London on business, Stead always attended. Each meeting opened with prayer and a reading from a sacred text of one of the world's religions. Meetings of 'Julia's Circle' sometimes included seances and attracted guest celebrity mediums, among them the American Mrs Etta Wriedt, who visited for several weeks in the spring of 1911, staying at Cambridge House. Stead claimed that the Bureau, as with *Borderland* in the 1890s, combined religious zeal with objective science. He described the bureau's work as 'experimental exploration', and compared telepathic messages sent by the spirits in the afterlife to the 'wireless communications' being sent by Marconi across the Atlantic.[80] And for him the religious aspect of the work was paramount. Speaking at the Spiritualists' National Union convention in Halifax on 4 July 1909, Stead insisted that 'the great mission of Spiritualism is to make men spiritual' and that in his version of Christian spiritualism, Jesus 'exists as our leader to a better world'. He now believed that his spiritual experience at Holloway

Gaol on New Year's Eve 1885—when he had heard the voice calling him to 'be a Christ'—had been his first experience as a medium, and he viewed his work with Julia's Bureau as his response to that divine call, by helping direct others to a higher and 'better world'.[81] 'To share "with another's need" his own joy,' Edith Harper observed of Stead at this time, 'to spread the knowledge that death is no dividing abyss, but the gateway, if we will, to closer communion, was his dearest wish.'[82]

As Roger Luckhurst noted in his fascinating *Mummy's Curse*, Stead was drawn still more deeply into the occult through his friendship with the spiritualist, Nile explorer, and amateur Egyptologist, Thomas Douglas Murray.[83] In 1903, Douglas Murray introduced Stead to hauntingly beautiful spirit drawings by the feminist painter and spiritualist, Anna Mary Howitt, who had died in 1884; Douglas Murray described them as 'automatic drawings', that is, drawings communicated by spirits in a similar manner to automatic writing.[84] In January 1909, at Douglas Murray's invitation, Stead dined with the Ghost Club, a secretive private club of about ten leading London spiritualists, included Sir William Crookes, the Rev Stainton Moses, Alfred Sinnett, and Laurence Oliphant, who shared ghost stories and held seances. Through the Ghost Club, Stead learned of the story of the haunted mummy lid of the priestess of Amen-Ra, a lid which Douglas Murray had brought back from Egypt and gifted to the Egyptian Room of the British Museum and which allegedly brought injury and death. Stead communicated the priestess's story to Julia, who assured him that by publicizing the story, he 'might be able to break the spell and help her [the priestess] escape from the self-created prison in which she lives'. Stead and Douglas Murray now began visiting the Egyptian Room, where they claimed that they could communicate with the spirits of the mummies.[85]

Stead's occult passions were raising questions about his mental balance. Surrounded by fellow enthusiasts in 'Julia's Circle', who filled his home, benefited from his largess and flattered his 'powers', and believing that he received continual direction from Julia's spirit, his views grew more and more extravagant. In the autumn of 1909, at seances conducted by 'Julia's Circle', Stead claimed to 'interview' the spirits of Disraeli, Gladstone, Manning, and other deceased public figures on such issues as the 'People's budget' and the reform of the House of Lords. He published some of these 'interviews' in such respected publications as the *Daily Chronicle, Fortnightly Review*, and *Contemporary Review*, suggesting that his spiritualism retained some credibility with the public.[86] But others shook their heads over Stead's 'spook exchange'.[87] As the critic Adolphe Smith noted, Stead's 'interviews' with the Disraeli and Gladstone spirits emulated the politicians' familiar speech patterns and ideas, but gave them nothing fresh or substantial to say. 'On earth,' Smith observed, 'these great men would have acquired new ideas and knowledge,' but 'in the spirit world they seem to stagnate where they do not deteriorate.'[88] An Italian journalist visited 'Julia's Bureau', and asked to be put in touch with the spirit of the celebrated Italian criminologist, Caesare Lombroso. The seance with a bureau medium was an embarrassment, as the 'Lombroso spirit' could not understand Italian or recall where he had lived.[89] Of the over 600 clients during the first three years, only about a third believed that they had established contact with deceased loved ones. The costs associated with 'Julia's Bureau', meanwhile, including salaries to the mediums and staff, and room rentals, were more than double the anticipated £1,000 a year and Stead could not continue to cover the costs. In March 1910, Stead was forced to give up the lease of Mowbray House, and Julia's Bureau lost its main offices. 'Julia's Circle' moved from daily to weekly meetings, now normally held on Wednesday evenings at Stead's Cambridge House home. On 18 May 1911 Stead sought to explain the relative lack of success of the Bureau, telling the Union of London Spiritualists that Julia recently confessed that she had been in error when she had said the spirits in the afterlife were eager to communicate with the living. 'After greater experience,' she wrote, 'she found that the number who wish for it is comparatively few.'[90]

'Stead's spiritualism,' observed Hugh Kingsmill, 'which towards the close of his life became the chief interest of his life, puzzled and alienated many of his supporters. They regarded his connection with Julia as an inexplicable aberration.'[91] This was certainly the case with his fellow Nonconformist journalist, William Robertson Nicoll, editor of the *British Weekly*. 'My violent dislike of the Spooks,' Nicoll confessed privately to a friend in May 1912, 'prevented us from having any really intimate intercourse for the last few years.'[92] And yet while friends and supporters were disappointed or perplexed by Stead's growing spiritualist commitments from the early 1890s, spiritualism for him was no aberration, but rather part of his lifelong commitment to seeking God's presence and serving God's will in the world. Stead longed to believe in a world saturated in divinity, a world created and sustained by God for a higher purpose, and watched over by a cloud of witnesses, including the spirits of the departed. For him, the communications from spirits in the modern world confirmed the accuracy of the biblical stories of spirits, demons, angels, and miracles, and showed that revelation, faith, and religion remained vital even in a materialist and sceptical age. The psychic phenomena challenged the increasingly prevalent materialism of his times and pointed to a divinely ordered creation in which not only spiritual forces, but also love, sacrifice, and martyrdom had transcendent and lasting meaning.

Spiritualism and theosophy had drawn his friend Annie Besant back from secularism and materialism and had given her life new direction through faith in divine forces governing the world. Spiritualism confirmed his own Christian beliefs and his sense of religious and moral mission. 'All my researches in spiritualism,' he told a Scottish clergyman in 1911, 'strengthen my faith in the essential doctrines of Christianity.'[93] It would be 'shameful', he once wrote of his absorption in spiritualism to Robertson Nicoll, 'that a Christian journalist should refuse to study the only proof of Christianity that can be offered to the human mind'.[94] It is significant that in 1904–5 Stead viewed the revival in Wales as an expression of psychical power or that in 1909 he looked back on his religious experience on New Year's Eve 1885 in Holloway Gaol—with its other-worldly voice calling him to 'be a Christ'—as his first experience as a medium. As his friend and fellow journalist, A. G. Gardiner observed of Stead, 'all that he did had its roots in the visionary. Spiritualism, automatic writing, telepathy, spirit photography, and the rest belonged to his later life, but they were inevitable developments of a mind whose allegiance was never to the five senses of the normal man, but always to some sixth sense that constituted for him the only valid governance of life.' 'Had he lived in an earlier age,' Gardiner added, 'he could have been the founder of a new religion or the furious Crusader on behalf of an old one.'[95]

## Notes

1. Roger Luckhurst, *The Invention of Telepathy 1870–1901* (Oxford, 2002), p. 1.
2. W. T. Stead, *Real Ghost Stories*, rev edn (London, 1897), p. x.

3. [W. T. Stead], 'Real Ghost Stories', *RoR* (December 1891), p. 574.

4. David G. Ritchie, 'The Logic of a Ghost's Advocate', *Westminster Review* 137 (1892), 1.

5. Edith K. Harper, *Stead, the Man: Personal Reminiscences* (London, 1918), 35.

6. Stead, *My Father*, pp. 96–103.

7. *PMG* (26 April 1884, 4 June 1884).

8. W. T. Stead to Olga Novikoff, 5 February 1886, Novikoff–Stead Corr., fos. 243–4.

9. Helena Blavatsky to W. T. Stead, 24 February 1888, Stead Papers, STED 1/5.

10. Stead, *M.P. for Russia*, vol. i, pp. 130–1.

11. [W. T. Stead], 'Madame Blavatsky', *RoR*, (June 1891), p. 549.

12. [Annie Besant], 'Among the Adepts. Madame Blavatsky on the "Secret Doctrine"', *PMG* (25 April 1889).

13. [W. T. Stead], 'Annie Besant', *RoR* (October 1891), p. 366.

14. Luckhurst, *Invention of Telepathy*, p. 126.

15. [W. T. Stead]. 'Wanted, a Census of Ghosts', *RoR* (September 1891), pp. 257–8.

16. [W. T. Stead], 'Real Ghost Stories', *RoR* (December 1891), p. 574.

17. [W. T. Stead], 'My Experience in Automatic Writing', *Borderland*, 1 (July 1893), 39.

18. Frances E. Willard, et al., *A Young Woman Journalist: A Memorial Tribute to Julia A. Ames* (Chicago, 1892), pp. 1–56.

19. Ibid., p. 67.

20. Ibid., 102–3; W. T. Stead, *The Story that Transformed the World; or the Passion Play at Ober Ammergau in 1890* (London, 1890), pp. 158–60.

21. Kingsmill, *After Puritanism*, pp. 218–19.

22. [W. T. Stead], 'Throughth; or, on the Eve of the Fourth Dimension', *RoR* (April 1893), p. 427.

23. Harper, *Stead, the Man*, p. 1.

24. Luckhurst, *Invention of Telepathy*, pp. 128–47.

25. W. T. Stead, 'Why I Believe in Immortality', *Borderland*, 2 (July 1895), p. 200.

26. Countess of Warwick to W. T. Stead, 10 September 1893, Stead Papers, STED 1/72.

27. Joseph O. Baylen, 'W. T. Stead's *Borderland:* A Quarterly Review and Index of Psychic Phenomena, 1893–97', *Victorian Periodicals Newsletter*, 4 (April 1969), pp. 30–5.

28. *Borderland*, 1 (July 1893), pp, 3, 5.

29. *Borderland*, 1 (July 1893), p. 6.

30. *Borderland*, 1 (July 1893), p. 7.

31. *Borderland*, 1 (October 1893), pp. 133–4.

32. *Borderland*, 3 (April 1896), pp. 130–8; 3 (October 1896), pp. 412–19.
33. *Borderland*, 2 (October 1895), p. 295.
34. Ibid., p. 303.
35. Ibid., p. 304.
36. Ibid., p. 308.
37. Ibid., p. 309.
38. *Borderland*, 3 (July 1896), pp. 297–303.
39. *Borderland*, 4 (October 1897), p. 343.
40. *Borderland*, 2 (January 1895), p. 8.
41. W. T. Stead, *Letters from Julia; or Light from the Borderland* (London, 1898).
42. Ibid., Appendix.
43. Quoted in Joseph O. Baylen, 'Sir Arthur Conan Doyle and W. T. Stead: The Novelist and the Journalist', *Albion*, 2 (1970), p. 11.
44. *Illustrated London News* (15 May 1897), 22; *The Times* (5 February 1898), p. 4.
45. Whyte, *Life of Stead*, vol. i, p. 338.
46. Sarah Crofton, '"Julia Says": The Spirit-Writing and Editorial Mediumship of W. T. Stead', *Interdisciplinary Studies in the Long Nineteenth Century*, 16 (2013), pp. 1–15; 2.
47. Kingsmill, *After Puritanism*, p. 216.
48. John L. Campbell and Trevor Hall, *Strange Things*, new edn. (Edinburgh, 2006), 142–3.
49. *Borderland*, 4 (October 1897), 368.
50. Campbell and Hall, *Strange Things*, p. 143.
51. *Borderland*, 4 (October 1897), , 341.
52. W. T. Stead to Frederic Myers, 2 October 1894, Myers Papers, Trinity College, Cambridge, 4/70.
53. [W. T. Stead], 'If a Man Dies Shall He Live Again?' *RoR*, 27 (March 1903), pp. 295–301.
54. Ibid., p. 300.
55. Stead, *My Father*, p. 279.
56. W. T. Stead, *The Revival of 1905* (London, 1905), pp. 3–11, quotations on pp. 10, 11.
57. Quoted in ibid., pp. 25, 26.
58. Ibid., pp. 98–9.
59. Ibid., pp. 38, 40.
60. Ibid. p. 54.
61. [W. T. Stead], 'Revival in the West', *RoR* (January 1905), p. 89.
62. Ibid., p. 89.
63. Stead, *Revival of 1905*, p. 32.

64. 'A World-Wide Revival', *RoR* (February 1905), p. 148.
65. 'The Religious Revival: Mrs. Annie Besant', *RoR* (August 1905), p. 135.
66. Stead, *My Father*, pp. 279–81.
67. Joseph O. Baylen, 'W. T. Stead and the Russian Revolution of 1905', *Canadian Journal of History*, 2 (1967), pp. 45–66.
68. *The Times* (26 September 1905), p. 8.
69. W. T. Stead, 'How I Know that the Dead Return', *Fortnightly Review*, 85 (January 1909), 64.
70. W. T. Stead, 'My Son', *RoR*, 37 (January 1908), pp. 23–30; F. Herbert Stead, 'His Work in Walworth', ibid., pp. 30–3.
71. Stead, 'How I Know that the Dead Return', p. 64.
72. Stead, *My Father*, pp. 284, 285.
73. Harper, *Stead, the Man*, p. 92.
74. Ibid., p. 119.
75. 'Messages from beyond the Grave', *RoR*, 38 (September 1908), p. 288.
76. W. T. Stead to Olga Novikoff, 11 October 1908, Novikoff–Stead Corr., fol. 262.
77. Harper, *Stead, the Man*, pp. 103–13.
78. W. T. Stead, 'The Exploration of the Other World', *Fortnightly Review*, 85 (May 1909), pp. 850, 858.
79. Justin Sausman, 'The Democratisation of the Spook: W. T. Stead and the Invention of Public Occultism', in Brake et al. (eds), *W. T. Stead: Newspaper Revolutionary*, p. 159.
80. W. T. Stead, 'When the Door Opened', *Fortnightly Review*, 86 (November 1909), p. 854.
81. Harper, *Stead, the Man*, pp. 158–61.
82. Ibid., 175.
83. Roger Luckhurst, *The Mummy's Curse: The True History of a Dark Fantasy* (Oxford, 2012).
84. T. Douglas Murray to W. T. Stead, 11 October 1903, Stead Papers, STED 1/55.
85. Luckhurst, *Mummy's Curse*, pp. 26–8, 38–9, 46–7, 54–5.
86. W. T. Stead, 'When the Door Opened', *Fortnightly Review*, 86 (November 1909), 853–74; W. T. Stead, 'Can Telepathy Explain All?', *The Contemporary Review*, 90 (July 1910), pp. 446–57.
87. 'Stead and his Spooks', *Washington Post* (28 November 1909), p. 13.
88. Adolphe Smith, 'A Spiritist Revival', *The Contemporary Review*, 98 (1910), p. 315.
89. Ibid., pp. 315–16; Sausman, 'Democratisation of the Spook', p. 161.
90. Harper, *Stead, the Man*, pp. 210–11.

91. Kingsmill, *After Puritanism*, p. 216.
92. W. Robertson Nicoll to A. H. Wilkerson, 1 May 1912, quoted in T. H. Darlow, *William Robertson Nicoll: Life and Letters* (London, 1925), pp. 224–5.
93. To Walter Wynn, quoted in Harper, *Stead, the Man*, p. 228.
94. W. Robertson Nicoll, 'W. T. Stead', *British Weekly* (25 April 1912).
95. Quoted in Whyte, *Life of Stead*, vol. i, p. 338.

# 5

# The Great Pacifist, 1894–1912

Stead's younger brother, Herbert, was a Christian mystic. In 1889, he resigned his Congregational pastorate in Leicester and moved with his wife to Oxford, where he pursued private theological study. While in Oxford, he experienced a vision of Christ; there could be no doubt, he wrote, of 'the certainty of His Self-manifestation'. Christ gave him no specific message, but 'He made me know Him to be the Present Companion, the Living Leader, the over-mastering Lover'. In the years that followed, Herbert became editor of the Congregationalist *Independent* newspaper and head of the Browning Hall mission in Walworth, while he assisted his brother with *The Review of Reviews*; he also grew increasingly obsessed with the arms race and horrors of war. One day in early 1894, while praying for peace, Herbert heard what he believed was a divine voice, telling him to 'Approach the Emperor of Russia: Through Him Deliverance will come'. The message seemed madness, as Herbert viewed the Tsar as 'the greatest War-lord on earth'. But recalling that his brother had once interviewed the Tsar, he wrote to William, who was then in Chicago. William responded on 20 February, observing that an approach to the Tsar would be futile. 'I am not in the habit of being daunted by impossibilities,' Stead reminded his brother. 'A Nonconformist who went to Rome to teach the Pope how to govern the Catholic Church is not likely to be deterred from proposing anything to anybody if there is a chance of a thousandth part of decimal one per cent of his advice being taken.' But Stead saw absolutely no chance of success in appealing to Tsar Alexander III to take up the cause of world peace.[1]

And yet, when Stead returned from the United States a few weeks later, his views had changed. He now told Herbert that he had received 'a Signpost and a half'—'Signpost' being Stead's term for an indication of the divine will—that the voice Herbert had heard was a divine revelation. Stead had also learned that Tsar Alexander was considering an appeal to the great powers for 'concerted disarmament'. Stead now took up the peace cause, calling in *The Review of Reviews* of April 1894 for a general European reduction of armaments and appealing for leadership to the Tsar, as 'the peace-keeper of Europe'.[2] Herbert continued telling his brother he must view the peace movement as his divine calling. In a letter to William on Christmas Eve 1895, he noted how William had already played 'a great part in staving off' two wars between Britain and Russia—in 1876–80 over the Balkans, and again in the Penjdeh incident of 1885 (when Britain had viewed Russia's capture of an Afghan border fort as threatening India's northwest frontier, and war was only narrowly averted when both sides agreed to negotiate). 'People think it a great deal to have saved one human life,' Herbert wrote, 'and so it is. But what greater honour it is to have saved the hundreds of thousands of lives which these wars would have sacrificed.' 'I am proud to think that the man so used of God to breathe peace and goodwill among the nations is my brother.' He was now convinced that God had been preparing William for the mission of world peace from their childhood: 'It is the old affection which made that home of ours at Howdon, with all its ructions and excitements, one of God's hotbeds of love, whence he had planted seedlings and saplings that have been for the shelter and healing of the nations.'[3]

From the mid-1890s, Stead fervently pursued the cause of world peace; it became the most prominent public activity of his final years. His peace activism included a leading role in opposing the South African War of 1899–1902, a role that made him for a time arguably the most hated person in Britain. Through his peace commitments he became an increasingly international figure, who from about 1903 moved beyond his belief in the divine mission of the 'English-speaking race'—now to denounce racism and call for justice for victims of Western imperialism in Africa and India. He entitled his autobiographical account of his later years 'The Great Pacifist' and portrayed his life as shaped by an unfolding ideal of peace leading ultimately to a 'World State whose tribunals would render the maintenance of armaments unnecessary'.[4]

## Stead in the Later 1890s and Early 1900s

As Stead reached his fiftieth birthday in 1899, he appeared older than his years. His hair was receding and his hair and beard had gone grey; his face was deeply lined and his once piercing blue eyes had faded to a light blue or grey. He was increasingly known among journalists as 'old Stead'. He remained careless about his dress, preferring ill-fitting old suits, which gave him a clumsy appearance; wearing new clothes, he confessed, left him feeling 'profoundly miserable'.[5] There was, one observer noted, 'nothing in his negligence of dress' that suggested the bohemian artist; rather, he resembled 'a country tradesman of the less pompous kind'.[6] He retained his remarkable memory. In social settings, he was a lively talker, with a rich store of anecdotes and stories, and he moved rapidly from topic to topic—great personages, ghosts, the Salvation Army, women's rights, imperial defence, Ireland, and peace—though it tended to be a monologue. He retained a lively sense of humour, and was ready to laugh at himself and his eccentricities. While he had been nervous speaking in public in his youth, he had developed into an engaging, often vehement public speaker, though some, among them George Bernard Shaw, were put off by his insistence on opening his speeches with prayer or his tendency to burst into prayer in the midst of a speech.[7]

He had relaxed his avoidance of alcohol, and enjoyed a glass of stout and even an occasional glass of wine; he also regularly smoked cigars, sometimes singeing his beard.[8] He enjoyed meals with friends and visitors at a restaurant in Holborn, where he always ordered the same—sole, macaroni and cheese, and fruit. He had a great love of flowers, and would buy roses or violets from flower-sellers on the Strand or bring them from his garden in Wimbledon to decorate *The Review of Reviews* office.[9] In his office, called 'The Sanctum'— where he spent much of his life—there were photographs of famous figures (among them James Russell Lowell) on the mantle over the fire, Scripture verses over the doors, a sofa covered with papers, and a bust of Cardinal Manning on his roll-top desk.[10] The mental stresses of his editorial work and reform campaigns took a toll on his health. He suffered a nervous breakdown in 1895, which necessitated a long period of rest. Following this, he purchased a seaside cottage, Holly Bush, with garden, on Hayling Island near Portsmouth; here he could escape for time with his family, for relaxation, or for longer writing projects. He enjoyed sailing, swimming, and camping with his children and their friends, and he and Emma would fill the Hayling house with young people during the summer months. He and his family worshipped at the Hayling Island Congregational church, a small village church with a membership of about fifty, and eventually he transferred his church membership there.[11] In 1895, he began the successful 'Masterpiece Library' to provide books, priced at a penny, for young people. Beginning with 'Penny Poets', he added 'Penny Novels' (abridgements of classic novels in one hundred pages) and then in 1896 began a series of illustrated children's books, 'Books for the Bairns', writing some of the stories himself.[12] They sold millions, and for many these 'penny Steadfuls' were their first exposure to literature. In a departure from the strict Nonconformist roots of his youth, he began attending the theatre in the summer of 1904. Believing that readers would be interested in his early impressions as a Nonconformist of the theatre, he provided a highly personal discussion, in twenty-five parts, in *The Review of Reviews* between July 1904 and January 1907. He wished to determine, he wrote, whether the theatre was an influence 'making for righteousness'.[13] But many Nonconformists had been attending the theatre for years, and most readers were simply bemused by his puritanical approach. 'We knew already that you were badly brought up,' George Bernard Shaw wrote him in response to the first article, 'and are a person of outrageously excessive temperament.'[14]

His marriage was often less than happy, and his wife Emma suffered bouts of depressive and physical illness. In September 1887, Stead confided to Olga Novikoff that Emma was 'very low in her mind' and was to be hospitalized for up to eight weeks. 'She has just told me,' he added, 'that she has never had a happy year since you saw me, that she has suffered agonies because of my having neglected her & ceased to love her.' She further told him, 'she will be my housekeeper nothing more.'[15] Yet there was also real affection in the marriage, and they enjoyed their family visits to Hayling Island. That said, tensions at home might help account for Stead's frequent travels from the late 1880s onwards. A major source of tension with Emma was over what she viewed as Stead's careless generosity with money; he gave large amounts to good causes, and was a notoriously easy touch for both men and women who came to his office with hard-luck stories. In promoting women's equality, he was generous in helping young female authors. In 1894, he provided Annie Holdsworth with a year's income, so that she could write her second novel. In 1900, he provided the London-based American actor, author, and suffragette, Elizabeth Robins, with funds to travel to the Alaskan gold fields to search for her brother and write about the gold rush. He also promoted the careers of young male authors, especially H. G. Wells, whose science fiction fascinated him.[16] He enjoyed flirting with attractive women. His friendship with 'OK' (Olga Kirieff) Novikoff was precious to him throughout his life; by 1908, he was signing his letters to her 'OW', for 'Old Willie'.

His Christian faith continued to inform his life and political activism. In his later years, he increasingly referred to God as the 'Senior Partner'. As he explained the term at a Silcoatian Old Boy's annual dinner in 1910 in Huddersfield, God was the 'Senior Partner' and all people were 'junior partners' in life's enterprise; God would do his share, and people must do their share, in the understanding that He would show people what their work was to be at the right time.[17] Stead's favourite Scriptural passage was Proverbs 3: 5–6 ('Trust in the LORD with all thine heart; and lean not unto thine own understanding. In all thy ways acknowledge him, and he shall direct thy paths'). These words, he insisted, had been 'imprinted on his mind before he was sixteen', he knew they had also been a favourite of General Gordon, and the passage would later be inscribed on the marble pedestal under Stead's bust in the Hall of Peace at The Hague. He viewed the passage as a call to action, a 'mental attitude of absolute readiness to obey the word of command with a passionate determination to do whatever is given us to do with our utmost strength and skill'.[18] He regularly attended Congregational services and weeknight prayer meetings at Worple Road church, Wimbledon, or at Hayling Island, joining in the singing zestfully (though badly out of tune), and he sometimes preached in mission halls. The hymn he had found most helpful in his life, he observed in his *Hymns That Have Helped* of 1897, was John Newton's 'Begone, Unbelief, My Saviour is Near', especially the verse:

> His love in time past
> Forbids me to think
> He'll leave me at last
> In trouble to sink.

'The rhyme,' he admitted, 'is bad enough, no doubt . . . but the verse as it is, with all its shortcomings, has been as a life-buoy, keeping my head above the waves when the sea raged . . . and when all else failed.'[19]

He no longer believed some of the Reformed doctrines in which he had been raised, especially the doctrine of everlasting punishment, and he accepted that critical biblical scholarship undermined the literal interpretation of much of Scripture, rendering 'the old attitude of blind and unhesitating and undiscriminating acquiescence in everything found inside of the Bible covers . . . all but impossible'.[20] The social gospel was central to his Christian faith and he viewed the Church as 'a Great Co-operative Society for Doing Good, an agency for promoting mercy, justice, righteousness, and humanity among the people'.[21] In the preface to *Here Am I, Send Me*, his semi-autobiographical Christmas annual for 1904 (reprinted in 1905 as *Which? Christ or Cain*), he argued that 'if any body of men and women associate together with the earnest purpose of raising the social and ethical status of their fellow-men, they will be led imperceptibly and unconsciously to evolve something that is practically identical with a Christian Church'.[22] He retained his belief in the Civic Church, with its ideal of 'the union of all who love in the service of all who suffer', and he continued dreaming of a 'Faith of the Future' that would unite all humanity and all major religions. In a perceptive brief overview of movements of religious thought, which he published in 1900 as part of a general account of the nineteenth century, Stead expressed agreement with notions of progressive revelation and evolving religious understanding that were drawing the main world faiths more closely together. 'The hope that we may be on the eve of the discovery of a wider synthesis,' he wrote, 'which will unveil to the wistful eye of man a real Catholicism, and display the essential unity which pervades all the religions of all the world, is in itself a prophecy of what may be in store for us.'[23] According to Harper, he came to view his own life's work as three-fold: 'He called it Peace, Woman, Spirit—terms for him synonymous, in their deepest meaning, with Love, Life, and Light.'[24]

## Arbitration and Armenian Massacres

The world was becoming more dangerous in the 1890s. Most European states, apart from Britain, Belgium, and the Netherlands, embraced economic protectionism from the 1880s. There was an upsurge in imperialism, reflected in the European 'scramble for Africa', with the European powers dividing up nearly all of the Continent. The German Empire, Austro-Hungarian Empire, and Italy entered into a military alliance, the Triple Alliance, in 1882. In response, France and the Russian Empire entered into a military alliance in 1894. Ambitious to enlarge its overseas empire, Germany began greatly expanding its navy from 1889, forcing Britain, France, and other powers to respond. Rapid developments in the design of warships and gunnery rendered existing ships obsolete, and required spiralling investment. Britain, which in 1889 adopted the 'two-power' policy (that its navy should be equal to the navies of any two other countries), struggled to meet the rising costs. Between 1889–90 and 1896–7, British naval expenditures rose by 65 per cent, and Gladstone resigned as prime minister in 1894 over the size of the naval estimates.[25] In 1898, the United States defeated Spain, took control of the Philippines, and emerged as a major imperial power. That same year, Britain and France nearly went to war over the Fashoda incident, involving control over the Sudan.

'The question of all questions,' Stead insisted in *The Review of Reviews* of May 1894, involved 'preparation for peace'. Burgeoning military expenditures not only made war more likely, but also swelled national debts and absorbed funds that might otherwise have gone to social reform. What was needed, he maintained, was an international agreement by which all nations would agree to a moratorium on any increase in military expenditures until at least 1900.[26] In June 1894, Stead threw *The Review of Reviews* behind a movement, initiated by the Arbitration Alliance of Great Britain, for a National Memorial in support of the international arms moratorium. The aim was to get signatures from political leaders and representatives of every church, labour union, and municipality in the United Kingdom and then to present the Memorial to the prime minister. Stead claimed that war budgets in the major European states had increased 23 per cent in the previous six years; it was time to end this madness in the name of 'civilisation and common sense'.[27] But the National Memorial failed to gain much support, prompting an angry outburst from Stead in *The Review of Reviews* of September 1894. Stead questioned Europe's claims to be a Christian civilization—lamenting how Christian nations were developing ever more sophisticated weaponry, including plans for military flying machines, to extend the work of slaughter. 'Even the Archbishop of Canterbury', Stead opined:

> cannot be induced to raise his voice in favour of an arrest of any further increase of armaments, and the prospect of arranging a Truce of God for the closing century seems to be remote. Mankind with its brutal animalism, its bloodshot eye and hereditary savagery, seems destined to groan for some time longer under the burden of the prince of the world, whose yoke is not easy, nor is his burden light.[28]

In early 1896, Stead took up the cause of arbitration as a means to settle international disputes peacefully. The occasion for this was the quarrel between Britain and the United States over a disputed border demarcation between Venezuela and British Guiana. The United States had sided with Venezuela and in December 1895, the American president Grover Cleveland threatened war if Britain did not accept arbitration. Stead knew that this was no empty threat. In *The Review of Reviews* of June 1895 and *The Contemporary Review* of September 1895, he had described a growing nationalist and anti-British sentiment in the United States, including demands by some American politicians for Britain to be ejected from its remaining colonies in the Americas.[29] While many believed Britain must not yield to American threats, Stead warmly supported an Anglo-American arbitration campaign launched in March 1896.[30] 'By public meetings and memorials,' Stead later wrote, 'we succeeded in producing such an expression of public opinion' that the British Government agreed to arbitrate.[31] In 1897 an arbitration tribunal was convened in Paris; it eventually agreed, in October 1899, a settlement of the Venezuelan dispute. Stead became a zealous advocate of the principle of arbitration, maintaining that every dispute between nations should go to arbitration. 'What we have to do is to sacrifice every doctrinaire scruple in order to get *all* questions sent to the Arbitration Court,' he assured James Bryce on 19 July 1896.[32] As he argued in a pamphlet of 1896, when two countries delayed military action, allowed tempers to cool, and presented evidence and arguments before an arbitration tribunal, it would almost invariably lead to a peaceful solution.[33] '"Always arbitrate before you fight",' he maintained, 'and in ninety-nine cases out of a hundred you will never fight at all.'[34]

Stead was not a pacifist and believed there was sometimes a need for military action, especially in defending a vulnerable people from oppression or genocide. He called passionately for armed intervention to halt the massacres of Armenian Christians, which began in the summer of 1894 in the Ottoman Empire, continuing for over two and a half years and claiming some 100,000 lives. Carried out by local mobs, with the apparent collusion of Ottoman officials, the massacres were accompanied by torture, rape, the burning of crops (to ensure the starvation of any survivors), and desecration of churches. There was a British public outcry against the atrocities from the autumn of 1895, with protest meetings and demonstrations across the country, similar to the protests over the Bulgarian atrocities of 1876. The agitation included significant church participation, with many veterans of the 1876 agitation, including Canons Malcolm MacColl and Henry Scott Holland, again prominent. Gladstone returned briefly from his retirement to denounce the horrors.

Stead provided harrowing, highly emotive depictions of the massacres in *The Review of Reviews* and in a pamphlet, *The Haunting Horrors of Armenia*. There must, he argued, be military intervention to stop the killings, and Britain had a special responsibility, because it had played a leading role in preserving the Ottoman Empire in the Crimean War of 1854–6, and again in the Eastern crisis of 1876–8. 'If there be such a thing as a Judgment Day . . . ,' he asked in February 1896, 'how can any one who makes no effort to have right done in this crisis escape from the haunting horror of the thought that he may be damned for this, and that his damnation would be just?'[35] The difficulty, however, was that amid the growing 'international turmoil' of the 1890s, there was no longer a Concert of Europe to act against the horrors. Russia had now taken on the role of protector of the Ottoman Empire, and France was allied with Russia. Germany was seeking economic concessions in the Ottoman Empire, so the German-led Triple Alliance would not intervene. The United States and Britain were divided over the Venezuelan controversy. In short, Britain was without allies and its naval power alone could not halt the massacres. Stead's proposed solution was joint British–Russian action and Russian occupation of Armenia, but this proposal found little support.[36] 'Poor Armenia,' Stead wrote to a correspondent in early 1896, 'she will be forgotten and her people exterminated, while all these questions which are matters of interest, and not "merely" of humanity and Christianity, hold the foreground.'[37]

## The Peace Campaign of 1894–9

Tsar Alexander III died in November 1894 and was succeeded by the young Nicholas II. Some four years later, on 24 August 1898, Nicholas surprised the world by issuing a rescript, proposing an international conference to discuss 'the most effectual means of insuring to all peoples the benefits of a real and durable peace', including putting a limit on the growth of armaments. Spiralling military spending, the Tsar insisted, was 'transforming the armed peace of our days into a crushing burden, which the peoples have more and more difficulty in bearing' and which threatened to bring cataclysmic war, 'the horrors of which make every thinking man shudder in advance'.[38] The Tsar's motives were mixed. Along with humanitarian concerns, he was all too aware that the Russian state could not meet the costs of equipping its vast army with the latest military technology while at the same time modernizing its economy and developing its territories in the Far East.[39] When the Tsar's rescript became public, Herbert Stead immediately reminded his brother of the divine call Herbert had heard in February 1894, to 'Approach the Emperor of Russia: Through Him Deliverance will come'. Europe now needed, Herbert insisted, a modern-day 'Peter the Hermit' who could rouse the nations for a 'crusade against war'. Stead responded that his brother's letter had come to him 'as a Call from the Highest'.[40] In *The Review of Reviews* of September 1898, Stead claimed the Tsar's rescript was a reason 'to thank God and take courage'. 'The disarmament of Europe is a long way off, but there is at least some hope for the human race when the master of so many millions undertakes in his own person the sacred Apostolate of Peace.'[41]

In mid-September 1898, Stead left London for a personal 'Pilgrimage of Peace' across Europe; his aim, he told his friend, Lord Esher, was 'to see the sovereigns and statesmen of Europe [and to] survey the present state of public opinion among those who are the leaders and directors of European thought'.[42] For the next two and a half months, he visited the major cities of Europe and met a number of political leaders. His pilgrimage included a visit to Russia, with stops at St Petersburg, Moscow, and finally Yalta, where he was twice received by the Tsar at his estate of Livadia. 'I am,' he wrote to Herbert on 14 November 1898, 'developing into the International Man for whose advent you prayed in 1894.' Stead's pilgrimage included a visit to Rome, where he hoped to convince the Pope to join with the Tsar in providing leadership to the Peace Crusade. 'Although I was born and I remain outside the Roman fold,' he wrote on 14 November in a letter intended for the Pope, 'I cannot resist the impulse to throw myself at the feet of the Holy Father and implore him to come to the help of a weary and war-torn world, by proclaiming to all men of goodwill in all lands and of all creeds, that the hour has come on the last year of the expiring century for a new Crusade, the Crusade of peace.'[43] He was not granted an interview.

Returning to London on 28 November, Stead took a leading part in a campaign to rouse British public opinion in support of the Tsar's rescript. The campaign began with a great public meeting on 'Peace Sunday', 18 December 1898, at St James's Hall, London, with Stead as one of the principal speakers. Over the next four months, Stead addressed over 200 town meetings. His *Review of Reviews* championed the peace campaign, and on 12 January 1899 Stead also began a weekly penny newsletter, *War against War: A Chronicle of the Peace Crusade*, to provide further publicity. The newsletter continued until the end of March 1899.[44] Stead called for a million volunteers to work for the movement.[45] For Stead, the campaign was God's work. 'It is odd, and yet not odd,' he confided to Herbert on 24 December 1898, 'that you should have called me to this work, and that it should have come to me with a power and to an extent of which none of us ventured to hope when you first wrote about it.' His peace meeting a few days earlier, he added, was marked by a 'manifest outpouring of the Divine Spirit'.[46] 'For the first time,' Stead insisted in *The Review of Reviews* for January 1899, 'the whole of the organised Christian Churches find themselves in hearty accord' with each other and also 'with all the humanitarian and non-theological organisations which seek for the improvement of the people'. It was a great struggle against the 'sword of Satan forged in the hell of national hatred and race prejudice'.[47] At the same time, the peace campaign had its critics, with many deriding it as hopelessly idealistic or as serving the interests of Tsarist autocracy.

What was becoming known as 'Stead's peace crusade' culminated in a National Convention on 21 March 1899 in London, with afternoon and evening meetings attended by some three thousand people.

In his address to the afternoon meeting, Stead called for a revival of 'national conscience' and warned of 'a terrible judgement to come' unless the British people overcame selfish interests and took up the cause of international peace and justice.[48] In May, Stead travelled to St Petersburg to present a British National Memorial in support of the rescript, with over 160,000 signatures bound in thirty volumes, to the Tsar.[49] While the peace crusade failed to inspire the great international groundswell for which Stead hoped, there were significant peace campaigns in the Netherlands, Belgium, Germany, and Austria.[50] In response to the Tsar's rescript and the popular agitation, the major powers of the world, some very reluctantly, accepted the invitation of Queen Wilhelmina of the Netherlands to meet as an international conference in her capital, The Hague, to discuss peace, arbitration, the limitation of armaments, and the laws that should govern warfare. Stead believed that he had been God's principal agent in bringing about the conference. 'Humanly speaking,' Stead later claimed, 'that Conference would never have assembled if it had not been for the Crusade of Peace which may be said in strict and literal truth to have been cradled in the office of *The Review of Reviews*.'[51] Stead had driven himself hard in the campaign, as noted by Henry Wickham Steed of *The Times* on 11 May: 'Twice across Europe and up and down England in six months is not a bad record for a man who is not a mere Queen's Messenger but a hard-working and overworked journalistic apostle.'[52]

The international peace conference, with representatives from twenty-six states, including the United Kingdom, convened on 18 May 1899 and continued until the end of July. Stead moved to lodgings on the outskirts of The Hague and stayed for the duration of the conference, providing publicity for its work and aims. His efforts helped ensure that this was the first intergovernmental conference to be accompanied by what Geoffrey Best described as 'a great show of organized public opinion', including fringe meetings and the lobbying of delegates.[53] Although the official meetings were private, Stead managed to garner inside information and wrote regular reports, which were published in English, Dutch, and French in the Dutch newspaper, *Dagblad*. He also published two books on the conference. The first, *The United States of Europe on the Eve of the Parliament of Peace*, explored the social, political, and historical background of the conference, portraying it is as part of a larger movement from primitive

armed conflict, the British state in 1881 recognized the independence of the Boer republics, under certain conditions, while claiming a vague suzerainty over them.

Tensions re-emerged in the mid-1880s following the discovery of massive gold deposits in the Transvaal. Gold mining brought the republics immense wealth, but also attracted a large influx of British and European entrepreneurs, speculators, adventurers, and labourers eager to make their fortunes. These foreigners, or uitlanders, demanded full rights of citizenship, including the vote, which threatened the ethnic identity of the Boer republics. Conflicts flared between Boers and uitlanders. Adding to the tensions was British fear that imperial competitors, especially Germany which claimed ethnic affinity with the Boers, would move to exert control over the region and its mineral resources. From the mid-1880s, the imperialist mining magnate, Cecil Rhodes (who became premier of the South African Cape Colony in 1890) pursued a policy of encircling the Boer republics with British territory. With his British South Africa Company (granted a royal charter in 1889) and its private army, Rhodes gained control of Matabeleland and also established a new colony, Rhodesia, to the north and west of the republics. His larger aim was for the Empire to absorb the Boer republics into a federal union of the British colonies in South Africa, with Britain then expanding its imperial control northwards in the African Continent.

In 1895, a group of uitlanders, with Rhodes' support, attempted the violent overthrow of the Boer government in the Transvaal. According to their plan, which had the sympathy of the British colonial secretary, Joseph Chamberlain, uitlanders in the Transvaal capital of Pretoria would stage a rising and seize control of the armoury. Then an armed mounted force of about five hundred South Africa Company police, led by Dr Leander Starr Jameson, a senior Company official, would dash into Pretoria 'to restore order', linking up with the insurgents and seizing control of the Transvaal. The insurgency in Pretoria, however, failed and the Jameson force, which invaded the Transvaal on 29 December 1895, was surrounded and forced to surrender on 2 January 1896. It was a humiliating debacle. A disgraced Rhodes now resigned his office of premier of the Cape Colony and returned to London to defend his actions. Jameson and prominent participants in the raid, including Rhodes's brother, were sent to England for trial. Initially given long prison sentences, they were released in June 1896. The Jameson Raid greatly added to tensions in South Africa; the Boer republics began importing weapons to defend themselves from further aggression, while in Britain many called for military action to defend the rights of uitlanders.

Stead had long taken a special interest in the affairs of South Africa, largely through his friendship with Cecil Rhodes. From the late 1880s, Stead promoted Rhodes's vision of the destiny of the English-speaking peoples to dominate the world; indeed, Stead's *Review of Reviews* was from its beginning in part a vehicle for disseminating Rhodes' ideas.[61] As Joseph Baylen observed, 'Stead not only became the confidant of Rhodes, but also the "most strenuous" propagandist of Rhodes and his ambitions in South Africa.'[62] In February 1896, Stead published a lengthy, flattering character sketch of Rhodes in *The Review of Reviews*. In supporting the Jameson Raid, Stead argued, Rhodes had been rightly responding to the threat of German intervention in support of the Boers. And even if Rhodes had acted rashly, he must be excused because his actions advanced the divine purpose. 'His objective,' Stead insisted, 'is the extension throughout the world of the great principles of peace, justice, and liberty, of which the English-speaking race may be regarded as in a special sense the standard-bearer of the Almighty.' Rhodes's grand designs for British dominance of Africa had a religious foundation—for God worked His will through chosen peoples, and the English-speaking peoples were 'the providential instruments for the betterment of the world'. 'Mr Rhodes,' he added, 'has no more doubt of the divine mission of the English folk than had Joshua of the Divine call of ancient Israel.' He had 'arrived at the conclusion that, if there be a God who ruleth over the nations of men and concerns Himself in the destinies of mortals, then it is impossible to serve Him better than by painting as much of the map British red as possible'.[63] Among Rhodes' grand designs for Africa was the creation of a 'United States of South Africa', to be achieved by uniting the Boer republics with the British Cape Colony and Natal. Stead insisted that the influx of uitlanders into the Boer republics represented progress in civilization, which the 'Boer oligarchy' must not be allowed to obstruct.[64]

Stead continued defending Rhodes over the coming months. He gathered evidence from government sources showing that the colonial secretary, Chamberlain (who publicly denied any prior knowledge of the Jameson Raid) had in truth encouraged the raid and must share responsibility for its failure. Stead, who had long distrusted Chamberlain, published his findings in the form of a comic story, *The History of the Mystery*, with the major actors behind the Jameson Raid appearing under names which made them easily identifiable. The story appeared as *The Review of Reviews* Christmas annual for December 1896 and received considerable attention.[65] While condemning Chamberlain, the story suggested that Rhodes had been morally right in attempting to overthrow Boer tyranny. 'Cecil Rhodes,' Stead insisted in the preface to *The History of the Mystery*, 'is the Abraham Lincoln of South Africa', working to create a United States of South Africa based on 'freedom, religious liberty and progress' against Boer republics that had 'slavery as [their] chief corner-stone'.[66] For Stead, the original Boer settlers 'had slaughtered the natives into submission' and now many Boers were determined 'to reduce the blacks to virtual slavery', reviving that 'foul blot' in part of the British Empire.[67]

Stead was delighted when in early 1897 his former assistant and protégé at the *Pall Mall Gazette*, Alfred Milner, was appointed high commissioner and governor of the Cape Colony. Since leaving the *Pall Mall* in 1885, Milner had become an effective imperial administrator, while he and Stead had remained friends. Stead warmly touted Milner's appointment. 'Sir Alfred Milner,' he asserted in *The Review of Reviews* of May 1897, 'is an Imperialist of the purest water and we can rely upon him' to make the whole of South Africa, including the Boer republics, 'as loyally British as Kent or Middlesex.' Milner would not impose 'Imperial unity' by force 'upon an unwilling population' but would achieve imperial unity by peaceful persuasion.[68] In the event, Stead was disappointed. As high commissioner, Milner made ever-increasing demands on the Boer republics to give full rights of citizenship to uitlanders, while moving troops to the borders of the Boer republics. Tensions culminated at a conference in Bloemfontein in late May and early June 1899, when Milner made demands that he knew the Transvaal president could not accept, ensuring that the negotiations would fail. Stead felt Milner had betrayed his confidence. On arriving in South Africa, he later observed, Milner 'suddenly changed front, and became the most ardent advocate for war'.[69] In Britain, there was a growing popular enthusiasm for war, promoted by nearly all newspapers. Britain would teach the Boers a lesson, ensure the rights of the uitlanders, and assert the power of Empire.

In the late summer of 1899, having recently returned from his attendance at The Hague Peace Conference (which he had viewed as divinely inspired), Stead set himself against the war fervour, and began calling loudly and urgently for peace. He broke from Rhodes and Milner. It was not only that he believed the case for war was weak, or that Britain refused any arbitration of the dispute. Stead had now become convinced that war in South Africa would be an act of national apostasy, a rejection of God and God's law. In late September, he issued a pamphlet, *Shall I Slay my Brother Boer? An Appeal to the Conscience of Britain*, in which he laid out his case against war. The language was prophetic in tone. Britain, 'fresh from the Peace Conference at the Hague', was preparing to 'suspend the Ten Commandments and let loose Hell in South Africa'. It would 'carry fire and sword through the Transvaal', pretending it was 'doing the will of God'. He noted the absurdity of the pro-war rhetoric, as 'a world-encircling empire, with 400,000,000 of population', claimed to represent a heroic ideal in moving to crush 'the tiniest Tom Thumb of a mannikin state . . . which cannot command the support of 100,000 whites, men, women and children included'. It was, Stead insisted, 'unholy and impious passions which are overpowering the wills and darkening the judgement of the crowds which cheer the departing troops and of the journalists who hound us on to war'. The pro-war jingoes effectively dismissed God; for them 'it does not matter how unjust our cause so long as we have the stronger battalions'. But, he insisted, there would be a divine judgement—because 'nations which forget God are turned into Hell—a very real Hell in this very modern world'.[70] Stead had this pamphlet, as he told a friend, 'sent by post to every minister of religion, every member of parliament, every peer, mayor, Chairman of County Council, Boards of Guardians, as well as the leading representatives of the Trades Unions in this country', and to every newspaper.[71] In October, Stead took the lead in organizing a National Memorial against the war, gathering over fifty thousand signatures within two weeks.[72] The pressing question, Stead thundered in *The Review of Reviews* of October, was 'not whether or not there will be war in the Transvaal, but how deep, or rather how thin, is the veneer of Christian morality over the mass of aboriginal savagery and blood-lust which has found such violent expression in our press'. The veneer of Christian civilization, he feared, was 'very thin'.[73]

The South African War began on 20 October 1899. Nearly all the British newspapers were pro-war, among them the *Daily Mail*, with its circulation in 1900 of over a million, the largest of any newspaper in the world.[74] While Stead's *Review of Reviews* opposed the war, as a monthly journal it lacked the popular clout of a newspaper. To assist the anti-war cause, Stead launched a penny weekly newspaper, *War against War in South Africa*, which began publication on 20 October and was a direct successor to his earlier *War against War: A Chronicle of the International Crusade for Peace*. As Ingrid Hanson has shown, Stead's penny weekly combined the sensationalist language of his 'Maiden Tribute' articles, with pronouncements of collective guilt and accountability before God. Each issue of the newspaper was subtitled 'Deliver us from Bloodguiltiness, O Lord!' (a slightly modified version of Psalm 51: 14), and headed by a short catechism of questions and responses, calling on readers to resist the war, in part by 'confessing our sins and doing right'. The cover of each issue included an illustration of the grim reaper with a harvest of skulls. The first issue observed how 'we stand on the shore of a sea of blood' with 'the stain of blood on our garments'.[75]

There was, it seemed, more behind Stead's vehemence than simply passionate conviction of the immorality of the war. There was also personal guilt. For had he not, by his claims that British imperialism represented a divine purpose and by his puffing up of Rhodes, contributed to the public mood that now exalted the war as just and righteous? Had not those writings of his helped send soldiers to South Africa to slay their Boer brothers? The men who brought Britain into the war, he later confessed, including Milner, Rhodes, Jameson, and others, 'were all my own personal friends, and it is not too much to say that they owed in no small measure of their position in public esteem to the way in which I had written about them in past years. They were enabled to avail themselves of the popular feeling against President Kruger which I had also done much to generate.'[76] Others shared this view, among them the pro-Boer journalist. A. J. Wilson. 'By popularising with your swift flowing pen,' Wilson wrote in a public letter to Stead in 1902, 'a monstrous conception of an imperial, bloody-minded Christ' and 'by ranting about England's destiny and mission',

Stead bore much of the blame for the war.[77] In September 1899, Stead had closed his pamphlet, *Shall I Slay my Brother Boer?* with a highly personal appeal to each person to do all they could to stop the war. Each must act, he wrote, as 'if you realised that you yourself individually may have to stand with hands reeking with your brother's blood before the judgment seat of God'.[78] The triple emphasis on 'you yourself individually', as Hanson observed, made Stead's appeal highly personal and imperative.[79] It was especially so for Stead, now driven to expiate the blood on his own hands. 'I may be a voice crying in the wilderness,' he wrote to an old friend, Ishbel Hamilton-Gordon, Countess of Aberdeen, on 8 January, 'woe is me if I keep silence'.[80] Very soon, Stead became one of the most hated men in a Britain that overwhelmingly supported the war.

From November, Stead helped form a Committee to co-ordinate the anti-war campaign. The initiative came from the popular novelist and former Methodist minister, Silas K. Hocking, but it was Stead who gave the Committee its uncompromising tone and provocative name, the 'Stop the War Committee'. The Committee was formally launched on 14 January at a conference at Exeter Hall, London, with Hocking as Chairman and Stead's long-term friend, the Christian Socialist Baptist minister, John Clifford, as president. The Stop the War Committee set up local branches around the country, circulated anti-war literature, and sent speakers to conduct anti-war meetings. Largely Nonconformist and middle class in membership, the Stop the War movement also received some socialist and labour support.[81] Stead and the Committee, moreover, worked to recruit women from all social classes and many women embraced the cause.[82] The Stop the War meetings, however, were violently broken up by jingo mobs, furious at what they called an anti-British, treasonous movement. Stead addressed several anti-war meetings, until the meetings had to be given up due to the violence. He was sickened by what he saw. In England, he complained to James Bryce on 9 March, 'we have a drunken mob established as absolute arbiter of the liberties of Englishmen. The public meetings have long been, and most private meetings are now being attacked, and what is worse, the policy of systematic outrage on the persons and property of friends of peace has been adopted without one word of protest from any leading politician either Liberal or Tory.'[83] He continued editing the weekly

*Stop the War* newspaper, and issuing leaflets and pamphlets. His was a voice of uncompromising moral condemnation of the war, with emphasis on the impending divine judgement. This war, he stated in a pamphlet in January 1900, 'is the greatest of all crimes, and may bring with it the greatest of all punishments. I am using no idle figure of speech when I say the curse of God rests heavily upon us every day that it continues. We have no reason to expect victory when we fight against God.'[84]

But at the end of 1900, Britain seemed close to complete victory. The imperial forces overran the capital cities of the South African republics. The main Boer armies surrendered or dispersed, the governments of the republics fled, and in late October, the Transvaal was formally annexed into the Empire. There were by now some 250,000 British and imperial troops occupying the republics. Stead's *War against War*, which had moved from a weekly to a monthly format in April, ceased publication at the end of August 1900. The Unionist government, sensing total victory was near, called a general election for September 1900. The Unionists secured an overall majority of 130 in the House of Commons, in what many viewed as a ringing popular endorsement of a successful war. During the summer, a despondent Stead made two trips to the Continent, speaking at a Peace Congress in Paris in early August, and attending the Passion Play at Oberammergau in September. At Oberammergau, he could not help but see the Passion Play as an allegory on the war, with Christ's crucifixion resulting from an alliance of priests and money-changers. 'It was the alliance,' he wrote, 'between the Sanhedrim and the traders of the Temple that was fatal to the Galilean, just as in our time it was an alliance between the clerics, the journalists, and the capitalists that brought on this war.' He felt a particular sense of betrayal from the British clergy, who on the whole firmly supported the war effort.[85] 'These ministers of Christ,' he raged, 'exult in combining Christ and Carnage...they say their prayers and sing their hymns and preach their sermons, and imagine it is religion.'[86] 'I have seen nobody since I came back from Ober Ammergau,' Stead wrote to Bryce on 26 September. 'When I was watching the Passion Play, I was thinking of nothing but the Boers. The story of the Passion is indeed a most extraordinary parallel to the General Election.'[87]

## Methods of Barbarism

The war in South Africa did not end as expected in the autumn of 1900. Thousands of Boer commandos in the field refused to surrender, and now carried on an effective guerrilla warfare against the occupying forces, attacking railway trains, supply columns, and encampments. In an effort to cut off the commandos' food supplies, the British forces began a 'scorched earth' policy—burning farms and crops and seizing or destroying livestock. Boer women and children, together with older or captured men, were rounded up and placed under armed guard in what were called concentration camps, where they lived in tents and were fed by the army. The conditions in the camps were appalling, with inadequate sanitation, food, shelter, and medical care. An estimated 18,000 to 28,000 Boer civilians, most of them children, died; far more civilians died in the camps than did soldiers on both sides in the fighting. Over 100,000 black Africans from the devastated countryside were also interned, placed in separate camps from the whites, and about 12,000 died.[88] In January 1901, the peace activist, Emily Hobhouse, travelled to South Africa on behalf of the South African Conciliation Committee, bringing clothing, blankets, and money for those interned in the camps. She was appalled by the conditions she found, and her harrowing letters home were published in the few anti-war newspapers. In June 1901, the Liberal Party leader, Sir Henry Campbell-Bannerman, furiously condemned what he described as 'methods of barbarism' in the British waging of war in South Africa.

Stead first learned of the policy of systematic farm burnings in late October 1900 from reports sent him by a serving British officer whose anonymity he protected. The reports included accounts of murders of civilians, the rape of women and girls, and of women and girls forced into prostitution for food. For Stead, such atrocities revived memories of the Maiden Tribute investigations, but now, he believed, the abuse of women and children was government policy. In early November 1900, Stead published a four-page broadside, *Hell Let Loose! What Is Now Being Done in South Africa*, presenting the accounts of farm burnings, rapes, and forced prostitution as evidence that 'our armies are deliberately violating laws of civilised War'. Every British citizen who had voted for a pro-war parliamentary candidate, he insisted, was 'personally responsible before God and his fellow-men' for the atrocities. If, he stated, 'some spark of manhood, some faint ray of Christian sentiment, should still linger amongst us, a cry for instant and searching inquiry will be raised in every newspaper and re-echoed from every pulpit and platform in the land'.[89]

Stead was widely denounced for the broadside, which for many had gone too far, especially in accusing British soldiers of atrocities. Undaunted, in December 1900 he responded to his critics with a pamphlet of over 100 pages, presenting graphic accounts of farm burnings, looting, and violence against civilians, drawn from the testimony of officers, soldiers, and newspaper correspondents.[90] He published further accounts of farm burnings in *The Review of Reviews* for December and January.[91] Early in July 1901, he issued another pamphlet, *Methods of Barbarism*, applauding Campbell-Bannerman's first use of the phrase and providing evidence of continuing atrocities. He insisted that 'multitudes' of women had been raped; most did not report their rapes to the British authorities, but would 'bury their shame in silence'. He closed by condemning the godlessness of it all. 'The fundamental fallacy upon which the whole of this war is based,' he insisted, 'has been the assumption cynically asserted in some quarters, tacitly accepted in others, that God Almighty does not count. The only God in whom this materialist generation believes is the God of the big battalions.'[92] Stead grew increasingly incensed. In August he attacked Campbell-Bannerman for not following up his condemnations of 'methods of barbarism' with forceful political action, describing him in a speech at Battersea as 'weaker than water'.[93] At an International Peace Congress in Glasgow on 12 September 1901, he embarrassed fellow delegates with a fevered speech, in which he declared Britain to be 'under the curse of civilisation' and 'excommunicate of humanity' for its crimes in South Africa'.[94]

In all Stead's passionate condemnations of the war, one theme was disturbingly absent: the suffering of black Africans. As Simon Potter has observed, Stead 'paid scant attention to the extreme violence meted out against Africans and Cape Coloured by Boer fighters'.[95] Nor did he refer to the high death rates of the black Africans interned in concentration camps. In his depictions of the violence against Boer women, Stead gave particular emphasis to allegations of rape by black

Africans, which he described as 'the worst outrage of all'.[96] 'The menacing figure of the Kaffir,' Stead wrote in early 1902, 'is never absent from the South African landscape.'[97] He was not alone among critics of the war in this lack of sympathy for the black majority, but he left the impression that he condemned this imperialist war largely because it was directed against white Boers.

The South African war finally came to an end in late May 1902, as the British state dropped previous demands for unconditional surrender and offered generous peace terms, which the Boer commandos accepted. By now the British public had largely lost interest in the war. Stead believed the Unionist government had needlessly prolonged the war by fifteen months, and sacrificed thousands more lives, by trying to secure an unconditional surrender, but at least it was over.[98] Stead's opposition to the war had been visceral. His writings on the war had been jeremiad sermons; he portrayed the war as a national sin, a rejection of God's law by a nation that was embracing materialism and no longer feared God. He was burdened by personal guilt and some continued blaming him for the war. 'The tragedy of it all,' his former friend, the Labour politician, John Burns, wrote to him with reference to the war on 15 June 1904, 'is that you and Rhodes are the real authors of this bad business.' 'Your "Big Navy", your "Anglo-Saxon Imperialism" . . . all those shibboleths, cries, and catchwords have been exploited to criminal ends.'[99] The South African novelist, Olive Schreiner, never forgave Stead for the 'harm he had done to South Africa' through his puffing up of Rhodes.[100] He also paid a price for his uncompromising opposition to the war. The circulation and advertising revenues of *The Review of Reviews* fell significantly as a result of his anti-war stand, and the journal never really recovered.[101] His homes in Wimbledon and on Hayling Island had been attacked and damaged by jingo crowds.[102] He experienced a break-up of friendships. This included an estrangement from the Methodist social reformer, Hugh Price Hughes, a strong supporter of the war.[103] Especially painful for Stead was the break with Rhodes, whom he had loved as a brother. Rhodes had removed him as a trustee from his will in late 1899 because of Stead's opposition to the war. But once the war was over, Stead was remarkably free of bitterness, and he sought to rebuild relationships and revive imperialist conceptions.

He tried to revive the ideal, which he had shared with Rhodes, of the civilizing mission of the English-speaking peoples. In early 1902, as the South African War was drawing to a close, Stead published a substantial book (*The Review of Reviews* Christmas annual), entitled *The Americanisation of the World or The Trend of the Twentieth Century*. In this work, he argued that the United States was coming to exercise a predominant influence over the world—economically, scientifically, religiously, and culturally—and that Britain should welcome this development, because 'the creation of the Americans is the greatest achievement of our race'. 'It was,' he maintained, 'the Puritan principles of free democracy which we exported in the *Mayflower* that fashioned and prepared...the American Commonwealth.' 'As it was through the Christian Church that the monotheism of the Jew conquered the world,' he insisted, 'so it may be through the Americans that the English ideals expressed in the English language may make the tour of the planet.' Stead viewed the United States as predominantly white and Anglo-Saxon, and he called for an ever-closer alliance, even a merger of the British Empire and the United States, in order 'to realise the great ideal of Race Union' which would lead to 'a new era of power and prosperity the like of which the race has never realised since the world began'. 'Many of the strongest imperialists,' he enthused, 'are heart and soul in favour of seeing the British Empire and American Republic merged in the English-speaking United States of the World.'[104] If Stead hoped to renew his former alliance with Rhodes by this revived appeal to imperialism and the destiny of the English-speaking peoples, it was not to be. Rhodes died in late March 1902 of heart failure, aged forty-eight, at his seaside home in the Cape Colony.

## New Perspectives on Imperialism and Race

In 1903, Stead revived his idea for a new London daily newspaper, *The Daily Paper*. His previous attempt to introduce *The Daily Paper* in 1893 had failed, but now he felt the time was right. He wanted to return to the work of editing a daily newspaper. Further, in the aftermath of the South African War, he believed there was a need for a new daily that would be bright, feminist, reforming, with a high moral and religious tone. Stead was discouraged by his friends, who noted there were already a number of London dailies. What they probably did not tell him was just how unpopular he had become over the war. But Stead persevered, borrowed heavily, recruited a team of reporters and writers, and launched *The Daily Paper* with great fanfare at the beginning of January 1904. It was an immediate failure. Deeply in debt and threatened with financial ruin, Stead suffered a nervous collapse on the first day of publication, and fell into a prolonged depression. The paper limped on for five weeks, ceasing on 9 February. His doctor recommended a long sea voyage for his recovery, and in mid-February he departed on a voyage to Australia via the Cape, accompanied by his daughter, Estelle. She recalled how he began the voyage withdrawn, silent, dejected, and despondent. But then, after some days at sea, he recovered his bearing, telling her that he now understood the failure of the newspaper was for a purpose, and they must remain for a time in South Africa. 'I feel,' he explained, 'there is work for me in South Africa—and so the Senior Partner is thus forcing me to go.'[105]

Arriving at the Cape on 6 March, Stead embarked on a campaign for 'peace and reconciliation'.[106] He travelled to the Boer republics, met with people on both sides in the war, and listened to their stories. He became convinced that what was needed was a commission that would interview veterans and victims of the war, loyalists and Boers, and take down their stories of sacrifice, suffering, loss, courage, and endurance. The accounts would be published in a multi-volume work, a 'Golden Book of South African Heroism', that would not only become a record of the war, but would also expose the war's cruelty and injustices, including the extent of the farm burnings and violence against non-combatants. It would be a sort of truth and reconciliation commission, leading to confessions of guilt, proper government compensation for war victims, forgiveness, and a real peace. While Boers were receptive to the idea, the loyalist press and the Cape Colony authorities, including Milner, viewed Stead's proposals as dangerous, even seditious. For them, such a commission would stir up bitter memories of the war and promote renewed unrest, not to mention suggesting a moral equivalency between Boer rebels and loyal supporters of the Empire. The Cape Colony government seriously contemplated charging him with sedition, but decided, as the governor informed Milner, that 'nothing would please Stead's vanity more than to be arrested'. Milner agreed and instead issued instructions that no colonial official was to meet Stead.[107] Stead, meanwhile, took some interest in the Chinese and black African labourers recruited to work in the mines, visiting their compounds and learning of the injustices they experienced. Then, feeling he had done all he could, Stead and his daughter abandoned their planned voyage to Australia, and departed South Africa for England on 21 April. On his return, Stead published a series of articles on his South African experience in *The Review of Reviews*.[108] He denied that he had meant to perpetuate the bitterness of the war, but insisted he had acted as a 'missionary of the British Empire', preaching its true ideals to Boers who had understandably come to view its flag as 'a symbol of grinning hate'.[109]

But while he revived his old imperialist language, Stead was in truth developing doubts about the new forms of imperialism that were becoming so pronounced in the world after 1900. Could this new imperialism, driven by finance capitalism, racial nationalism, and militarism—building tariff walls, carving up the world, and seizing resources—be seen even remotely as part of the providential plan to spread civilization and elevate humankind? In 1902–3, Stead felt the chill of imperialism's heart of darkness when he learned of the horrors behind the lucrative rubber trade in the Congo Free State. The Congo Free State had been created in 1885 by the great powers at the Congress of Berlin, and placed under the control of King Leopold II of Belgium. Intended as a great philanthropic and civilizing venture that would end the slave trade and bring the benefits of free trade to Central Africa, the Congo Free State was in truth Leopold's personal colony, and it degenerated into a brutal regime in which Leopold's officials employed a mercenary army of Africans to torture, mutilate, and murder villagers—including the severing of hands and feet—in order to terrorize them into collecting rubber resin without payment for the state-run rubber monopoly. The Congo atrocities were exposed by the British journalist, E. D. Morel, in a series of investigative articles beginning in 1900.

Stead was initially sceptical about Morel's claims, but he became convinced and threw *The Review of Reviews* behind a public campaign to expose the practices. In February 1903, he published an article under the title, 'Cannibal Christendom in West Africa', presenting, in graphic language, the grim findings of Morel and other investigators—including evidence that the mercenaries employed to enforce rubber collection also engaged in cannibalism. The Congo brought to mind the horrors of the Bulgarian and Armenian massacres, only now it was not Ottoman Turks, but European imperialists who were behind the atrocities, with profit as their motivation. Stead's Nonconformist conscience was aroused, and he now saw the Congo horrors as yet another ugly chapter in a centuries-old saga of European cruelty towards black Africans. Since the beginnings of the slave trade, he insisted, 'Christendom may be said to have gorged itself with the flesh and blood of thirty millions of the African brothers and sisters of Christ. What a cannibal repast!—a kind of Gargantuan parody of the Last Supper.'[110] In June 1903, Stead wrote for his *Review of Reviews* a devastating 'Character Sketch' of King Leopold, accusing him 'of having established in the name of civilisation a veritable Empire of Hell in the heart of Africa'. Leopold then used his ill-gotten wealth to buy off potential critics, making generous donations to missionary and anti-slavery societies. As a result, 'he receives eulogistic addresses from Baptist missionaries in Brussels at the very moment that his agents are despatching cannibal hordes throughout the Congo region in order to compel the unhappy natives to bring in rubber'.[111] In May 1903, the British House of Commons passed a resolution protesting the human rights violations in the Congo, and calling for an official investigation. 'When I felt I had won you over,' Morel wrote to Stead on 22 May 1903, 'I felt I had done the best day's work since starting the palaver— some four or five years ago.' 'I shan't forget,' he added, 'and I am sure no one will forget, how you flung yourself into the fray—once you were convinced—and what a powerful lever that has been.'[112] Within a few years, mounting international pressure forced changes in the government of the Congo.

Stead was also developing doubts about providence and British imperial rule in India. Influenced by the writings, especially *Prosperous British India* (1901), of the English journalist and reformer, William Digby, Stead began seeing the extreme poverty of the Indian masses, the chronic malnutrition, and the periodic famines that claimed millions of lives as forming a devastating indictment of the Empire.[113] In July 1903, Stead argued in *The Review of Reviews* that Britain's misgovernment of India had two main causes. First, Britain was over-taxing the largely impoverished Indian population in order to maintain and equip a standing Indian army of some 300,000 men. This army, paid for by the Indian poor, existed to serve Britain's imperial interests, including what Stead viewed as unnecessary confrontations with Russia along the northwest frontier. If Britain would adopt policies of peace and arbitration, this army could be considerably reduced in size and the tax burden on the Indian people eased. 'We have gained nothing, absolutely nothing,' he insisted, 'by the sedulous cultivation of hatred, malice and all uncharitableness towards our northern [Russian] neighbour. But the luckless natives of India have had to pay for all our follies and our crimes.'[114]

The second major cause of imperial misgovernment, Stead believed, was racism, which led to British callousness towards Indian suffering. This 'spread of race pride' among the British rulers, he insisted in December 1901, was 'the very incarnation of Satan'. A first step towards any improvement for the people of India was 'the duty of recognising that these immense masses of humanity are composed of our own brothers and sisters, each of whom is our equal in the eye of the Almighty'. If the British could only overcome the racial barrier, they would also discover in India, and indeed across Asia, a spirituality that would provide a powerful antidote to the materialism that was becoming so pervasive in Western societies.[115] The highest duty of Britain's Indian Raj, he observed in 1906, was now 'to dig its own grave with maximum despatch' so that India would become unified and independent.[116] Stead's writings on their affairs were well received in India, and many educated English-speaking Indians grew to value *The Review of Reviews* for its global perspectives. He was invited to preside at the assembly of the Indian National Congress meeting in December 1903 at Madras. When he had to decline due to pressure of work, the invitation was renewed in 1907; again, he had to decline.[117]

Stead was embracing more global perspectives and moving beyond the racial discourse that had informed his imperialist visions of the 1890s. In a 'Retrospect' on his first fourteen years as editor of *The Review of Reviews*, published in December 1903, he noted that he had undergone one major change in attitude: he no longer believed that the English-speaking peoples, by which he had meant white British and American peoples, were chosen by God to lead the world. He had lost his 'complacent faith in the English-speaking man', and learned to appreciate the qualities of other peoples (though he would continue advocating closer union between the English-speaking peoples).[118] Following the early Japanese victories in the Russo-Japanese War of 1904–5, Stead published a review of recent literature on race, noting how 'the triumph of Japan sounds the death knell of the ascendancy of the white race' and 'we whites have to learn to treat our darker-skinned fellow-mortals as brethren'. He dismissed 'scientific' claims, including those of Arthur de Gobineau and Benjamin Kidd, for the superiority of any race, and denounced the 'race-mania' of the late Cecil Rhodes. Looking at the recent history of imperialism, he noted how the 'idea of the innate superiority of the white race, and especially of the Anglo-Saxon race, is used or abused as the justification for every species of injustice and abomination'.[119] Six years later, he commissioned an English translation of a French work against 'pseudo-scientific' racism, with a preface in which Stead lamented how 'the so-called Science of Race... became the plausible justification for every infamy', including denying some peoples 'the inalienable rights belonging to the human family'.[120]

## The Hague Conference of 1907 and 'The Coming Parliament of Man'

In the spring of 1906, on the suggestion of President Theodore Roosevelt, Tsar Nicholas II called for a second Hague Peace Conference, to provide a 'fresh development to the humanitarian principles which served as a basis for the great international meeting of 1899'.[121] The initiative was in response to continuing international tensions and growing armaments expenditures. Over the coming months, the plans took shape. While twenty-six states had participated in the Conference of 1899, forty-six states, representing nearly every state in the world, were invited to the second Conference, which was to be held in June 1907. Stead threw himself into the cause with renewed, even ecstatic, hope. For him, it was to be not only a peace conference, but a 'coming Parliament of Man', promising to bring 'a great International Pact of Peace'. It was also an opportunity for Britain, 'the chief sinner against the Hague convention... to repair so far as possible' the immense damage done by her 'faults and follies' in the South African

War.[122] He devoted January 1907 to touring Europe, meeting with political leaders and promoting the cause in the capital cities of the great powers. On returning, he called for a 'world's pilgrimage of peace'. His plan was for each nation to form a deputation of distinguished public leaders. The pilgrimage would begin with the deputation from the United States travelling to England, where it would be joined by the British deputation. After public meetings in London, the two deputations would travel to France, where they would be joined by the French deputation for meetings in Paris, and so forth, until the combined deputations of the various states finally reached The Hague for the start of the Conference.

In late March 1907, Stead and his wife, Emma, travelled to the United States, where Stead had been invited to speak at the first Arbitration and Peace Conference of America, hosted by the steel magnate and philanthropist, Andrew Carnegie. It was Emma's first trip to America. Stead combined the Conference with a speaking tour of the United States and Canada, aimed at rousing support for The Hague Conference and his world pilgrimage of peace. Arriving in New York on 3 April, he travelled to Washington, Pittsburgh, Chicago, Toronto, and Boston, speaking to civic associations, peace societies, church groups, and university students, including meetings at Harvard, Yale, and Vassar. He met with President Roosevelt, received an honorary doctorate from Western Pennsylvania University, and enjoyed himself immensely. Before accepting any speaking invitation, he first insisted that the meeting must be open to women. 'No women, no Stead,' he telegraphed on more than one occasion. Fired up by the cause, Stead could be abrasive, even offensive, directing biting sarcasm at churches and peace societies for not being more forceful in working for peace. 'A lot of you ethical folks,' he told a meeting of the Society for Ethical Culture in New York on 14 April, 'will get together and you will express admirable sentiments, but you will never do a single thing to carry them out.'[123] He lambasted one church meeting for their pious 'amens', which led to a newspaper headline, 'Stead damns Amen'. A cartoon in a Minneapolis newspaper portrayed a wild, rampaging Stead in a highland kilt and carrying a club. 'If he's like this as a peace representative,' observed a nervous Uncle Sam, 'heaven preserve us from a visit from Mr. Stead in any other capacity.' 'As Richard Wagner,' observed the *New York Times*, 'invented the continuous . . . opera, so W. T. Stead has invented the continuous speech, which he considers the groundwork of universal peace.'[124]

Stead returned to Britain in mid-May. Later that month, he travelled to Germany for ten days of meetings. This was part of an exchange of newspaper editors between Britain and Germany that Stead had helped initiate for promoting understanding and peace between the two rival countries; the German editors had visited Britain in 1906 and the Germany hosted the British editors in 1907. From Germany, Stead proceeded to The Hague, where he remained for four months (with occasional trips back to Britain). At The Hague Conference, Stead produced at his own expense the daily *Courrier de la Conference*, an illustrated four-page newspaper that became the unofficial organ of the Conference. The actual work of the Conference was in many respects disappointing, as there was no real commitment among the great powers to either disarmament or compulsory arbitration. The main contributions were on the rules of naval warfare, but even here there were few significant advances.

Stead none the less believed that the Conference, with representation from nearly every state in the world, marked a new beginning for humankind. At The Hague, he observed in *The Contemporary Review*, he enjoyed 'close relations with as varied and as capable a collection of my fellow-men as have ever come together under one roof'. The Conference confirmed for him St Paul's message 'that God hath made of one blood all nations of men' and had demonstrated conclusively that 'differences of colour, of race, of religion, of culture, of continent, of civilisation did not go much deeper than the skin'. He was encouraged by how 'the fetich of race superiority received scant respect at The Hague' and how people of different races discussed matters as equals and became friends. He was impressed by how 'there was no perceptible difference in the moral standpoint of Christians or non-Christians'. He was, to be sure, disappointed by 'the singularly small part played by women'. There were no women among the 200 delegates, and with the exception of social functions, 'one-half of the human race might have had no existence so far as the Conference was concerned'. Despite this failing, Stead believed that the Conference, 'as the first attempt ever made to assemble the representatives of the whole world in a single Chamber, must be pronounced a remarkable success', forming a 'conspicuous landmark in the progress of mankind towards the realisation of the Federation of the World'.[125]

Stead revived his call for a 'world-wide pilgrimage' to follow on from The Hague Conference. His idea now was for a group of about twelve 'missioners', respected international figures, to travel together around the world from city to city, holding public meetings with churches, civic associations, women's groups, and educational institutions, explaining what the Second Hague Conference had done and promoting the cause of a future united nations. It was to be an evangelistic mission, lasting for six months in the first instance. 'We have,' he insisted, 'a definite faith to proclaim: the Federation of the World is at hand.' And because 'the Press is the Pulpit of the Modern World', he personally felt a special calling to preach for 'the conversion of all nations'.[126] He hoped to finance the pilgrimage from a grant from the Nobel Prize Committee. Stead had been nominated for the Nobel Peace Prize in 1901 and there were rumours that Stead would receive the Prize in 1908.[127] He intended to lead the pilgrimage, while his son, Willie, would edit *The Review of Reviews* in his absence.

There was, however, little support for his proposed world pilgrimage; nor was he awarded the Nobel Peace Prize. Public interest in the Second Hague Peace conference soon waned. The great powers continued amassing armaments and preparing for war. The formation of the Triple Entente of France, Russia, and Britain in 1907 greatly heightened international tensions, as Germany and the Austro-Hungarian Empire felt encircled and threatened. But perhaps most significantly for Stead, in December 1907 his favourite son, Willie—who had shared his father's religious and moral commitments and who Stead had viewed as his successor—suddenly and unexpectedly died, leaving Stead devastated. 'The death of my eldest son,' he later wrote, 'rendered it impossible for me to leave London as I had done before, so the idea [of the pilgrimage] came to nothing.'[128] As was noted in the previous chapter, Stead devoted much of the year 1908 to writing the two-volume biography of his intimate friend, Olga Novikoff—his last major book. Later in 1908, he experienced a period of 'unusual psychic activity', leading to the formation of 'Julia's Bureau' in January 1909. He continued to write on a wide range of issues in *The Review of Reviews* and elsewhere, supporting social reform, old age pensions, labour rights, and votes for women, and he did not cease his efforts for peace. In 1911, concerned over the warfare in the Balkans and then the war between Italy and Turkey, Stead felt called by the 'Senior Partner' twice to visit Constantinople, interviewing the Sultan, pressing the case for arbitration, and speaking, he believed, with the same 'mandate' as an ancient 'Prophet of Israel'.[129] He even proposed a pilgrimage of peace by Ottoman subjects to the capitals of Europe. But his international efforts had little impact. Increasingly, as his dreams for world unity and world peace receded, he spent more and more time in the world of the spirits and 'Julia's Circle'.

### The 'Martyrdom of Man'

In the summer of 1910, Stead made his third pilgrimage to Oberammergau, to view again the celebrated Passion Play that was performed every tenth year. When he had first attended the Passion Play in 1890, the dramatic enactment of Christ's passion and crucifixion had reminded him of the great political struggles that he had known in his life—the campaigns for the liberation of Bulgaria, for better housing for the London poor, for an end to child prostitution, for the rights of free speech and assembly at Trafalgar Square, and for justice in Ireland. He had thought of those willing to lay down their lives, to be martyrs and Christs, in the cause of those who suffered; he saw 'the perpetual re-incarnation of God's Messiah in the great causes of Justice, Freedom, and Humanity'.[130] When he attended his second Passion Play in 1900, it had been for him an allegory on the South African War and the general election of that year, when the electorate had returned a majority of pro-war MPs. For him, the money-lenders and high priests who had sought Christ's death were the same types as the capitalists and the Churches supporting the war; for him, the crowds calling for Christ's crucifixion were typical of the crowds which broke up anti-war meetings and were drunk with imperialist pride. The experience had been one of enduring sadness.

At Oberammergau in 1910, Stead came to a new understanding of Christ's passion, bringing him a fresh sense of joy and hope. A question that had long troubled him, he confessed, was why the unjust killing of one man should have formed the foundation of a religion that transformed the world. The killing of Jesus was, after all, 'but a passing incident in the unceasing martyrdom of man'. So many who sought to alleviate suffering or end injustices met violent deaths. Most left no record; they were simply the 'myriad nameless dead, who are even now perishing at some point on the earth's surface—innocent martyrs for great causes—which they water with their blood'. In comparison to the prolonged, agonizing deaths of many, Christ's final sufferings had been comparatively short: 'They were soon over, and they were much less horrible than those to which myriads have been exposed.' The prolonged human suffering experienced in the sex trafficking of children or rubber extraction in the Congo seemed worse. But now he believed he understood, aided by his work among the spirits. It was Christ's Resurrection from the dead that was 'the key to the mystery', for it was Christ's Resurrection that demonstrated conclusively that there was a spiritual life beyond this material world. The Resurrection showed that there was a higher purpose to life—that the universe was 'ordered by Infinite Wisdom for the ends of Infinite Love'—and this in turn gave meaning to human history, with all its striving and suffering, and showed that each life, no matter how short or full of suffering, had an eternal value. Through the Resurrection, 'untold millions of men and women in endless succession, as generations follow generations and centuries mount up to millenniums, have been helped the better to bear their sorrows and to face more bravely their death'. 'So it came to pass,' Stead observed, 'that the third seeing of the Passion Play left me with quite a different set of impressions.' 'I was no longer sorry for Christ. On the contrary, I felt like heartily rejoicing in His joy over the success with which he had carried out his demonstration'—a demonstration that there was a life beyond.[131]

Stead's life's work in journalism had represented an abiding commitment to unifying society around shared moral and spiritual values. The son of a Congregational minister and devout mother, his early life had been shaped by strict Nonconformity, and he grew to adulthood under the influence of Cromwell's Puritanism, the Revival of 1859–62, and the evangelical anti-slavery movement. In the 1870s, he emerged as a prominent voice of the Nonconformist Conscience, seeking to make the *Northern Echo* a pulpit for preaching God's purpose for society, calling readers to moral action, and reviving the Puritan ideal of the godly commonwealth. At the *Pall Mall Gazette* in the 1880s, he pioneered the New Journalism, with its emotive investigative reporting, innovative newspaper formatting, sense of moral mission, and use of sensationalism. His bold and engaging prose style was infused with belief in transcendent values and a sense of himself as God's vehicle, called to 'be a Christ' in a secularizing, materialist world. From the later 1880s, he endeavoured through books on Russia, Rome, 'Darkest England', and Chicago, and *The Review of Reviews*, to proclaim a social gospel based on sacrifice for others, and an inclusive, this worldly Civic Church that would unite 'all who love in the service of all who suffer'. He remained in many respects a conscientious Nonconformist, with fervent beliefs in the Bible, the Cross, the evil of sin, and Christian social activism. But he also grew increasingly open to other religious movements, coming to look on High Anglicans, the Salvation Army, Roman Catholics, Russian Orthodox, Welsh revivalists, agnostics, spiritualists, and theosophists with respect, even admiration. His version of Christian spiritualism was rooted in a genuine belief in paranormal forces, and also a sense that if people in a more secular, materialist age could receive clear proof of an afterlife, they would return to faith in God, in Christ and His call to sacrificial love, and in a transcendent meaning to existence. In his later peace campaigns and work for world federation, he combined condemnations of nationalistic warfare with an enthusiasm for humanity, increasingly global perspectives, growing denunciations of racism, and millenarian hopes for world unity.

Stead had little formal education and no theological training. His religious views were a mixture of childhood training, and elements picked up from various sources (including sermons) and his theological views became increasingly eclectic and 'broad church' as he aged. His religious thought was highly influenced by individuals whom he respected—his parents, Oliver Cromwell, Thomas Carlyle, James Russell Lowell, Josephine Butler, Olga Novikoff, Henry Parry Liddon, Charles Gordon, Henry Manning, Catherine Booth, Annie Besant, Julia Ames—and he took aspects of their often very different theological positions and tried to combine them. There was an element of hero worship. He was not a critical thinker, he could be highly credulous in his beliefs, and his thinking moved rapidly, drawing connections and analogies, but lacking sustained analysis. His

Christianity was focused on service to others, and at the foundation of his faith was belief in the martyr Christ, laying down His life in love and service to those who suffered. This belief shaped his writing and his activism. He was a regular churchgoer, normally attending two services each Sunday (not always Congregational services), and finding comfort in hymns. His religious faith also gave him an independence as a journalist; he belonged to no political party or interest, and, believing he had an obligation to God to speak what he sincerely believed to be true and righteous, he held nothing back. Whether through the Nonconformist conscience, the social gospel, his enthusiasm for humanity, his Civic Church, his spiritualism, or his peace campaigns, he sought to make religion live as a social force in the world. He viewed the newspaper as the Bible of the new era, a further testament being written in a world where revelation was ongoing. He saw the world as a place of collective spiritual pilgrimage for humankind, and he came to view different religions as paths to spiritual truth, drawing people towards a Universal Church of the Future. For all his human weaknesses and errors, his writing conveyed a deep and abiding empathy for others, a sensitivity to human suffering, and a capacity to grow in understanding. His view of journalism as a pulpit to reach tens of thousands with religious and moral instruction reflected how newspapers were replacing churches as moral voices in late Victorian Britain.

In March 1912, Stead was invited by cable to travel to the United States to speak at the conference of the 'Men and Religion Forward Movement' to be held in Carnegie Hall in New York City. This Movement had been initiated in the summer of 1911, in part as a response to the drift of young men away from church membership. The aim was to appeal to men with calls to practical Christian service from an evangelical perspective. It would be, Stead believed, a version of his Civic Church idea. Stead was invited to speak at the session on world peace on 21 April. Other speakers at the conference were to be William Howard Taft (president of the United States), James Bryce (British ambassador to the United States), Booker T. Washington (African-American educator and public intellectual) and William Jennings Bryan (Democratic politician and former presidential candidate). Stead readily accepted the invitation. 'I expect to leave by the *Titanic* on April 10th,' he informed his *Review of Reviews* readers 'and hope I shall be back in London in May.'[132] He travelled by himself. He perished when the *Titanic* struck an iceberg and sank in the early hours of 15 April. There were several dubious 'last sightings' of him by survivors; some recalled him either reading quietly, or helping others into the lifeboats, or standing at the rails of the sinking ship, 'in silence and what seemed . . . a prayerful attitude, or one of profound meditation'.[133] One survivor was certain that it was Stead who had the ship's eight-man orchestra play 'Nearer my God to Thee', although it is not certain that the orchestra actually played this piece. In truth, there are no reliable accounts of his last hours, and his body was never found.

## Notes

1. F. Herbert Stead, *The Unseen Leadership: A Word of Personal Witness* (London, 1922), pp. 15–33.
2. [W. T. Stead], 'Progress of the World', *RoR* (April 1894), pp. 329–31.
3. F. Herbert Stead to W. T. Stead, 24 December 1895, Stead Papers, STED 1/66.
4. W. T. Stead, 'The Great Pacifist', *RoR* (June 1912), p. 620.
5. Harper, *Stead: The Man*, pp. 142–3.
6. E. T. Raymond, *Portraits of the Nineties* (London, 1921), p. 174.
7. Whyte, *Life of Stead*, ii, pp. 72–4; i, p. 305.
8. Ibid., ii, p. 56; Harper, *Stead: The Man*, pp. 59, 142.
9. Harper, *Stead: The Man*, pp. 65, 150.
10. Whyte, *Life of Stead*, ii, pp. 54–5.
11. *Congregational Year Book* (1913), pp. 8, 242.
12. Joseph O. Baylen, 'Stead's Penny "Masterpiece Library"', *Journal of Popular Culture*, 9 (1975), pp. 710–25.
13. W. T. Stead, 'First Impressions of the Theatre', *RoR* (July 1904), p. 32.
14. Quoted in 'First Impressions of the Theatre', *RoR* (August 1904), p. 143.
15. W. T. Stead to Olga Novikoff, 12 September 1887, Novikoff–Stead Corr., fol. 246.
16. Joseph O. Baylen, 'W. T. Stead and the Early Career of H. G. Wells, 1895–1911', *Huntington Library Quarterly*, 38 (1974), pp. 53–79.
17. Graham McClelland, 'W. T. Stead: The Formative Years', *News-Stead*, 11 (Fall 1997), p. 8.
18. Harper, *Stead: The Man*, p. 10.
19. W. T. Stead (ed.), *Hymns That Have Helped*, 2nd edn (New York, 1898), pp. 19–20.

20. [W. T. Stead], 'The Old Book after the Deluge of the New Criticism', *RoR* (June 1896), pp. 551–62, 562.

21. W. T. Stead, 'Character Sketch: Oliver Cromwell and the National Church', *RoR* (May 1899), p. 433.

22. W. T. Stead, *Which? Christ or Cain?* (London, 1905), p. iii–iv.

23. W. T. Stead, *'Lest We Forget': A Keepsake from the Nineteenth Century* (London, 1901), p. 71.

24. Harper, *Stead: The Man*, p. 255.

25. G. R. Searle, *A New England? Peace and War 1886–1918* (Oxford, 2004), pp. 246–7.

26. [W. T. Stead], 'Progress of the World', *RoR* (May 1894), p. 446.

27. [W. T. Stead], 'The Arrest of Armaments', *RoR* (June 1894), pp. 580–1.

28. [W. T. Stead], 'Progress of the World', *RoR* (September 1894), p. 212.

29. [W. T. Stead], 'Anti-English Feeling in the United States', *RoR* (June 1895), pp. 523–5; W. T. Stead, 'Jingoism in America', *The Contemporary Review*, 68 (1895), pp. 334–47.

30. Whyte, *Life of Stead*, ii, pp. 86–7.

31. Stead, 'The Great Pacifist', p. 612.

32. W. T. Stead to James Bryce, 19 July 1896, Bryce Papers, fol. 114.

33. W. T. Stead, *Always Arbitrate before You Fight* (London, 1896).

34. Stead, 'The Great Pacifist', p. 612.

35. W. T. Stead, *The Haunting Horrors in Armenia* (London, 1896), p. 5.

36. [W. T. Stead], 'Wanted, an Anglo-Russian Entente', *RoR* (February 1896), pp. 149–51; [W. T. Stead], 'The Eastern Ogre; or, St George to the Rescue', *RoR* (October 1896), pp. 355–61.

37. Quoted in Whyte, *Life of Stead*, ii, p. 79.

38. 'Rescript of the Russian Emperor', in James Brown Scott (ed.), *Texts of the Peace Conferences at the Hague, 1899 and 1907* (Boston, 1908), pp. 1–2.

39. Geoffrey Best, 'Peace Conferences and the Century of Total War: The Hague Conference and What Came After', *International Affairs*, 75 (1999), pp. 621–2.

40. Stead, *Unseen Leadership*, p. 42.

41. [W. T. Stead], 'Progress of the World', *RoR* (September 1898), p. 219.

42. W. T. Stead to Lord Esher, 3 September 1898, quoted in Daniel Hucker, 'British Peace Activism and "New" Diplomacy: Revisiting the 1899 Hague Peace Conference', *Diplomacy and Statecraft*, 26 (2015), p. 409.

43. Whyte, *Life of Stead*, ii, p. 143.

44. Martin Ceadel, *Semi-Detached Idealists: The British Peace Movement and International Relations, 1854–1945* (Oxford, 2000), 152–3; *The Times* (19 December 1898), p. 12.

45. Hucker, 'British Peace Activism and "New" Diplomacy', p. 409; Laity, *The British Peace Movement*, pp. 146–50; Whyte, *Life of Stead*, ii, pp. 147–8.

46. Stead, *Unseen Leadership*, pp. 44–5.

47. [W. T. Stead], 'International Crusade of Peace', *RoR* (January 1899), p. 25.

48. 'International Crusade of Peace', *Leeds Mercury* (22 March 1899).

49. W. T. Stead, 'Some Pages of a Busy Life', *RoR* (June 1899), pp. 536–43.

50. Stead, 'The Great Pacifist', p. 614.

51. [W. T. Stead]. 'Vindication: Tardy But Complete', *RoR* (November 1904), pp. 485–6.

52. H. Wickham Steed to W. T. Stead, 11 May 1899, Stead Papers, STED 1/66.

53. Best, 'Peace Conferences and the Century of Total War', p. 623.

54. W. T. Stead, *The United States of Europe on the Eve of the Parliament of Peace* (London, 1899); W. T. Stead, *The Parliament of Peace and its Members* (London, 1899).

55. Quoted in Paul Laity, *The British Peace Movement 1870–1914* (Oxford, 2002), p. 151.

56. T. P. O'Connor, 'Mr W. T. Stead', *Daily Telegraph* (17 April 1912).

57. Whyte, *Life of Stead*, ii, p. 153.

58. [W. T. Stead], 'The Topic of the Month', *RoR* (August 1899), pp. 147–8.

59. [W. T. Stead], 'Internationalism: An Ideal for the New Century', *RoR* (January 1901), p. 35.

60. Stead, *Unseen Leadership*, pp. 46–7.

61. John Marlow, *Cecil Rhodes: The Anatomy of Empire* (London, 1972), p. 210; Joseph O. Baylen, 'W. T. Stead and the Boer War: The Irony of Idealism', *Canadian Historical Review*, 40 (1959), p. 305.

62. Joseph O. Baylen, 'W. T. Stead's History of the Mystery and the Jameson Raid', *Journal of British Studies*, 4 (1964), p. 105.

63. [W. T. Stead], 'Character Sketch. Cecil Rhodes of Africa', *RoR* (February 1896), pp. 120, 121.

64. Ibid., p. 130.

65. Baylen, 'W. T. Stead's History of the Mystery', pp. 105–32.

66. Quoted in Simon J. Potter, 'W. T. Stead, Imperial Federation, and the South African War', in Lauren Brake, E. King, R. Luckhurst, and J. Mussell (eds), *W. T. Stead: Newspaper Revolutionary* (London, 2012), p. 124.

67. [W. T. Stead], 'The Progress of the World', *RoR* (February 1896), p. 106; 'The Progress of the World', *RoR* (October 1897), p. 330.

68. J. Lee Thompson, *A Wider Patriotism: Alfred Milner and the British Empire* (London, 2007), p. 37; 'Progress of the World', *RoR* (May 1897), p. 416.

69. Stead, 'Great Pacifist', p. 613; Baylen, 'W. T. Stead and the Boer War', pp. 310–11.
70. W. T. Stead, *Shall I Slay my Brother Boer?* (London, 1899), pp. 5, 8, 61, 62.
71. W. T. Stead to James Bryce, 9 December 1899, Bryce Papers, fol. 129.
72. Laity, *The British Peace Movement*, p. 153.
73. 'Shall We Let Hell Loose in South Africa?' *RoR* (October 1899), p. 356.
74. Kenneth O. Morgan, 'The Boer War and the Media (1899–1902)', *Twentieth Century British History*, 13 (2002), pp. 2–5.
75. Ingrid Hanson, ' "God'll Send the Bill to You": The Costs of War and the God Who Counts in W. T. Stead's Pro-Boer Peace Campaign', *Journal of Victorian Culture*, 20 (2015), pp. 170–7.
76. Stead, 'Great Pacifist', p. 615.
77. Quoted in Baylen, 'W. T. Stead and the Boer War', p. 314.
78. Stead, *Shall I Slay my Brother Boer?* p. 64.
79. Hanson, ' "God'll Send the Bill to You" ', p. 176.
80. Quoted in Baylen, 'W. T. Stead and the Boer War', p. 314.
81. Arthur Davey, *The British Pro-Boers 1877–1902* (Cape Town, 1978), 85–6; Ceadel, *Semi-Detached Idealists*, p. 157.
82. Eliza Riedi, 'The Women Pro-Boers: Gender, Peace and the Critique of Empire in the South African War', *Historical Research*, 86 (2013), pp. 98–9.
83. W. T. Stead to James Bryce, 9 March 1900, Bryce Papers, fol. 133.
84. W. T. Stead, *Are We in the Right?* 2nd edn. (London, 1900), p. 96.
85. Mark D. Chapman, 'Theological Responses in England to the South African War, 1899–1902', *Zeitschrift für Neuere Theologiegeschichte*, 16 (2009), 181–96.
86. Whyte, *Life of Stead*, ii, pp. 183, 181.
87. W. T. Stead to James Bryce, 26 September 1900, Bryce Papers, fol. 134.
88. Thomas Pakenham, *The Boer War* (London, 1979), pp. 572–3.
89. W. T. Stead, *Hell Let Loose! What Is Now Being Done in South Africa* (London, 1900), p. 1.
90. W. T. Stead, *The War in South Africa: How Not to Make Peace* (London, 1900).
91. 'How to Make Peace in South Africa', *RoR* (December 1900), 540–7; 'How We Are Waging War in South Africa', *RoR* (January 1901), pp. 154–5.
92. W. T. Stead, *The War in South Africa: 'Methods of Barbarism'* (London, 1901), pp. 77, 92.
93. Davey, *The British Pro-Boers*, p. 87.
94. *Western Daily Press* (13 September 1901), p. 3; Ceadel, *Semi-Detached Idealists*, p. 158; Laity, *British Peace Movement*, pp. 160–1.
95. Potter, 'W. T. Stead, Imperial Federation, and the South African War', pp. 127–8.

96. Stead, *The War in South Africa. How Not to Make Peace*, p. 50.

97. W. T. Stead, *The Americanisation of the World* (London, 1902), p. 33.

98. 'Progress of the World', *RoR* (June 1902), pp. 553–4.

99. John Burns to W. T. Stead, 15 June 1904, BL, Burns Papers, Add MS 46287, fol. 246.

100. Clare Gill, ' "I'm Really Going to Kill him This Time": Olive Schreiner, W. T. Stead, and the Politics of Publicity in the *Review of Reviews*', *Victorian Periodicals Review*, 46 (2013), p. 203.

101. Davey, *The British Pro-Boers*, p. 87; O'Connor, 'Mr. W. T. Stead'; Baylen, 'W. T. Stead as Publisher and Editor of the "Review of Reviews" ', p. 78.

102. Robertson, *Life and Death of a Newspaper*, p. 224n.

103. [W. T. Stead], 'Character Sketch: Two High Churchmen', *RoR* (January 1905), p. 32.

104. Stead, *Americanisation of the World*, pp. 5, 19, 7, 153.

105. Stead, *My Father*, pp. 274–5.

106. Joseph O. Baylen, 'W. T. Stead's Controversial Visit to South Africa, 1904', *History Today*, 30 (1980), pp. 11–15.

107. Ibid., p. 13.

108. [W. T. Stead]. 'South Africa and its Problems', *RoR* (June 1904), pp. 560-8; 'The Most Pressing Question in South Africa Today', *RoR* (July 1904), pp. 33–6; 'What South Africa Expects from the Liberal Government', *RoR* (August, 1904), pp, 146–9.

109. [Stead], 'What South Africa Expects', p. 147.

110. [W. T. Stead], 'Cannibal Christendom in West Africa', *RoR* (February 1903), pp. 183–7, 183.

111. [W. T. Stead], 'Character Sketch: Leopold, Emperor of the Congo', *RoR* (June 1903), pp. 562–70, 565, 569.

112. Quoted in Whyte, *Life of Stead*, ii, p. 219.

113. [W. T. Stead], 'Prosperous British India', *RoR* (January 1902), pp. 84–5.

114. [W. T. Stead], 'Our Grand Monarque in India', *RoR* (July 1903), p. 81.

115. [W. T. Stead], 'What Is My Duty to the People of India?', *RoR* (December 1901), p. 616.

116. [W. T. Stead], 'India: A Nation', *RoR* (April 1906), p. 389.

117. Whyte, *Life of Stead*, ii, p. 225.

118. [W. T. Stead], 'Retrospect: After Fourteen Years', *RoR* (December 1903), p. 571.

119. [W. T. Stead], 'Are There Any Superior Races?' *RoR* (May 1905), pp. 538, 539, 540.

120. W. T. Stead, Preface, Jean Pinot, *The Death-Agony of the 'Science' of Race*, trans. Constance A. Grande (London, 1911), pp. 5, 6.

121. A. J. A. Morris, 'The English Radicals Campaign for Disarmament and the Hague Conference of 1907', *Journal of Modern History*, 43 (1971), p. 374.
122. [W. T. Stead], 'The Coming Parliament of Man', *RoR* (February 1907), pp. 145, 146.
123. 'Stead Talks War to Ethical Society', *New York Times* (15 April 1907), p. 2.
124. [W. T. Stead], 'Notes on my American Tour', *RoR* (June 1907), pp. 597, 596, 600.
125. W. T. Stead, 'Impressions from the Hague', *The Contemporary Review*, 92 (1907), pp. 721, 722, 724, 730.
126. [W. T. Stead], 'After the Hague: A World-wide Pilgrimage', *RoR* (June 1907), pp. 647, 648.
127. M. Maartens to W. T. Stead, 30 November 1907, Stead Papers, STED 1/48.
128. Stead, 'The Great Pacifist', p. 619.
129. Stead, *My Father*, pp. 318–34, quotation on p. 324; Harper, *Stead: The Man*, p. 216.
130. Stead, *Story That Transformed the World*, p. 158.
131. [W. T. Stead], 'Ober Ammergau: For the Third Time', *RoR* (July 1910), pp. 36–7.
132. [W. T. Stead], 'Progress of the World', *RoR* (April 1912), p. 350.
133. Quoted in Eckley, *Maiden Tribute*, p. 380.

# Select Bibliography

Ausubel, Herman, 'General Booth's Scheme of Social Salvation', *American Historical Review*, 56 (1951), pp. 519–25.

Battiscombe, Georgina, *Shaftesbury: A Biography of the Seventh Earl*. London, 1974.

Baylen, Joseph O., 'Olga Novikov, Propagandist', *American Slavic and East European Review*, 10 (1951), pp. 255–71.

Baylen, Joseph O., 'W. T. Stead and the Boer War: The Irony of Idealism', *Canadian Historical Review*, 40 (1959), pp. 304–14.

Baylen, Joseph O., 'A Victorian's "Crusade" in Chicago, 1893–1894', *Journal of American History*, 51 (1964), pp. 418–34.

Baylen, Joseph O., 'W. T. Stead's History of the Mystery and the Jameson Raid', *Journal of British Studies*, 4 (1964), pp. 104–32.

Baylen, Joseph O., 'W. T. Stead and the Russian Revolution of 1905', *Canadian Journal of History*, 2 (1967), pp. 45–66.

Baylen, Joseph O., 'W. T. Stead's *Borderland:* A Quarterly Review and Index of Psychic Phenomena, 1893–97', *Victorian Periodicals Newsletter*, 4 (April 1969), pp. 30–5.

Baylen, Joseph O., 'Sir Arthur Conan Doyle and W. T. Stead: The Novelist and the Journalist', *Albion*, 2 (1970), pp. 3–16.

Baylen, Joseph O., 'The "New Journalism" in Late Victorian Britain', *Australian Journal of Politics and History*, 18 (1972), pp. 367–85.

Baylen, Joseph O., 'W. T. Stead and the Early Career of H. G. Wells, 1895–1911', *Huntington Library Quarterly*, 38 (1974), pp. 53–79.

Baylen, Joseph O., 'Stead's Penny "Masterpiece Library"', *Journal of Popular Culture*, 9 (1975), pp. 710–25.

Baylen, Joseph O., 'W. T. Stead as Publisher and Editor of the "Review of Reviews"', *Victorian Periodicals Review*, 12 (1979), pp. 70–84.

Baylen, Joseph O., 'W. T. Stead's Controversial Visit to South Africa, 1904', *History Today*, 30 (1980), pp. 11–15.

Baylen, Joseph O., 'Politics and the "New Journalism": Lord Esher's Use of the *Pall Mall Gazette*', *Victorian Periodicals Review*, 20 (1987), pp. 126–41.

Bebbington, David, *The Nonconformist Conscience: Chapel and Politics 1870–1914*. London, 1982.

Best, Geoffrey, 'Peace Conferences and the Century of Total War: The Hague Conference and What Came After', *International Affairs*, 75 (1999), pp. 619–34.

Booth, Bramwell, *Echoes and Memories* (1925). London, 1977.

Booth, William, *In Darkest England and the Way Out*. London, 1890.

Brake, Laurel, 'Journalism and Modernism, Continued: The Case of W. T. Stead', in Ann Ardis and Patrick Collier (eds), *Transatlantic Print Culture, 1880–1940* (Basingstoke, 2008), pp. 149–66.

Brake, Laurel, 'W. T. Stead and Democracy: The Americanization of the World', in Ella Dzelzainis and Ruth Livesay (eds), *The American Experiment and the Idea of Democracy in British Culture* (Farnham, 2013), pp. 161–78.

Butler, Josephine, *Rebecca Jarrett*. London, [1885].

Campbell, John L. and Trevor Hall, *Strange Things: The Story of Fr Allan McDonald, Ada Goodrich Freer, and the Society for Psychical Research's Enquiry into Highland Second Sight*, new edn. Edinburgh, 2006.

Campbell, Kate, 'W. T. Stead, Matthew Arnold and a New Journalism: Cultural Politics in the 1880s', *Victorian Periodicals Review*, 36 (2003), pp. 20–40.

Ceadel, Martin, *Semi-Detached Idealists: The British Peace Movement and International Relations, 1854–1945*. Oxford, 2000.

Chadwick, Owen, *A History of the Popes 1830–1914*. Oxford, 1998.

Chapman, Mark D., 'Theological Responses in England to the South African War, 1899–1902', *Zeitschrift fur Neuere Theologiegeschichte*, 16 (2009), pp. 181–96.

Christian, R. F., 'The Road to Yashnaya Polyana: Some Pilgrims from Britain and their Reminiscences', *Slavonic and East European Review*, 66 (1988), pp. 526–52.

Crofton, Sarah, '"Julia Says": The Spirit-Writing and Editorial Mediumship of W. T. Stead', *Interdisciplinary Studies in the Long Nineteenth Century*, 16 (2013), pp. 1–15.

Darlow, T. H., *William Robertson Nicoll: Life and Letters*. London, 1925.

Davey, Arthur, *The British Pro-Boers 1877–1902*. Cape Town, 1978.

De Nie, Michael, 'W. T. Stead, Liberal Imperialism, and Ireland', in Karen Steele and Michael de Nie (eds), *Ireland and the New Journalism* (Basingstoke, 2014), pp. 101–18.

Downey, D. B., 'William Stead and Chicago: A Victorian Jeremiah in the Windy City', *Mid-America*, 68 (1987), pp. 153–66.

Downey, D. B., *A Season of Renewal: the Columbia Exhibition and Victorian America*. Westport, Connecticut, 2002.

Eckley, Grace, *Maiden Tribute: A Life of W. T. Stead*. Philadelphia, 2007.

Gill, Clare, '"I'm Really Going to Kill Him This Time": Olive Schreiner, W. T. Stead, and the Politics of Publicity in the *Review of Reviews*', *Victorian Periodicals Review*, 46 (2013), pp. 184–210.

Goldsworthy, Simon, 'English Nonconformity and the Pioneering of the Modern Newspaper Campaign', *Journalism Studies*, 7 (2006), pp. 387–402.

Goodwyn, Helena, 'A "New" Journalist: The Americanization of W. T. Stead', *Journal of Victorian Culture*, 23 (2018), pp. 405–20.

Gorham, Deborah, 'The "Maiden Tribute of Modern Babylon" Re-examined: Child Prostitution and the Idea of Childhood in Late-Victorian England', *Victorian Studies*, 21 (1978), pp. 353–79.

Graybar, Lloyd J., *Albert Shaw of the Review of Reviews*. Lexington, 1974.

Hale, Ann M., 'W. T. Stead and Participatory Reader Networks', *Victorian Periodicals Review*, 48 (2015), pp. 15–41.

Handy, Robert T., 'George D. Herron and the Kingdom Movement', *Church History*, 19 (1950), pp. 97–115.

Hanson, Ingrid, ' "God'll Send the Bill to You": The Costs of War and the God Who Counts in W. T. Stead's Pro-Boer Peace Campaign', *Journal of Victorian Culture*, 20 (2015), pp. 168–85.

Harper, Edith K., *Stead, the Man: Personal Reminiscences*. London, 1918.

Hattersley, Roy, *Blood and Fire: William and Catherine Booth and their Salvation Army*. London, 1999.

Hucker, Daniel, 'British Peace Activism and "New" Diplomacy: Revisiting the 1899 Hague Peace Conference', *Diplomacy and Statecraft*, 26 (2015), pp. 405–23.

Inglis, K. S., *Churches and the Working Classes in Victorian England*. London, 1963.

Jenkins, Roy, *Sir Charles Dilke: A Victorian Tragedy*, 2nd edn. London, 1965.

Jordan, Jane, *Josephine Butler*. London, 2001.

Kingsmill, Hugh, *After Puritanism 1850–1900*. London, 1929.

Laity, Paul, *The British Peace Movement 1870–1914*. Oxford, 2002.

Larkin, Emmet, *The Roman Catholic Church and the Plan of Campaign 1886–1888*. Cork, 1978.

Leslie, Shane, *Henry Edward Manning: His Life and Labours*. London, 1921.

Luckhurst, Roger, *The Invention of Telepathy 1870–1901*. Oxford, 2002.

Luckhurst, Roger, 'W. T. Stead's Occult Economies', in Louise Henson et al. (eds), *Culture and Science in Nineteenth-Century Media* (Aldershot, 2004), pp. 125–35.

Luckhurst, Roger, *The Mummy's Curse: The True History of a Dark Fantasy*. Oxford, 2012.

Lunn, H. S., *Chapters from my Life with Special Reference to Reunion*. London, 1918.

Marlow, John, *Cecil Rhodes: The Anatomy of Empire*. London, 1972.

Matthew, H. C. G., *Gladstone 1809–1898*. Oxford, 1997.

McClelland, V. A., *Cardinal Manning: His Public Life and Influence 1865–1892*. Oxford, 1962.

McCormack, Kathleen, 'Sundays at the Priory: Olga Novikoff and the Russian Presence', *George Eliot—George Henry Lewes Studies*, 67 (2015), pp. 30–42.

Morgan, Kenneth O., 'The Boer War and the Media (1899–1902)', *Twentieth Century British History*, 13 (2002), pp. 1–16.

Morley, John, *Recollections*, 2 vols. London, 1917.

Morris, A. J. A., 'The English Radicals Campaign for Disarmament and the Hague Conference of 1907', *Journal of Modern History*, 43 (1971), pp. 367–93.

Mulpetre, Owen, 'W. T. Stead and the New Journalism'. University of Teeside MPhil thesis, 2010.

Mussell, James, ' "Of the Making of Magazines There Is No End": W. T. Stead, Newness, and Archival Imagination', *English Studies in Canada*, 41 (2015), pp. 69–91.

Nethercot, Arthur H., *The First Five Lives of Annie Besant*. London, 1961.

Oldstone-Moore, C., 'The Forgotten Origins of the Ecumenical Movement in England: The Grindelwald Conferences, 1892–95', *Church History*, 70 (2001), pp. 73–97.

Pakenham, Thomas, *The Boer War*. London, 1979.

Pimlott, J. A. R., *Toynbee Hall: Fifty Years of Social Progress 1884–1934*. London, 1935.

Potter, Simon J., 'W. T. Stead, Imperial Federation, and the South African War', in Lauren Brake, E. King, R. Luckhurst and J. Mussell (eds), *W. T. Stead: Newspaper Revolutionary* (London, 2012), pp. 115–32.

Purcell, E. S., *Life of Cardinal Manning*, 2 vols. London, 1896.

Raymond, E. T., *Portraits of the Nineties*. London, 1921.

Reid, T. Wemyss, *Memoirs of Sir Wemysss Reid 1842–1885*, ed. Stuart J. Reid. London, 1905.

Riedi, Eliza, 'The Women Pro-Boers: Gender, Peace and the Critique of Empire in the South African War', *Historical Research*, 86 (2013), pp. 92–115.

Robertson Scott, J. W., *The Life and Death of a Newspaper*. London, 1952.

Robinson, W. Sydney, *Muckraker: The Scandalous Life and Times of W. T. Stead*. London, 2013.

Rouse, R. and S. C. Neill (eds), *A History of the Ecumenical Movement 1517–1948*. London, 1954.

Sandford, E. G. (ed.), *Memoirs of Archbishop Temple*, 2 vols. London, 1906.

Sausman, Justin, 'The Democratisation of the Spook: W. T. Stead and the Invention of Public Occultism', in Lauren Brake, E. King, R. Luckhurst and J. Mussell (eds), *W. T. Stead: Newspaper Revolutionary* (London, 2012), pp. 149–65.

Schults, Raymond L., *Crusader in Babylon: W. T. Stead and the* Pall Mall Gazette. Lincoln, Nebraska, 1972.

Scotland, Nigel, *Squires in the Slums: Settlements and Missions in Late Victorian London*. London, 2007.

Seager, R. H., *The World's Parliament of Religions*. Bloomington, Indiana, 1995.

Searle, G. R., *A New England? Peace and War 1886–1918*. Oxford, 2004.

Shannon, Richard, *Gladstone and the Bulgarian Agitation*, 2nd edn. Hassocks, 1975.

Shannon, Richard, *Gladstone: Heroic Minister 1865–1898*. London, 1999.

Smith, Gary Scott, 'When Stead Came to Chicago: The "Social Gospel Novel" and the Chicago Civic Federation', *American Presbyterians*, 68 (1990), pp. 193–205.

Stead, Estelle W., *My Father*. London, 1913.

Stead, F. Herbert, *The Unseen Leadership: A Word of Personal Witness*. London, 1922.

Stead, W. T., *Truth about Russia*. London, 1888.

Stead, W. T., *The Pope and the New Era, being Letters from the Vatican in 1889*. London, 1890.

Stead, W. T., *If Christ Came to Chicago! A Plea for the Union of All Who Love in the Service of All Who Suffer*. London, 1894.

Stead, W. T. (ed.), *Hymns that Have Helped*. New York, 1898.

Stead, W. T., *The Parliament of Peace and Its Members*. London, 1899.

Stead, W. T., *The United States of Europe on the Eve of the Parliament of Peace*. London, 1899.

Stead, W. T., *Life of Mrs Booth, the Founder of the Salvation Army*. New York, 1900.

Stead, W. T., *The Americanisation of the World*. London, 1902.

Stead, W. T., *The Last Will and Testament of Cecil John Rhodes with Elucidatory Notes*. London, 1902.

Stead, W. T., *The Revival of 1905*. London, 1905.

Stead, W. T., *Which? Christ or Cain?* London, 1905.

Stead, W. T., *The M.P. for Russia, Reminiscences and Correspondence of Madame Olga Novikoff*, 2 vols. London, 1909.

Stead, W. T., *Real Ghost Stories* (1890), new edn. New York, 1921.

Stevenson, John S., *The Reverend William Stead and his Family: An Eulogy*. Newcastle-upon-Tyne, 1987.

Taylor, A. J. P., *The Trouble Makers: Dissent over Foreign Policy 1792–1939*, 2nd edn. London, 1993.

Thompson, J. Lee, *A Wider Patriotism: Alfred Milner and the British Empire*. London, 2007.

Walker, Pamela J., *Pulling the Devil's Kingdom Down: The Salvation Army in Victorian Britain*. Berkeley, California, 2001.

Walker, Pamela J., 'The Conversion of Rebecca Jarrett', *History Workshop Journal*, 58 (2004), 246–58.

Walkowitz, Judith R., *City of Dreadful Delight: Narratives of Sexual Danger in Late-Victorian London*. London, 1992.

Walsh, Patrick J., *William J. Walsh: Archbishop of Dublin*. Dublin, 1923.

Waugh, Benjamin, *William T. Stead: A Life for the People*. London, [1885].

Whyte, Frederic, *Life of W. T. Stead*, 2 vols. London, 1925.

Willard, Frances E. et al., *A Young Woman Journalist: A Memorial Tribute to Julia A. Ames*. Chicago, 1892.

Willey, Basil, *More Nineteenth Century Studies*. London, 1956.

# Index